A CONCEPTUAL GUIDE TO STATISTICS USING SPSS

ELLIOT T. BERKMAN
University of Oregon

STEVEN P. REISE
University of California, Los Angeles

Los Angeles | London | New Delhi
Singapore | Washington DC

Los Angeles | London | New Delhi
Singapore | Washington DC

FOR INFORMATION:

SAGE Publications, Inc.
2455 Teller Road
Thousand Oaks, California 91320
E-mail: order@sagepub.com

SAGE Publications Ltd.
1 Oliver's Yard
55 City Road
London EC1Y 1SP
United Kingdom

SAGE Publications India Pvt. Ltd.
B 1/I 1 Mohan Cooperative Industrial Area
Mathura Road, New Delhi 110 044
India

SAGE Publications Asia-Pacific Pte. Ltd.
33 Pekin Street #02-01
Far East Square
Singapore 048763

Acquisitions Editor: Christine Cardone
Editorial Assistant: Sarita Sarak
Production Editor: Eric Garner
Copy Editor: Liann Lech
Typesetter: C&M Digitals, (P) Ltd.
Proofreader: Wendy Jo Dymond
Indexer: Brian Clark
Cover Designer: Gail Buschman
Marketing Manager: Liz Thornton
Permissions Editor: Karen Ehrmann

Copyright © 2012 by SAGE Publications, Inc.

Printed in the United States of America

Library of Congress Cataloging-in-Publication Data

Berkman, Elliot T.

A conceptual guide to statistics using SPSS / Elliot T. Berkman, Steven P. Reise.

p. cm.

ISBN 978-1-4129-7406-6 (pbk.)

1. SPSS for Windows. 2. Statistics—Computer programs. 3. Social sciences—Statistical methods—Computer programs. I. Reise, Steven Paul II. Title.

HA32.B47 2012
005.5'5—dc22
2011009895

This book is printed on acid-free paper.

11 12 13 14 15 10 9 8 7 6 5 4 3 2 1

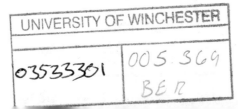

Contents

Preface

This book grew out of our experiences across many years of teaching introductory statistics to graduate students and advanced undergraduates in psychology. We noticed that our students faced a special set of challenges in learning statistics compared to other topics covered in the psychology curriculum. It was often the case that our students had little or no background in statistics and were consequently unfamiliar with thinking about the world in statistical or probabilistic terms. Even when they were familiar with statistics, our students often just *didn't like* it. And to make matters worse, in addition to their usual course load, they were also busy completing heavy research expectations (for graduate and honors students) or assisting faculty with their research. The dilemma for these students became how to simultaneously learn the challenging theoretical material taught in statistics class and to come away with the practical computational skills needed to advance their research?

The current text proposes to aid students by drawing clear connections between the theoretical and computational aspects of statistics, emphasizing the importance of understanding theoretical concepts during computation, and demonstrating how and where they fit in to SPSS, an IBM Company*. The text not only demonstrates how to use SPSS to advanced computation but also aids students' understanding of the theoretical concepts by teaching them in another, more practical context.

Our goal in this book is to clearly map the theories and techniques taught in a statistics class to the procedures in SPSS. The text teaches students how to perform standard and advanced statistical tests using both the point-and-click menus and syntax functions and how to integrate the SPSS functions with the statistical theory taught in class. The theoretical foundation underlying each topic are introduced before the computational steps in order to remind students of the logic of each statistical test. In this way, a conceptual link is created between the statistical test and the computational steps, and attention is drawn to test-specific issues. Presenting the material in this way also helps to give students a better understanding of the test output because they know which parameters were used "behind the scenes" in the computation. To better fit the material to the needs of a graduate-level audience, advanced options and variations on each test are discussed, and the syntax commands are presented. This gives students more flexibility in tailoring their analyses to a wide variety of experimental paradigms.

It was impossible to cover all of the many statistical tests offered in the SPSS package. Instead, our goal was to provide coverage on any statistical test that might

---

*Note: SPSS was acquired by IBM in October 2009.

appear in a peer-reviewed psychology journal article. The text features detailed chapters on the tests most commonly used by psychologists, as well as several newer tests that are increasing in popularity. Each chapter is structured similarly so students familiar with the text will be able to quickly flip open the book to learn a new topic.

The book is organized in parallel to many standard statistics textbooks covering correlation, *t*-tests, ANOVA and MANOVA, multiple regression, and nonparametric tests. Each chapter begins with a brief conceptual introduction featuring test assumptions and a sketch of the mathematical operations behind a procedure. This is followed by an illustrated and annotated step-by-step guide to computation with references back to the introduction where possible and concludes with a discussion of the output.

Target Audience

This book is intended for anyone who not only wants to know how to use SPSS to compute a variety of statistical tests, but who also wants to understand the reasons behind each step and the conceptual meaning of the output. This includes advanced undergraduates in the social sciences; master's students in psychology, education, economics, public health, biological sciences, and counseling psychology; PhD students in the social sciences; and faculty in all these fields seeking a deeper understanding of SPSS than that offered by the usual step-by-step procedural guides. Most of the examples are drawn from research in social and personality psychology, but the tests used are common across many fields that make use of empirical behavioral data.

This text is sufficiently detailed to serve as a stand-alone guide to SPSS, but also is intended to complement a statistics textbook for a variety of undergraduate and graduate statistics courses in the social sciences. Because we cover topics ranging from *t*-tests and regression to factor analysis and matrix algebra, and because we describe both basic and advanced features of SPSS for each, we are confident that SPSS users at all levels of expertise will find something new and useful in this book.

Special Features

Behind the Scenes

The *Behind the Scenes* sections explain the conceptual machinery underlying the statistical tests. In contrast to merely presenting the equations for computing the statistic, these sections describe the idea behind each test in plain language. In writing these sections, we sought to answer, in conceptual terms, the questions, What does SPSS do with your data to transform it into the test statistic? Which parts of the data are important for this calculation? and How does the output relate to the meaning of the test? After that, and only where it is helpful to building a conceptual understanding, we give the equation for the test and explain each part in terms of the idea behind the test. Several *Behind the Scenes* sections also contain schematic diagrams that are intended to clarify how different patterns of data relate to key ideas in the test. These sections were written specifically for introductory students seeking to make a connection between the ideas taught in a statistics course or textbook and the SPSS procedure.

Connections

The *Connections* sections use SPSS to demonstrate the equivalence among tests that are often treated as distinct. Particularly for introductory students, the syllabus of a statistics course can seem like a laundry list of unrelated tests. The layout of SPSS also supports this impression by segregating similar tests into different menus. The purpose of the *Connections* sections is to provide a "bigger picture" perspective by highlighting the conceptual similarities across tests. We do this by showing commonalities within a family of tests (e.g., those based on the general linear model) and by relating entirely different types of tests to each other (e.g., between nonparametric tests and ANOVA-based tests). We also use the *Connections* sections to point out similarities in the SPSS output across different but related statistical tests.

A Closer Look

The *A Closer Look* sections feature advanced topics that are beyond the scope of other introductory SPSS books. These sections teach the reader how to use SPSS to compute tests or display output that is can be important to report in a research paper but that SPSS does not compute or display by default. Though the topics are more advanced or specialized, the *A Closer Look* sections are nonetheless written so that introductory students can understand when and why they might want to use them and that more advanced students can quickly learn how to compute them. Topics covered in *A Closer Look* sections include custom hypothesis tests among group means in ANOVA, assumption checking in the General Linear Model, and saving predicted scores in multiple regression.

Making the Most of Syntax

In the *Making the Most of Syntax* sections we describe statistical tests and output options that are exclusive to syntax. These include extensive treatment of custom hypothesis testing in ANOVA, MANOVA, ANCOVA, and regression, and an entire chapter on the advanced matrix algebra functions available only through syntax in SPSS. Our emphasis on the powerful capacity of the syntax functions is unique among introductory SPSS books. In order to help the reader learn how to use syntax in your own research, we provide the general form and also a specific example of each syntax function. As always, we emphasize conceptual understanding by linking the specifics of the syntax functions to the general idea behind the test.

This section also highlights the value of using syntax for all statistical tests even when other options are available. Syntax is the easiest way to rerun statistical tests with slight variations or with different variables. And by describing the syntax corresponding to every topic, this book teaches the reader to create a syntax log that provides a complete record of your data analysis process from data cleaning all the way through to figures for publication.

Data Files

Each of the statistical tests covered here is accompanied by an example data set, and the screenshots and output that are shown in each chapter are based on these data sets. Our intention is that the reader can follow along and practice analysis using these data sets, so we have made the data files available on the book webpage at www .sagepub.com/berkman. We hope it is clear from the content of the data sets that they are simulated and intended for illustrative purposes only.

Acknowledgments

We would like to acknowledge the insightful feedback from our brilliant colleagues in statistics education, Emily Falk and Hongjing Lu, as well as the willingness of many of our students to serve as proofreaders and guinea pigs for this book over the last few years. We also appreciate helpful comments from several expert reviewers in the field. They made our jobs easier and improved the book substantially.

About the Authors

Elliot T. Berkman is Assistant Professor of Psychology and director of the Social and Affective Neuroscience Laboratory at the University of Oregon. He has been teaching statistics to graduate students using SPSS for the past six years. In that time, he has been awarded the UCLA Distinguished Teaching Award and the Arthur J. Woodward Peer Mentoring Award. He has published numerous papers on the social psychological and neural processes involved in goal pursuit. His research on smoking cessation was recognized with the Joseph A. Gengerelli Distinguished Dissertation Award. He received his PhD in 2010 from the University of California, Los Angeles.

Steven P. Reise is professor, chair of Quantitative Psychology, and codirector of the Advanced Quantitative Methods training program at University of California, Los Angeles. Dr. Reise is an internationally renowned teacher in quantitative methods; in particular, the application of item response theory models to personality, psychopathology, and patient reported outcomes. In recognition of his dedication to teaching, Dr. Reise was named "Professor of the Year" in 1995–96 by the graduate students in the psychology department at UC Riverside, and was awarded the 2008 Psychology Department Distinguished teaching award. Most recently, in recognition of his campus-wide and global contributions, Dr. Reise was awarded the University of California campus-wide distinguished teaching award. Dr. Reise has spent the majority of the last twenty years investigating the application of latent variable models in general and item response theory (IRT) models in particular to personality, psychopathology and health outcomes data. In 1998, Dr. Reise was recognized for his work and received the Raymond B. Cattell award for outstanding multivariate experimental psychologist. Dr. Reise has over 70 refereed publications, including, two Annual Review Chapters, two contributions to American Psychological Association Handbooks, several articles in leading journals such as *Psychological Assessment* and *Psychological Methods*, and, finally, along with Dr. Susan Embretson, Dr. Reise has the leading textbook on item response theory called *Item Response Theory for Psychologists* (2000 and forthcoming). He received his PhD from the Department of Psychology at the University of Minnesota in 1990.

Introduction

Goal of This Book: Conceptual Understanding

Chances are that if you are just beginning to learn SPSS, then you are also beginning to learn statistics. It can often be challenging to map the concepts you're learning in statistics class onto the functions and outputs of SPSS when learning both at the same time. A typical course will teach you to compute statistics based on formulas, whereas SPSS uses point-and-click menus and syntax to compute tests; statistical calculations often involve a number of steps with a variety of quantities being computed, whereas SPSS displays only limited output that may or may not contain the numbers that you would have used to find the end result. A larger challenge still is that learning to compute statistics by hand or with SPSS can encourage rote, step-by-step memorization without developing an underlying conceptual foundation.

The goal of this book is to help you develop a conceptual understanding of a variety of statistical tests by linking the ideas you learn in statistics class or from a traditional statistics textbook with the computational steps and output from SPSS. Learning how statistical ideas map onto computation in SPSS will help you build your understanding of both. For example, seeing exactly how the concept of *variance* is used in SPSS—how it is converted into a number based on real data, with which other concepts it is associated, and where it appears in various statistical tests—will not only help you understand how to use statistical tests in SPSS and how to interpret their output but also will teach you about the concept of variance itself.

In line with this goal, we focus on the core ideas behind each statistical test covered in this book and try to relate it as clearly and directly as possible to how the test is computed in SPSS. Because this book is intended to be a guide to SPSS and not a statistics text per se, we omit details that are important for statistical calculation but are not relevant to their computation in SPSS. We use formulas and equations sparingly, and when we do, we display them in their most general form rather than a specific instantiation in order to describe more clearly how each term in the equation contributes to the conceptual meaning of the whole.

Chapter Organization

Each chapter begins with a plain-language explanation of the concept behind each statistical test and how the test relates to that concept. Then we walk through the steps to compute the test in SPSS and the output, pointing out wherever possible how the SPSS procedure and output connects back to the conceptual underpinnings of the test. Each of the steps is accompanied by annotated screen shots from SPSS, and relevant components of output are highlighted in both the text and the figures.

We assume that you have access to an introductory statistics textbook and that you have a basic understanding of the purpose of each test, but each chapter is written to be accessible to someone with no prior knowledge of how to run the test covered in the chapter. This text is sufficiently detailed to serve as a stand-alone guide to SPSS, but also is intended to complement a statistics textbook for a variety of undergraduate and graduate statistics courses in the social sciences. Because we cover topics ranging from *t*-tests and regression to factor analysis and matrix algebra, and because we describe both basic and advanced features of SPSS for each, we are confident that SPSS users at all levels of expertise will find something new and useful in this book.

Features That Will Help You in This Book

This book has a number of unique features among SPSS guides in addition to a conceptual focus on a broad range of topics.

Behind the Scenes

The *Behind the Scenes* sections explain the conceptual machinery underlying the statistical tests. In contrast to merely presenting the equations for computing the statistic, these sections describe the idea behind each test in plain language. In writing these sections, we sought to answer, in conceptual terms, the following questions: What does SPSS do with your data to transform them into the test statistic? Which parts of the data are important for this calculation? and How does the output relate to the meaning of the test? After that, and only where it is helpful to building a conceptual understanding, we give the equation for the test and explain each part in terms of the idea behind the test. Several *Behind the Scenes* sections also contain schematic diagrams that are intended to clarify how different patterns of data relate to key ideas in the test. These sections were written specifically to help you make the connection between the ideas and SPSS procedures.

Connections

The *Connections* sections use SPSS to demonstrate the equivalence among tests that are often treated as distinct. Particularly for introductory students, the syllabus of a statistics course can seem like a laundry list of unrelated tests. The layout of SPSS also supports this impression by segregating similar tests into different menus. The purpose of the *Connections* sections is to provide a "bigger picture" perspective by highlighting the conceptual similarities across tests. We do this by showing commonalities within a family of tests (e.g., those based on the general linear model) and by relating entirely different types of tests to each other (e.g., between nonparametric tests and ANOVA-based tests). We also use the *Connections* sections to point out similarities in the SPSS output across different but related statistical tests.

A Closer Look

The *A Closer Look* sections feature advanced topics that are beyond the scope of other introductory SPSS books. These sections will teach you how to use SPSS to compute tests or display output that can be important to report in a research paper but that SPSS does not compute or display by default. Although the topics are more advanced or specialized, the *A Closer Look* sections are nonetheless written so you can understand when and why you might want to use them and learn how to compute them if you wish. Topics covered in *A Closer Look* include custom hypothesis tests among group means in ANOVA, assumption checking in the GLM, and saving predicted scores in multiple regression.

Making the Most of Syntax

In the *Making the Most of Syntax* sections, we describe statistical tests and output options that are exclusive to syntax. These include extensive treatment of custom hypothesis testing in ANOVA, MANOVA, ANCOVA, and regression, and an entire chapter on the advanced matrix algebra functions available only through syntax in SPSS. Our emphasis on the powerful capacity of the syntax functions is unique among introductory SPSS books. In order to help you learn how to use syntax in your own research, we provide the general form and also a specific example of each syntax function. As always, we emphasize conceptual understanding by linking the specifics of the syntax functions to the general idea behind the test.

This section also highlights the value of using syntax for all statistical tests, even when other options are available. Syntax is the easiest way to rerun statistical tests with slight variations or with different variables. And by describing the syntax corresponding to every topic, this book will teach you to create a syntax log that provides a complete record of your data analysis process from data cleaning all the way through to figures for publication.

A Note on Data Files

Each of the statistical tests covered here is accompanied by an example data set, and the screenshots and output that you see in each chapter are based on these data sets. Our intention is that you can follow along and practice analysis using these data sets, so we have made the data files available on the book webpage at www.sagepub.com/berkman. We hope it is clear from the content of the data sets that they are simulated and intended for illustrative purposes only.

2

Descriptive Statistics

Introduction to Descriptive Statistics

Before we get into the formal "hypothesis testing" type of statistics that you're used to seeing in research articles, we will briefly cover some *descriptive statistics*. Descriptives are numbers that give you a quick summary of what your data look like, such as where the middle of the distribution is and how much the observations are spread around that middle.

Why should you be interested in these things? First, looking at descriptives is an excellent way to check for errors in data entry (which is especially important if you employ undergraduate research assistants!) and other irregularities in the data such as extreme outliers. Second, because good science involves making small improvements over what has been done before, most researchers tend to use the same measures over and over. Carefully examining your raw data is one of the best ways to familiarize yourself with measures and subject populations that you will use repeatedly. Knowing roughly what the distributions of those things should be and being able to recognize when they look unusual will make you a better researcher and enable you to impress your colleagues with your vast knowledge of bizarre data tics. For example, did you know that many scales of the trait "self-monitoring" have a two-humped (bimodal) distribution? Finally, sometimes your data analysis can start and end with descriptive statistics. As we will see, one measure in particular—the standard error of the mean—plays an important role in hypothesis testing. Often, when the standard error is very small (or, sadly, at times very large), we need not bother even doing hypothesis testing because our conclusions are foregone. In this way, descriptives can give you a fast "sneak peak" not only at your data but also at what conclusions you might draw from them.

Computing Descriptive Statistics in SPSS

We will practice descriptive statistics using the data set "Descriptives.sav" on the course website (see Chapter 1). Once the file is open and you have access to the data, you can get just about any information about them from the **Descriptive Statistics** menu. Click on **Analyze → Descriptive Statistics** to pull this up.

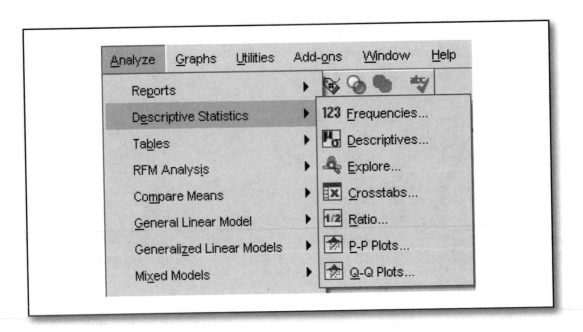

The first decision to make is whether the variable you'd like to examine is *categorical* or *continuous*. *Categorical* variables are made up of distinct groups that differ qualitatively rather than quantitatively, such as sex or experimental treatment condition. *Continuous* variables are those with a natural underlying metric, such as height, or those that vary along a continuum, such as happiness. To tell the difference, the key question to ask is, "Does it make sense to say that one level of my variable is greater than another?" If so, then your variable can likely be treated as continuous; otherwise, it is categorical. For example, it makes sense to say that a height of 6 ft is greater than a height of 5 ft, but not that Drug A is greater than Drug B.

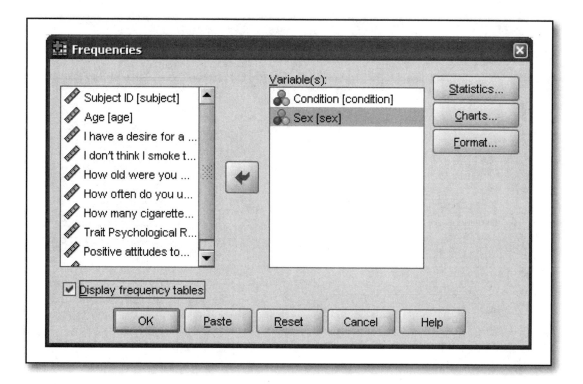

If you're dealing with a categorical variable, you'll want to click on **Frequencies**. In the window that opens, move all of the variables of interest into the right window. By default, this will display a frequency table for each selected variable that tells you how many observations and which percentage of the total are in each category. And that's pretty much everything that you'd want to know about your categorical variables.

The syntax for getting frequencies on these two categorical variables is as follows:

```
FREQUENCIES VARIABLES=condition sex .
```

For continuous variables, both the **Frequencies** and the **Descriptives** options are useful. In **Frequencies**, clicking on the **Statistics** tab brings up a variety of options for summarizing your data. For example, we can get lots of information about the variable *age* such as the average (mean, median, mode, sum), variability (including the standard error of the mean mentioned previously); and shape of the distribution (skewness and kurtosis). You can also get SPSS to find the cut points to divide your continuous variable into any number of equal groups (use "Quartiles" for four) or groups based on percentiles.

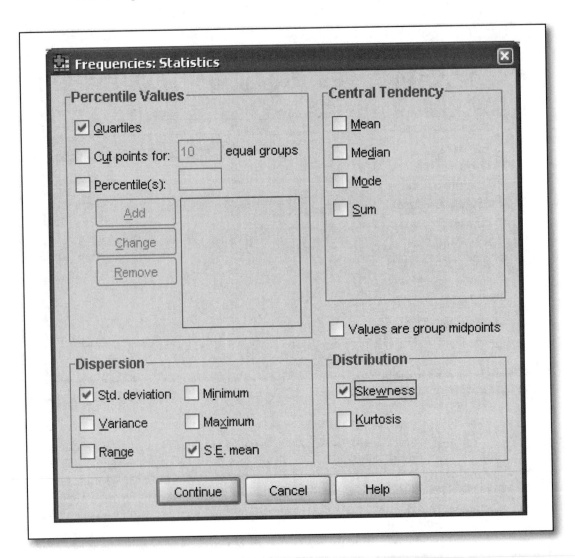

The last really cool thing that **Frequencies** can give you is a histogram of the distribution. Along with the skewness and kurtosis, this can give you a sense of whether your variable is approximately normally distributed (which we will see is one of the assumptions that we make about our data that should be checked). In the **Frequencies** menu, click on **Charts**, and select "Histograms: With normal curve." Then click "Continue."

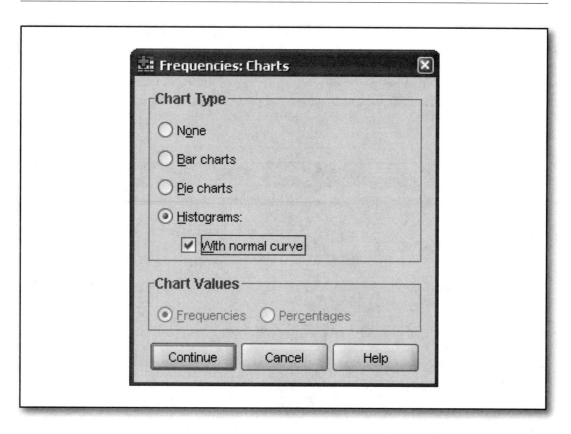

One thing to remember when using **Frequencies** with continuous data is to uncheck the "Display frequency tables" button on the main window. Otherwise, your output screen will be slammed with a large table with one entry per value of your variable. The syntax for this is as follows:

```
FREQUENCIES VARIABLES=age

/FORMAT = NOTABLE      /* Remove the large frequency table

/NTILES = 4            /* Use "4" for quartiles

/STATISTICS = ALL      /* Get every statistic in the book

/HISTOGRAM NORMAL .    /* Histogram with normal curve
```

Finally, if you are working with continuous data, you might want to transform the data into *standard units,* which have a mean of 0 and a standard deviation of 1. Values that are in standard units are said to be "standardized" and are called "z-scores." You can get z-scores of any variable one of two ways: the hard way using the **Compute** function (Chapter 1) or the easy way using the **Descriptives** function. Click on **Analyze** → **Descriptives**, put your continuous variable in the box on the right, and check the "Save standardized values as variables" box. You can peek into the **Options** menu if you want, but there's nothing in there that you can't get in from **Frequencies**. In fact, **Frequencies** offers a far more complete set of descriptive statistics than **Descriptives** does!

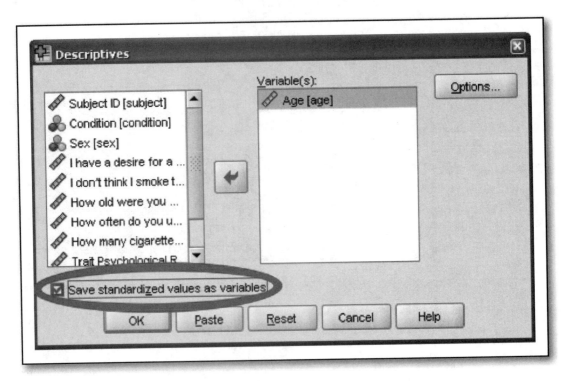

The syntax for this is simply

```
DESCRIPTIVES VARIABLES=age /SAVE .
```

After you run this syntax, notice that there will be a new variable in your "Variable View" spreadsheet called "Zage" corresponding to the z-score of age.

We can now run all three of these commands at once by highlighting them in the syntax window and clicking the run button.

Interpreting the Output

In this experiment (data available on the website under the name "Reactance.sav"), male and female cigarette smokers viewed a cigarette advertisement that either did or did not contain the Surgeon General's warning (SGW). As you can see, about half (53%) of the participants saw the version with no warning, and 28% of the participants were men.

Condition

		Frequency	Percent	Valid Percent	Cumulative Percent
Valid	No SGW	53	52.0	52.0	52.0
	SGW	49	48.0	48.0	100.0
	Total	102	100.0	100.0	

Sex

		Frequency	Percent	Valid Percent	Cumulative Percent
Valid	Male	28	27.5	27.5	27.5
	Female	74	72.5	72.5	100.0
	Total	102	100.0	100.0	

As for our continuous variable, notice the hearty statistics table that results from the syntax "/STATISTICS=ALL":

Age

N	Valid	102
	Missing	0
Mean		32.05
Std. Error of Mean		1.911
Median		27.00
Mode		24
Std. Deviation		19.295
Variance		372.305
Skewness		6.484
Std. Error of Skewness		.239
Kurtosis		54.597
Std. Error of Kurtosis		.474
Range		182
Minimum		16
Maximum		198
Sum		3269
Percentiles	25	23.00
	50	27.00
	75	37.00

Below that, we can see a rather unusual-looking histogram:

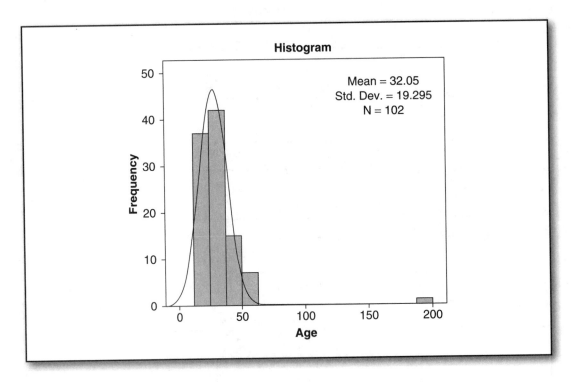

So what's going on here? If you look carefully at the histogram, it looks like there is a single 198-year-old person in the sample. That is rather old, especially given the known health risks of smoking. This outlier is confirmed by examining the range in the statistics table: from 16 to 198. On inspecting the original logbooks, we found that (surprise, surprise) our research assistant made a typo when entering this participant's data; the correct age should be 19. Upon fixing this error, the updated histogram looks much better.

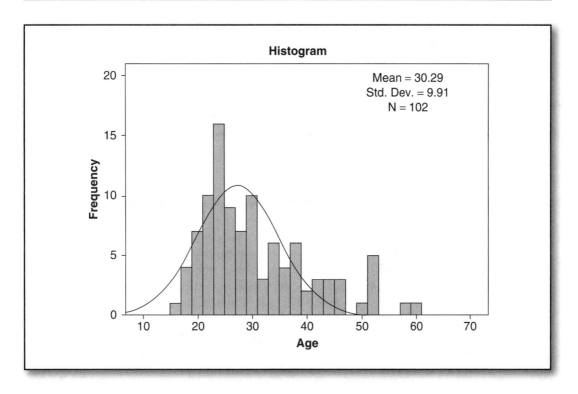

A CLOSER LOOK: EYEBALLING A HYPOTHESIS TEST

Although we will cover formal hypothesis testing in detail for most of the rest of the book, we want to note here that some simple hypothesis tests (e.g., differences between independent means) can be gleaned quite easily from descriptive statistics alone.

The key is that the so-called critical value in hypothesis testing, or the value that your observed test statistic must exceed in order to be called "significant," depends upon only two things: the Type I error rate, called α (*alpha*), and the sample size, N. In the social sciences, alpha is typically 0.05. And it turns out that the critical value is more or less the same for sample sizes larger than about 20. This magical critical value is 2, as in any value greater or less than 2 times the standard error from the mean of a variable will be called "significantly different" from that mean.

From the descriptives, we get a report of the mean of a variable (e.g., the mean of *age* is 30.29) and the standard error around that mean (.981). Here, we can tell that any value smaller than 30.29 − 2*.981 = 28.33, or larger than 30.29 + 2*.981 = 32.25, will be significantly different from our mean of 30.29. So if we had hypothesized that the mean of the sample would be 25, we can tell right away that that hypothesis would be rejected.

If you have a very small sample (e.g., $N = 6$), or want to be super-conservative, a critical value of 2.5 should do the trick.

A CLOSER LOOK: ASSESSING FOR NORMALITY

As we mentioned earlier, one of the key assumptions of almost all of the statistics that researchers use is that their dependent measures are normally distributed. The histogram provides a nice visual way to tell if your data are normal. Another way to check for normality is with a "probability-probability" plot, usually denoted as a "P-P" plot. Instead of plotting the frequency at each value of the variable as in the histogram, the P-P plot shows the expected *cumulative* probability at each value of the variable against the expected cumulative probability of a comparison distribution. If your data are perfectly normally distributed, then the P-P plot will be a straight, 45-degree line. If your data deviate from normal, the plot will fluctuate around the line. By convention, a straight line is displayed on the P-P plot to make these fluctuations more obvious. For example, if the distribution of your variable has fat tails and is more flat in the middle than a normal distribution (called *platykurtic*), then the 10th percentile of your data will correspond to a lower value than the 10th percentile of the normal distribution. Thus, the points on the plot will be below the straight line.

To generate a P-P plot in SPSS, click on **Analyze → Descriptive Statistics** and choose the **P-P Plots** function. It will bring up a window where you can select your continuous dependent variable (e.g., *age*) and plot it against any one of a number of distributions. The default is "Normal."

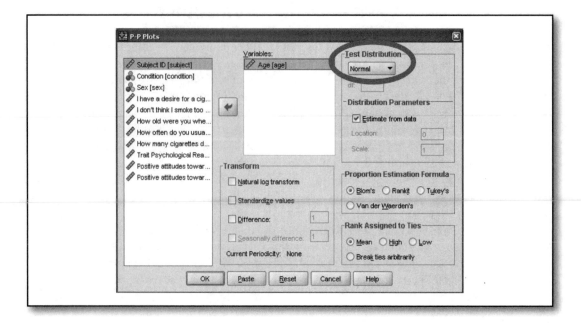

The P-P plot itself is a little tricky to read. SPSS plots the observed distribution on the *x*-axis, and the plot expected under the normal distribution (or whichever distribution you chose) on the *y*-axis. When the data points (i.e., the open circles) are *above* the straight line, it means that there are *fewer* than expected observations by that percentile, and vice versa. So, in the distribution of age, we can tell that the tails are too thin because the points are above the line at the ends. Likewise, the middle is too tall because the points are below the line there.

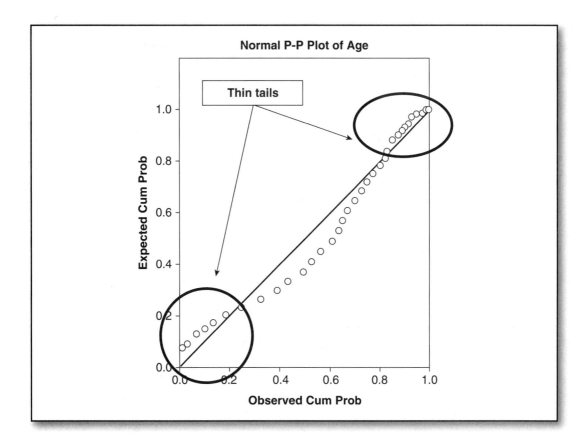

The good people at SPSS must agree with us that the observed-by-expected version of the P-P plot is confusing, so they did us the favor of providing a "detrended" version that follows in the output. In this version, the *x*-axis is the same as above (observed cumulative probability), but the *y*-axis has been redrawn to represent the deviation from normality at each percentile. Thus, positive values mean too many observations at that point, and negative values mean too few. It is more clear from the detrended plot that our distribution has thin tails and a fat middle (hey, just like my cats!).

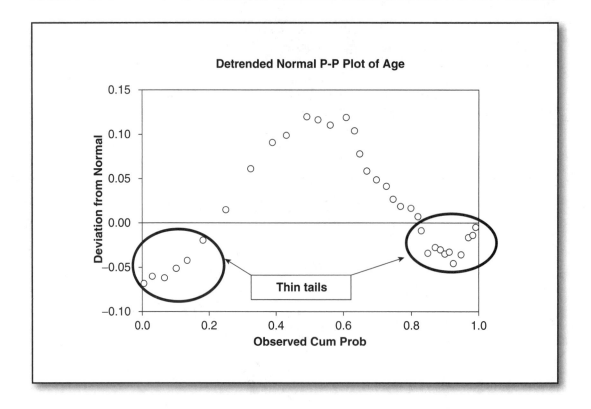

So far, we have covered only visual ways of testing for normality. There are also a handful of more formal ways to check this assumption. The parameters *skewness* and *kurtosis* provide quantitative measures of the shape of a distribution. Positive skew values mean the distribution has a long tail to the right; negative skew values mean the distribution has a long tail to the left. Positive values of kurtosis mean the distribution has a high peak (*leptokurtic*), and negative values of kurtosis mean the distribution has a relatively flat peak above (*platykurtic*).

SPSS provides the skewness and kurtosis values, along with their standard errors, as part of the output from the **Frequencies** function.

Statistics

Age

N	Valid	102
	Missing	0
Mean		30.29
Std. Error of Mean		.981
Median		27.00
Mode		24
Std. Deviation		9.910
Variance		98.210
Skewness		.957
Std. Error of Skewness		.239
Kurtosis		.272
Std. Error of Kurtosis		.474
Range		43
Minimum		16
Maximum		59
Sum		3090
Percentiles	25	23.00
	50	27.00
	75	36.25

A perfectly normal distribution has a skewness of 0 and a kurtosis of 0. So, using what we learned in this chapter about eyeballing a hypothesis test, you can conclude that your distribution is not significantly different from normal if the skewness and kurtosis are within about twice their respective standard errors from zero. In this case, the skewness is probably significantly positively different from normal (because 0.96 is more than 2*0.24 away from 0), but the kurtosis is not (because 0.27 is within 2*0.47 from 0).

KEYWORDS

descriptive statistics	frequencies	kurtosis
categorical variable	normal distribution	
continuous variable	skewness	

The Chi-Squared Test for Contingency Tables

Introduction to the Chi-Squared Test

In the chapter on descriptive statistics, we drew a distinction between categorical and continuous variables. Most of the inferential statistics we discuss in this book assume that your outcome variable is continuous. However, sometimes we have outcomes that fall into categories (e.g., was someone on trial for a crime convicted or not? Or did a participant choose to open door number one, two, or three?). In these cases, and when our predictor variable is also categorical, the chi-squared test is appropriate.

The raw data typically analyzed using the chi-squared test are *counts* of the same outcome in each of two or more conditions. For example, if you wanted to know whether gender affected traffic court convictions, you could tally up the number of men who were and weren't convicted on a given day, then separately tally up the number of women who were and weren't convicted on that same day. Those four counts would then be entered into a chi-squared analysis, and it would tell you whether the proportion of men who were convicted that day was different from the proportion of women who were convicted.

The chi-squared test can also be used to answer questions about proportions within a single variable. In other words, the test can be used to tell you whether the percentage of cases in each category differs from some hypothesized distribution. Suppose that a court claims that it convicts 90% of people who come up with a traffic violation. If you tallied the number of people who were convicted or not for a given period, the chi-squared test could tell you whether the proportion of people convicted in that period was significantly different from 90%.

We mentioned above that most inferential tests described in this book assume that your dependent measure is continuous. These tests make several more important assumptions, and we'll get to those later on. One of the nice features of the chi-squared test is that it doesn't make many assumptions about your data. For this reason, the chi-squared test is sometimes called a "nonparametric" test, including in SPSS. However, this is not literally true. The chi-squared test is computed by coming up with an "expected" count for each cell and comparing it to the actual, "observed" value count for each cell according to the following equation:

$$\chi^2 = \sum_{cells} \frac{(O - E)^2}{E}.$$

What this equation says is that, for each cell, the difference between the observed count and the expected count is squared, then that number is divided by the expected count. These values are added up across all the cells; then the total is compared to the chi-squared distribution with $(r-1)*(c-1)$ degrees of freedom, where r is the number of rows and c is the number of columns in the contingency table. So this test does make the assumption that the summed value across all cells of the above equation is chi-square distributed.

Computing the Chi-Squared Test in SPSS

Even though it is an inferential statistic, chi-squared can be found in SPSS by clicking on **Analyze → Descriptive Statistics → Crosstabs**. This crosstabs function will generate a table of tallies (i.e., frequencies) of cases in your data set that fall into each of the cells defined by the rows and columns you specify. Using the same data set from Chapter 2 (now called "Reactance.sav" on the website), we might want to know whether smokers had high or low desire for a cigarette (*desire*: 0 = Low, 1 = High) following exposure to a cigarette advertisement that either had or did not have a Surgeon General's Warning condition (*condition:* 0 = No warning label, 1 = Warning label). We will arbitrarily display *condition* as columns and the *desire* as rows, but this choice does not affect the actual statistics—it just changes how the data are displayed.

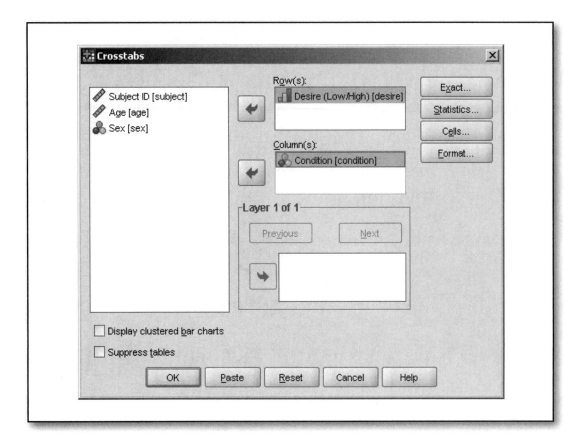

This setup will merely generate the tallies in each cell. These counts make up the raw data on which the chi-squared statistic is computed. In order to actually get SPSS to compute the test, you need to click on the **Statistics** button, then check "Chi-square."

We know that SPSS can get the observed value in each cell based on the data. You can also get SPSS to tell you what the expected values are (in the **Crosstabs** box, click the **Cells** button; then check "Expected," and "Observed" will be checked by default).

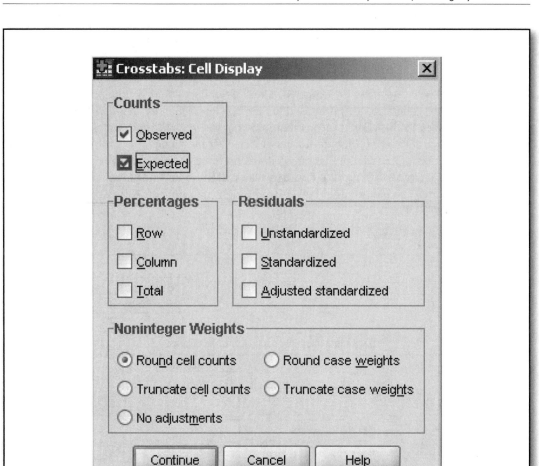

With all of these options selected, the syntax to generate a chi-squared test based on a contingency table is as follows:

```
CROSSTABS
/TABLES=desire BY condition
/FORMAT=AVALUE TABLES
/STATISTICS=CHISQ
```

```
/CELLS=COUNT EXPECTED
/COUNT ROUND CELL.
```

Where does it get the expected values? To understand this, it helps to recall that the null hypothesis of this test is that there is *no systematic relationship between the variables*. In this case, it means that knowing to which group someone was randomly assigned tells us nothing about his or her desire for a cigarette. Instead of using the condition as a predictor (which contains no information under the null hypothesis), the expected distribution of desire in each condition depends instead on the *base rates* of desire. The base rates are given in the right margin of the crosstab in the column titled "Total":

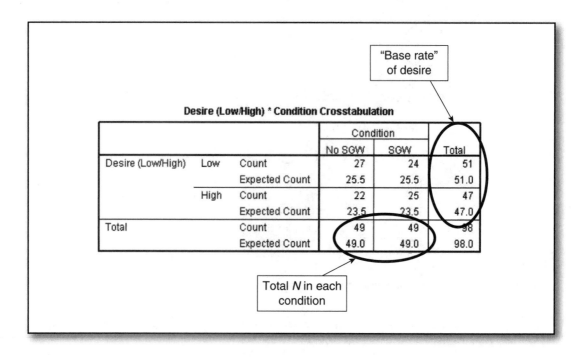

Here, summing across both conditions, a little more than half of the subjects (51/98, or 52%) have low desire, and a little less than half (47/98, or 48%) have high desire. So if the null hypothesis is correct and the two conditions do not differ on desire, then a little more than half (52%) of all the subjects in the "No SGW" condition should have low desire and the rest should have high desire. Similarly, 52% of all the subjects in the "SGW" condition should have low desire and the rest should have high desire. Because we know that there are 49 subjects in each condition (given in the bottom margin of Figure 3.4), we can compute the expected value in each of the four cells. For example, for the "No SGW" condition, 52% of the total should be in the low desire condition. The expected value in that cell is 52% of 49, or 25.5.

Once we have the observed and expected counts in each of the four cells, we can compute a chi-squared value based on the equation shown on the previous page. SPSS computes this value for you and reports it in the table labeled "Chi-Square Tests" as the Pearson Chi-Square Value. Furthermore, SPSS also tests this value against the chi-squared distribution with $(r - 1)*(c - 1)$ degrees of freedom, and reports the p value of that test under "Asymp. Sig. (2-sided)":

Chi-Square Tests

	Value	df	Asymp. Sig. (2-sided)	Exact Sig. (2-sided)	Exact Sig. (1-sided)
Pearson Chi-Square	.368[a]	1	.544		
Continuity Correction[b]	.164	1	.686		
Likelihood Ratio	.368	1	.544		
Fisher's Exact Test				.686	.343
Linear-by-Linear Association	.364	1	.546		
N of Valid Cases	98				

a. 0 cells (.0%) have expected count less than 5. The minimum expected count is 23.50.

b. Computed only for a 2x2 table

A CLOSER LOOK: FISHER'S EXACT TEST

As we noted earlier, Pearson's chi-squared test isn't truly nonparametric because it assumes data are distributed according to the chi-squared distribution, which is governed by one parameter—the degree of freedom. There is another test that can be computed on a contingency table that *is* truly nonparametric called "Fisher's Exact Test." This test is computed by listing all of the possible 2×2 tables given the observed base rates (also known as "marginals"). For example, in our data, there were 49 people in the "No SGW" group, so their distribution into low/high desire groups, respectively, could have been 0/49, 1/48, 2/47, and so on. Fisher's Exact Test assesses *how extreme* the observed distribution was (27/22 for "No SGW"; 24/25 for "SGW") compared to all other possible breakdowns. This test is also reported in the "Chi-Square Tests" box shown in Figure 3.5.

You may notice that Fisher's Exact Test reports both one- and two-tailed p values. As with the t-tests we will discuss later, the difference between these tests corresponds to the difference between asking, "Is my distribution *greater than* the null would predict?" and "Is my distribution *different from* what the null would predict (either greater or lesser)?" In the case of contingency tables, we might predict before even running the experiment that the distribution of cravings in the SGW group would be *higher* than the base rate, in which case we would use the one-tailed test. In other cases, the two-tailed test might be more appropriate. Either way, the two-tailed test is always more conservative (as demonstrated by the fact that the *p* value in the two-tailed test is the larger of the two).

The last thing to note about Fisher's Exact Test is that it will be reported in SPSS only for 2×2 contingency tables. There is no good theoretical reason for this limitation in SPSS—it just happened to be the case that the test was implemented in the program only for a 2×2 table. But there is a good reason for *you* to look at a 2×2—it is the cleanest and most unambiguous way to interpret statistics based on a contingency table. Sometimes, this might mean recoding a variable that has many levels into a new variable that has only two levels, or excluding all of the levels except for two.

For example, suppose we wanted to examine the relationship between age (divided into four quartiles) and desire for a cigarette. We could compute a crosstabulation between these two variables:

Desire (Low/High) * Age (quartiles) Crosstabulation

			Age (quartiles)				Total
			Q1	Q2	Q3	Q4	
Desire (Low/High)	Low	Count	16	6	12	17	51
		Expected Count	14.1	12.0	12.5	12.5	51.0
	High	Count	11	17	12	7	47
		Expected Count	12.9	11.0	11.5	11.5	47.0
Total		Count	27	23	24	24	98
		Expected Count	27.0	23.0	24.0	24.0	98.0

and then compute the chi-squared test on that table:

Chi-Square Tests

	Value	df	Asymp. Sig. (2-sided)
Pearson Chi-Square	10.207[a]	3	.017
Likelihood Ratio	10.547	3	.014
Linear-by-Linear Association	1.360	1	.244
N of Valid Cases	98		

a. 0 cells (.0%) have expected count less than 5. The minimum expected count is 11.03.

There are a few important things to note about this analysis. First, the significance value of the chi-squared test (Figure 3.7) indicates that there is a significant relationship between age and desire. Second, it is difficult to tell from the crosstabulation which cells are driving that significant effect. Although the deviations from the expected values are larger in some cells than others, the chi-squared test on its own cannot tell us which cells are causing the effect—only that there is a relationship between the variables. Third, the table in Figure 3.7 does not include Fisher's Exact Test because the table is larger than 2×2.

Suppose we wanted to obtain Fisher's Exact Test for this analysis, and we wanted to be able to make a more conclusive statement about how age relates to desire for cigarettes. We could rerun the test by limiting our analysis only to the 2nd and 4th quartiles (using **Select Cases**), which are the cells that show the greatest deviation from the null distribution. The crosstabulation looks like this:

Desire (Low/High) * Age (quartiles) Crosstabulation

			Age (quartiles)		
			Q2	Q4	Total
Desire (Low/High)	Low	Count	6	17	23
		Expected Count	11.3	11.7	23.0
	High	Count	17	7	24
		Expected Count	11.7	12.3	24.0
Total		Count	23	24	47
		Expected Count	23.0	24.0	47.0

And rerunning the chi-squared test yields the following results:

Chi-Square Tests

	Value	df	Asymp. Sig. (2-sided)	Exact Sig. (2-sided)	Exact Sig. (1-sided)
Pearson Chi-Square	9.411[a]	1	.002		
Continuity Correction[b]	7.705	1	.006		
Likelihood Ratio	9.758	1	.002		
Fisher's Exact Test				.003	.002
Linear-by-Linear Association	9.210	1	.002		
N of Valid Cases	47				

a. 0 cells (.0%) have expected count less than 5. The minimum expected count is 11.26.

b. Computed only for a 2x2 table

As is often the case, Fisher's Exact Test and Pearson's chi-squared test both imply the same conclusion. Namely, there is a significant relationship between age and desire and specifically that younger people tend to have more desire and older people tend to have less desire. Retabulating our data into a 2×2 form allowed us to make this more detailed inference.

The Chi-Squared Test for Testing the Distribution of One Categorical Variable

So far, we have described how to use the chi-squared test to examine the relationship between two categorical variables. The same test statistic can also be used to compare the distribution of a single categorical variable to an expected distribution that you specify. Often, this distribution is *uniform,* meaning that each group is expected to have approximately the same number of participants. For example, an experimenter might want to check that her 30 participants were distributed into three even groups, so she would set her expected values for each group to 10. Other times, the test distribution might be nonuniform to match a known population distribution. Suppose we wanted to test whether U.S. presidents are left-handed more often than would be expected by chance. We know that in the U.S. population, approximately 8.5% of individuals are left-handed, and 91.5% are right-handed, so we would generate our expected counts based on that ratio. Out of the 14 most recent presidents for whom handedness is known, 6 were left-handed (where 8.5% of 14 is about 1.2) and 8 were right-handed (and 91.5% of 14 is about 12.8).

The test statistic is computed exactly the same way as before, by squaring the differences between observed and expected, dividing by the expected values, then summing across all cells. In the case of the presidential handedness example:

$$\chi^2 = \sum_{cells} \frac{(O - E)^2}{E} = \frac{(6 - 1.2)^2}{1.2} + \frac{(8 - 12.8)^2}{12.8} = 21$$

And a chi-squared value of 21 with 1 degree of freedom corresponds to a p value well under .001. We can conclude that the proportion of lefty presidents is higher than would be expected if they were drawn randomly from the population of the United States.

Suppose we wanted to examine whether our sample for the reactance experiment was approximately half women and half men. We could compute this test in SPSS by clicking **Analyze → Nonparametric Tests → Chi-square.**

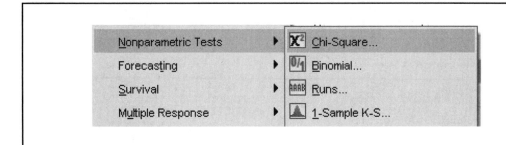

Next, select the variable that we want to test, *Age*. In the "Expected Values" box below the test variable list, select "All categories equal" to test an even distribution (default) or enter the proportion values individually to test a skewed distribution. For example, if we wanted to test whether our sample handedness deviated from the population distribution of 8.5/91.5%, we would enter ".085" then click "add," then ".915" and "add" again. These proportions should be entered in ascending order of the variable level values; in the hypothetical variable called *Handedness*, lefties might be coded as "1" and righties might be coded as "2," so the expected proportion of lefties would come first.

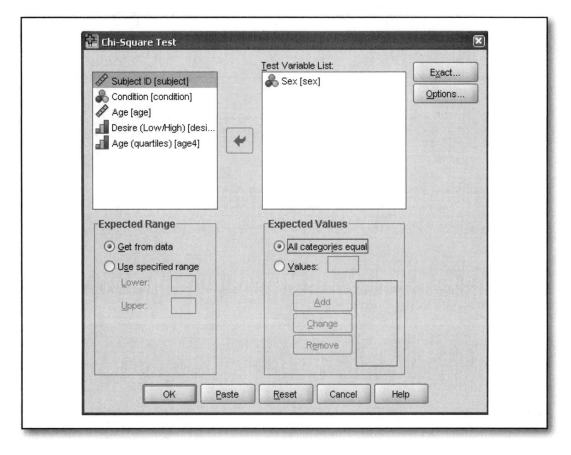

The syntax for this test is

```
NPAR TESTS
/CHISQUARE=sex
/EXPECTED=EQUAL
/MISSING=ANALYSIS.
```

If we wanted to test a different proportion of men to women, we would change the "EXPECTED" value to be a series of proportions ranging from 0 to 1 that together sum to 1. For example, to test whether the ratio of men to women was 40/60, we would write:

```
/EXPECTED = .4 .6
```

Assuming that men were the first group in the *Sex* variable. Hence, the syntax above would produce exactly the same output if "EQUAL" were replaced by "0.5 0.5."

The output of this version of the chi-squared test produces a contingency table with the observed frequencies in the data and the expected frequencies based on the proportions we provided.

Sex

	Observed N	Expected N	Residual
Male	25	49.0	-24.0
Female	73	49.0	24.0
Total	98		

Finally, the chi-squared test based on the table is reported, along with its degree of freedom and associated *p* value.

Test Statistics

	Sex
Chi-Square	23.510[a]
df	1
Asymp. Sig.	.000

KEYWORDS

count variable	marginal means	uniform distribution
crosstabs	exact test	

Correlation

BEHIND THE SCENES: CONCEPTUAL BACKGROUND OF CORRELATION

Correlation has many definitions, and we'll give you a few different ones, but the only one that you really need to know is this: the degree of the *linear* relationship between two variables. One reason people often get confused about correlation is that the equation used to compute it has no intuitive relationship to the conceptual meaning of "linear relationship between two variables." So we will begin this chapter by providing (or at least attempting to provide) an intuitive explanation of how the formula for a *correlation coefficient* relates to the concept of a correlation.

To do this, it is helpful to first understand *covariance*. In class or in your textbook, you may have learned that the covariance between two variables, *X* and *Y*, is defined as

$$COV(X,Y) = E(XY) - E(X)E(Y),$$

where

$$E(XY) = \sum_i \sum_i x_i y_i P(X = x_i, Y = y_i),$$

$$E(X) = \sum_i x_i P(X = x_i), \text{ and}$$

$$E(Y) = \sum_i y_i P(Y = y_i).$$

In English, this says that the covariance between X and Y is the difference between the expected value of their products and the product of their expected values. In order to simplify this, suppose for now that both X and Y are centered around 0 (i.e., we have subtracted the mean from each observation). Furthermore, suppose that X and Y are distributed symmetrically around the (zero) mean.

Now, look again at the equations for $E(X)$ and $E(Y)$. These quantities are the sum of the products of each value with its probability. Under the assumptions that we made (observations are centered symmetrically around the zero mean), each positive value in the distribution is mirrored by a negative value, and each has the same probability of appearing in a sample. For example, in a symmetric distribution around zero, if the probability that $X = 5$ is 0.3, then the probability that $X = -5$ is also 0.3. When this is true, then the sum of all such products—that is, the sum of $x_i^* P(X = x_i)$ for all i—will be 0. This is a long-winded way of saying that the expected value for a distribution symmetrically distributed around zero is zero. For our purposes, $E(X) = E(Y) = 0$.

Now, given these assumptions, the covariance of X and Y reduces to just

$$COV(X, Y) = E(XY) = \sum_i \sum_i x_i y_i P(X = x_i, Y = y_i).$$

So what is $E(XY)$? To help understand this, let's make one further assumption—that the probability of any x,y pair is equal for all pairs (i.e., uniform probability distribution). Thus, $P(X = x_i, Y = y_i) = 1/n$ for each value of i. So now, the equation for covariance reduces even further:

$$COV(X, Y) = E(XY) = \sum_i \sum_i x_i y_i * \frac{1}{n} = \frac{\sum_i \sum_i x_i y_i}{n}.$$

In English, this equation says that the covariance of X and Y is the average product of the x,y pairs (when X and Y are uniformly distributed around 0). The following chart will help illustrate the implications of this formula.

As you can see in the chart, any given observation x_i, y_i can fall into one of four quadrants. The covariance is the average product of all the observations (i.e., average of all $x_i{}^*y_i$). Thus, if most of the values fall into the top-right and the bottom-left quadrants, the average $x_i{}^*y_i$ will be strongly positive. Indeed, the strongest possible covariance between two variables would be a straight line going from the bottom left to the top right—the canonical correlation of +1. Conversely, the covariance would be negative if most of the observations fall in the top-left and bottom-right quadrants.

All covariances can be described as some mixture of positive and negative $x_i{}^*y_i$ products. For example, imagine a situation in which X and Y have no systematic relationship. In this case, data points would be scattered approximately equally throughout the four quadrants, resulting in an average product of about 0.

As a thought experiment, use the average-product method described here to figure out what the covariance would be between X and Y if their relationship were a perfectly symmetrical U-shape starting in the top-left quadrant, dipping through the bottom two quadrants, and ending in the top-right quadrant? Even though there does appear to be a systematic relationship between X and Y (described by the "U"), the covariance is 0 because there are equal numbers of data points in the positive and negative product quadrants.

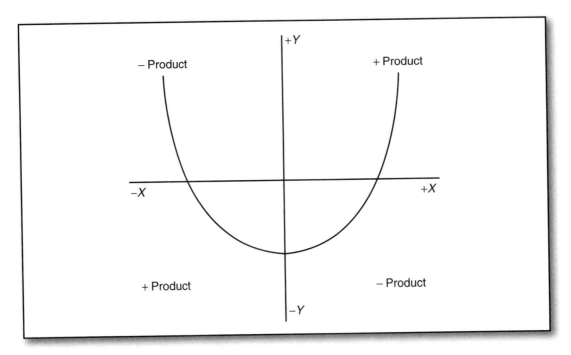

This thought experiment illustrates a critical point about covariances, which is that they describe the degree of *linear* relationship between two variables. Many other relationships (e.g., the "U"-shaped quadratic) might give the same degree of prediction accuracy but still yield a zero covariance. For example, in Figure 4.2, even though we can know with certainty which value *Y* will take for any given value of *X*, the covariance between the two is still zero.

Covariance Versus Correlation

So far we've been talking about covariances, but what about correlations? The two concepts are intimately linked. We could go into far more detail on this topic, but we'll leave that for another longer and more boring book. For now, what you need to know is that a *correlation coefficient is a standardized covariance*. In other words, a correlation is a covariance between two variables that have been converted into *z*-scores. As you learned in Chapter 2, you can standardize a centered variable by dividing it by its standard deviation. Similarly, a covariance can be "standardized" by dividing by the product of the standard deviations:

$$CORR(X, Y) = \frac{COV(X, Y)}{SD(X) * SD(Y)}.$$

We can take away a few lessons from this. First, as with raw variables, the process of standardization discards any sense of scale. For example, although the covariance between dollars of income and days of education might be in the tens of thousands, their correlation will always be between −1 and 1. In fact, all correlations range from −1 to 1. Second, because standard deviations are always positive numbers, the *numerical sign* of a correlation will always be equivalent to the sign of the covariance.

Computing Correlation (and Covariance) in SPSS

Now that you have some conceptual idea of what a correlation is, you might want to know how to compute one in your sample using SPSS. To practice this, open the data set called "Reactance.sav" (found on the website) and click on **Analyze → Correlate → Bivariate**. Although correlations are always computed between exactly two variables (hence the *bi*variate), you may notice that you can enter more than two variables for analysis in the "Variables" list. SPSS will compute the bivariate correlation between every possible pair of the variables that you enter here. So if you put in only two variables, you'll get one correlation. But if you put in three variables, you'll get three correlations; four variables yields six correlations, and so on. For now, let's examine the correlations between current desire for a cigarette (*desire_now*), age at smoking onset (*smkage*), and frequency of smoking (*smkoft*).

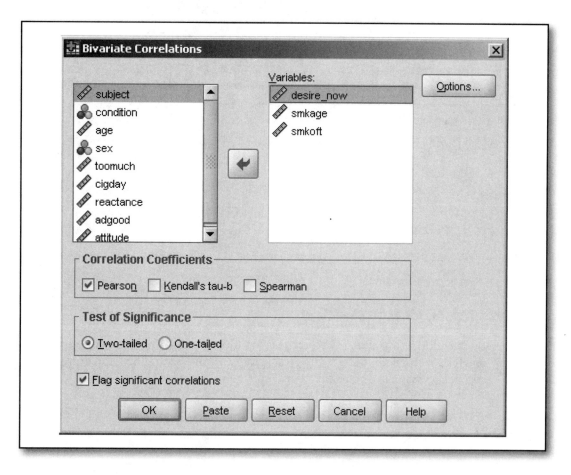

Running this function as is will produce the correlation between each pair of variables and their associated sample sizes and *p* values. However, sometimes we might want to know the covariances as well. To get these, click on "Options" and check the "Cross-product deviations and covariances" option.

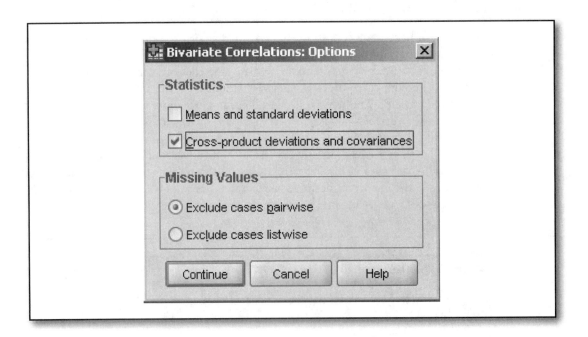

The final syntax for this command is

```
CORRELATIONS

/VARIABLES=desire_now smkage smkoft

/PRINT=TWOTAIL NOSIG

/STATISTICS XPROD

/MISSING=PAIRWISE.
```

Interpreting the Correlation Output

By default, SPSS will give us the correlation coefficient (called the "Pearson Correlation") and its associated sample size and *p* value for each pair of variables. And as we further specified, SPSS also outputs the covariances.

Correlations

		I have a desire for a cigarette right now.	How old were you when you first smoked? (in years)	How often do you usually smoke tobacco?
I have a desire for a cigarette right now.	Pearson Correlation	1	-.136	.414**
	Sig. (2-tailed)		.182	.000
	Sum of Squares and Cross-products	147.388	-50.857	37.531
	Covariance	1.519	-.524	.387
	N	98	98	98
How old were you when you first smoked? (in years)	Pearson Correlation	-.136	1	-.153
	Sig. (2-tailed)	.182		.125
	Sum of Squares and Cross-products	-50.857	974.667	-36.667
	Covariance	-.524	9.650	-.363
	N	98	102	102
How often do you usually smoke tobacco?	Pearson Correlation	.414**	-.153	1
	Sig. (2-tailed)	.000	.125	
	Sum of Squares and Cross-products	37.531	-36.667	58.873
	Covariance	.387	-.363	.583
	N	98	102	102

**. Correlation is significant at the 0.01 level (2-tailed).

The first statistic to be listed for each pair is the correlation (circled), and its significance value is directly beneath it (boxed). Note that there is a significant positive correlation between current desire for a cigarette and frequency of smoking (.414) and that this correlation is "starred" because its significance value is less than .001. Note also that the correlations are all between −1 and 1, and the correlations along the diagonal of the 3 × 3 graph—representing the correlation of each variable with itself—are all "1"s. Finally, notice that the sample sizes vary slightly across the correlations. This is because of the line from our syntax, "/MISSING=PAIRWISE," indicating to exclude subjects with missing data *only from the pair of variables being computed,* and not from missing data anywhere in the list. By examining the different *N*s, we see that there were 98 subjects who completed the *desire_now* variable, and 102 who completed the others. Thus, the correlations involving *desire_now* contain only 98 observations, but the correlations between the other two contain 102. In contrast, substituting the command "/MISSING=LISTWISE" into the syntax would instruct SPSS to exclude subjects who had any missing data from *any of the variables in the list,* rather than on a pair-by-pair basis. Thus, there would be *N* = 98 for all three correlations.

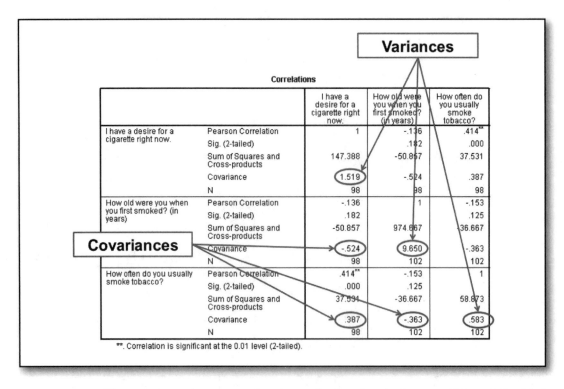

Correlations

		I have a desire for a cigarette right now.	How old were you when you first smoked? (in years)	How often do you usually smoke tobacco?
I have a desire for a cigarette right now.	Pearson Correlation	1	-.136	.414**
	Sig. (2-tailed)		.182	.000
	Sum of Squares and Cross-products	147.388	-50.857	37.531
	Covariance	1.519	-.524	.387
	N	98	98	98
How old were you when you first smoked? (in years)	Pearson Correlation	-.136	1	-.153
	Sig. (2-tailed)	.182		.125
	Sum of Squares and Cross-products	-50.857	974.667	36.667
	Covariance	-.524	9.650	-.363
	N	98	102	102
How often do you usually smoke tobacco?	Pearson Correlation	.414**	-.153	1
	Sig. (2-tailed)	.000	.125	
	Sum of Squares and Cross-products	37.531	-36.667	58.873
	Covariance	.387	-.363	.583
	N	98	102	102

**. Correlation is significant at the 0.01 level (2-tailed).

The covariances between each pair are also listed at the bottom. Although the label says "covariance," the three values along the diagonal represent the covariance of each variable with itself, which is more commonly known as the variance. Notice that the scale of the variances/covariances depends on the units of measurement. For example, smoking onset age is measured in years with a range of 7 to 26 and a variance of 9.77, and smoking desire is measured on a 1-to-5 Likert scale and thus has a variance of 1.52. The fact that the variance of smoking onset age is relatively large is reflected in the covariance of the two variables (−.52) but not in the correlation (−.14), which is independent of the units. Indeed, the largest correlation in this table is between desire and smoking frequency (.41), and it corresponds to the smallest absolute covariance (.39)!

A CLOSER LOOK: PARTIAL CORRELATIONS

A common form of the correlation is the *partial correlation,* which represents the linear relationship between two variables while controlling for one or more other variables. Partial correlations are closely linked to partial regression coefficients, which we will cover in more detail in the chapter on regression. For now, you can think of partial correlation coefficients as the linear relationship between two variables that is not accounted for by a third.

The partial correlation can be obtained from SPSS by clicking **Analyze** → **Correlate** → **Partial**. As with standard correlation, put the two or more variables to be correlated in the "Variable" list, and put the third (and fourth, etc.) variable to control for in the "Controlling for" box. For example, suppose we wanted to know whether the significant positive correlation between desire and smoking frequency that we observed earlier remained significant when controlling for smoking onset age.

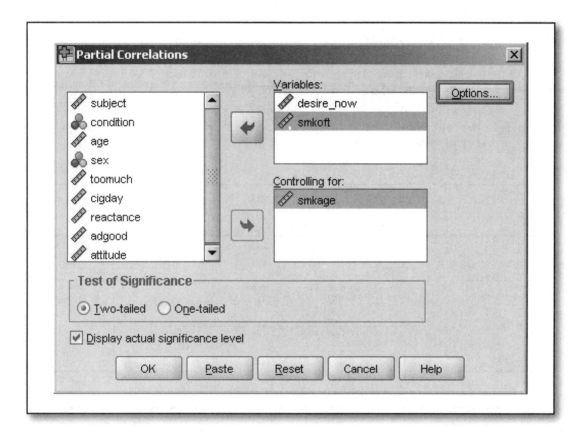

The syntax for this function is similar to the syntax for correlation except the command name is "PARTIAL CORR" instead of "CORRELATIONS," and the "/VARIABLES" tag has an additional command, "BY," at the end. Any variables listed after the "BY" will be (simultaneously) controlled for in the reported correlations. For example, if your "/VARIABLES" line was "var_A var_B BY var_C var_D var_E," then SPSS would report one correlation between variables A and B, controlling for variables C, D, and E all at once. Finally, notice that the "/MISSING" tag will default to "LISTWISE" for partial correlations (instead of "PAIRWISE") because valid data are required from each participant in all three variables (i.e., the two correlated variables and the third control variable).

```
PARTIAL CORR

/VARIABLES=desire_now smkoft BY smkage

/SIGNIFICANCE=TWOTAIL

/MISSING=LISTWISE.
```

The output from the partial correlation is similar to the output from the standard correlation. SPSS reports the partial correlation coefficient (.40) and its associated p value ($< .001$). Instead of reporting the sample size, N, here, SPSS reports the degrees of freedom (df), which is typically equal to ($N - 1$)—(# predictors + # control variables). In this case, $N = 98$, and there is 1 predictor (which there always will be in correlation) and 1 control variable, so $df = 98 - 1 - 2 = 95$. In case you were curious, the df for standard correlation will always be $N - 2$ ($N - 1 - 1$).

Correlations

Control Variables			I have a desire for a cigarette right now.	How often do you usually smoke tobacco?
How old were you when you first smoked? (in years)	I have a desire for a cigarette right now.	Correlation	1.000	.400
		Significance (2-tailed)	.	.000
		df	0	95
	How often do you usually smoke tobacco?	Correlation	.400	1.000
		Significance (2-tailed)	.000	.
		df	95	0

Based on this analysis, we can conclude that the positive correlation between current desire for a cigarette and frequency of smoking is still significant when controlling for smoking onset age.

Visualizing Correlations

There is no more compelling way to visualize a significant correlation than a scatterplot. Not only can a scatterplot depict a pleasing linear association between two variables, but also, by showing the raw data values, a scatterplot can prove to your readers that your correlation is not driven by an outlier.

To generate one, click on **Graphs** → **Legacy Dialogs** → **Scatter/Dot**.

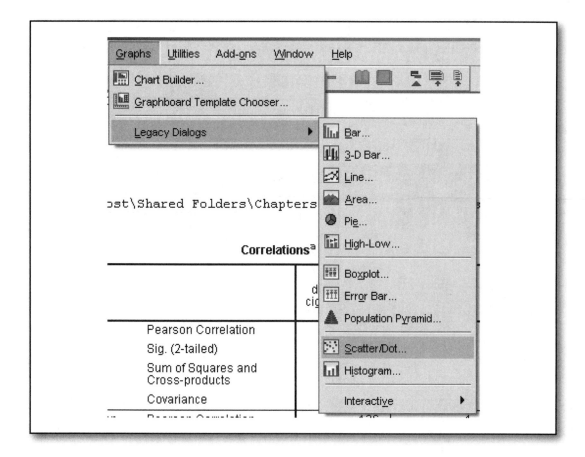

This will bring up another dialogue box with a few more options. Click on "Simple Scatter."

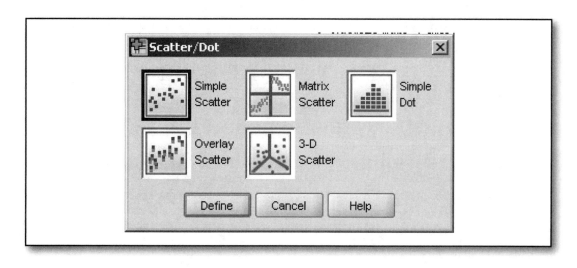

Don't be intimidated by the "Simple Scatterplot" box, which appears far from simple. In practice, you won't need most of these options. The first ones that you will need are the "Y Axis" and "X Axis" fields. Put your two main correlated variables there, such as smoking frequency (*smkoft*) in the "X Axis" and cravings (*desire_now*) in the "Y Axis" field.

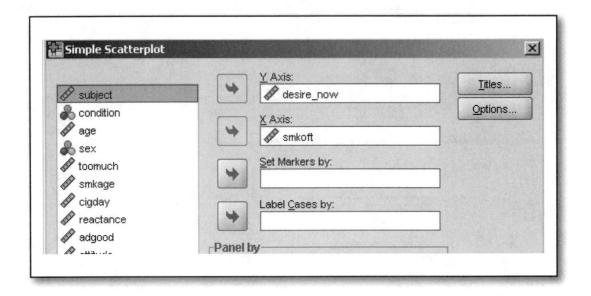

The syntax for this maneuver is simple, and can be written in only one line:

```
GRAPH /SCATTERPLOT(BIVAR) = smkoft WITH desire_now .
```

For most continuous variables, this command will be fine. However, because of the restricted number of levels for both of these variables (five for *desire_now* and only three for *smkoft*), the scatterplot looks a little odd because of the overlapping observations:

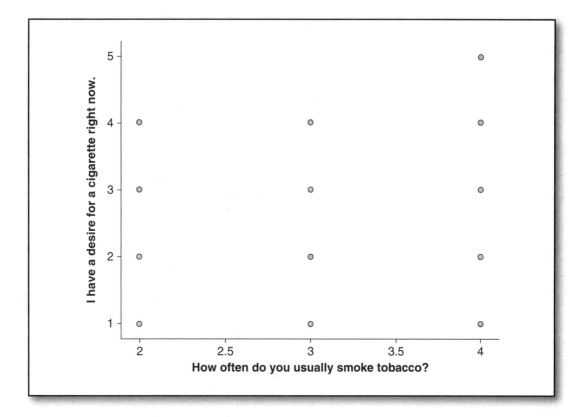

There are several options for how to proceed in this case. The first is to use the "bin intensity" function to show that there are more observations in some of the points and fewer in others. **Double-click on the graph** in the output window to bring up the Chart Editor; then select the "bin element" button (circled).

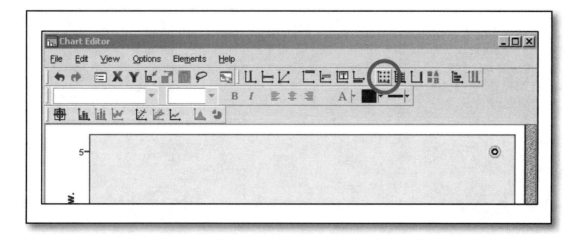

This will bring up the useful Properties window, from where you can select to have the scatter dots vary either by size or by color intensity to depict frequency.

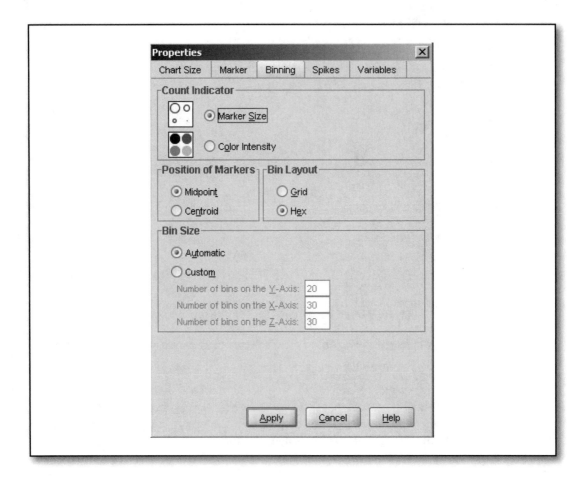

If you choose "Marker Size," then larger dots will indicate that there are more observations in that location and smaller dots indicate fewer observations. SPSS also inserts a "Scale" legend to help readers interpret the meaning of the various marker sizes.

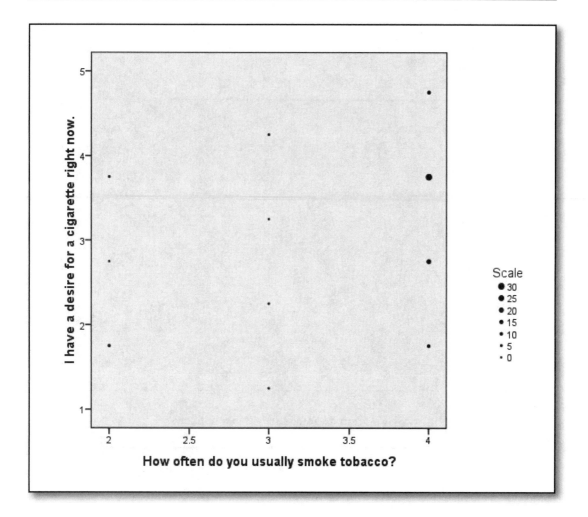

The second option is to "jitter" the observations on the chart so that they no longer overlap. To do this, we must use the "interactive" chart feature, which can be accessed only through syntax:

```
IGRAPH /X1 = smkoft /Y = desire_now /
        SCATTER COINCIDENT = JITTER .
```

This is similar to plotting using the "GRAPH" command, but instead we specify which variable goes on the x-axis and which on the y-axis by using the commands "/X1" and "Y." The "/SCATTER COINCIDENT = JITTER" command tells SPSS to jitter the observations when they overlap (i.e., are "coincident" with one another). Run this command to see the jittered scatterplot.

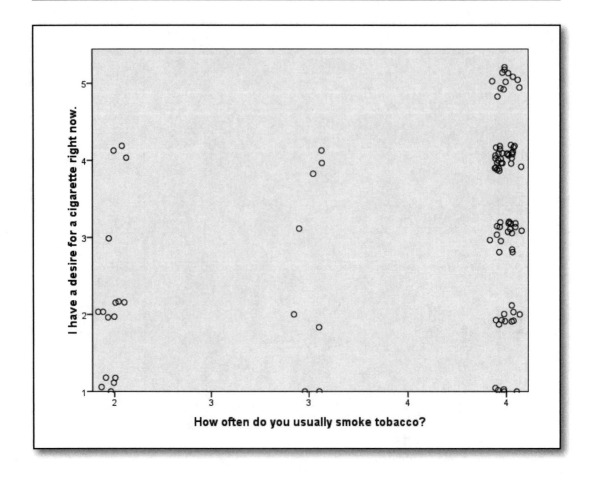

As you can see, it is far easier to view the positive correlation with the jittered observations.

Finally, inserting a linear fit line is an excellent way to emphasize the link between the (jittered) raw data shown in the graph and the correlation coefficient that we estimated previously. Once again, **double-click on the graph** in the output window to bring up the Chart Editor; then click on the "add fit line at total" button (circled).

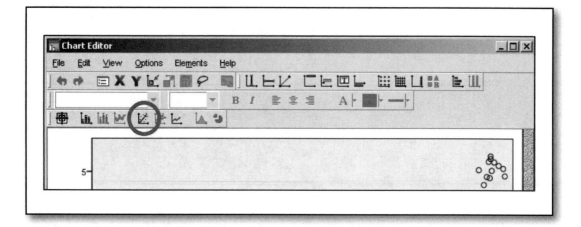

Selecting this option will insert a fit line into your graph and will bring up the "Properties" window that allows you to make changes to the graph and the fit line.

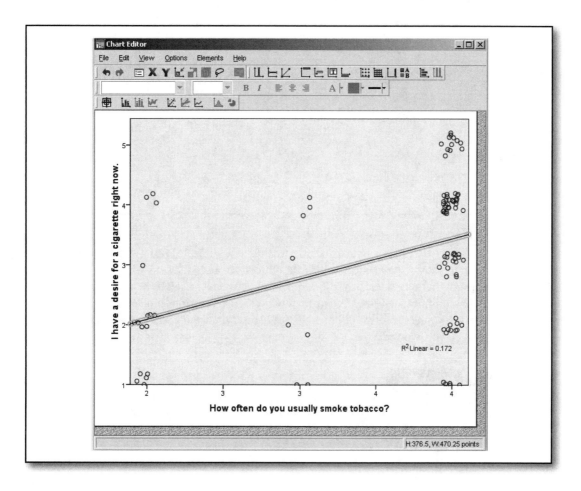

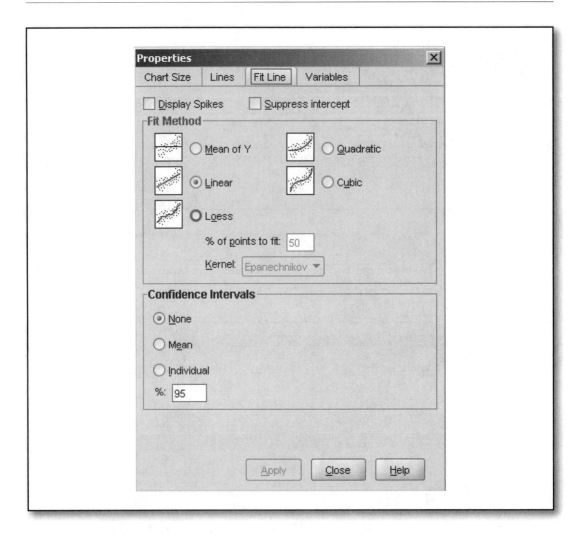

Notice that the fit line also comes with a new statistic, "R^2 Linear." This R-squared value is most often associated with regression analysis (see Chapter 11), and its presence here underscores the similarity between correlation and regression. We discuss this similarity further in the chapter on regression, but for now, simply note that the value given for R-squared, 0.172, is literally the square of the correlation between the two variables, 0.414^2.

KEYWORDS

linear correlation   covariance   scatterplot

correlation coefficient   partial correlation

5

One- and Two-Sample *t*-Tests

Conceptual Background of the *t*-Test

Earlier, we discussed the distinction between categorical and continuous variables, and we showed how chi-squared tests and correlation can be used to examine the relationship between two categorical and continuous variables, respectively. But what if you have one continuous and one categorical variable? The next several chapters—on *t*-tests and ANOVA—deal with this case.

The *t*-test is a simple and elegant way to examine the difference between two groups, defined by a categorical independent variable, on a continuous independent variable. In its most basic, one-sample form, the *t*-test simply asks whether the mean of a dependent variable for a single group is different from some value (usually zero).

With slight modification, the two-sample version of the *t*-test asks whether the *difference* between the means of two groups is different from zero (i.e., whether the group means are equal). The two-sample version can be further modified to look at differences between two groups that are related to each other (e.g., couples in a relationship or the same individual across two different conditions).

BEHIND THE SCENES: THE *T*-RATIO

How does a *t*-test "work"? In its essence, a *t*-test is a signal-to-noise ratio. The *t* value is a single number that captures the ratio of the "signal," typically a mean or difference between means, relative to the "noise," or some measure of the standard error. Hence, the most general equation for testing whether the "signal," *M*, is greater than zero, is

$$t = \frac{signal}{noise} = \frac{M}{SE},$$

where *M* can be a mean, a difference between means, or even a difference between a mean and some hypothesized value, and *SE* is the corresponding standard error. The really amazing part is that, if certain assumptions are met (which we'll discuss later), and for any given sample size, the probability of obtaining an observed *t* value or more is known! In other words, once you compute a *t* value based on your data set, you can simply look it up in the Student's *t* distribution table to find out the associated cumulative probability. As it turns out, a signal-to-noise ratio of about 2:1 (equivalent to a *t* value of 2) is significantly unlikely to occur by chance (at the .05 significance level, two-tailed) for samples of about 25 or more. This is the source of the "quick and dirty" significance test for a mean that we mentioned in the chapter on descriptive statistics.

The fact that the *t*-test yields a measure of signal-to-noise along with a probability value, not to mention that it is quite simple, makes it one of the most basic and commonly used statistics in the social science toolbox. In this chapter, we'll show you how to compute several types of *t*-tests using SPSS, describe how the *t*-test is related to other statistics, discuss some of the assumptions and limitations, and present several ways of graphing the results of a *t*-test.

Computing the One-Sample *t*-Test Using SPSS

We will be using a new data set, called "Motivation.sav" on the website, to practice *t*-tests. These data are measures of *approach motivation* from 132 women and men before and after an induction of approach motivation. The induction is expected to increase levels of approach motivation, but we want to make sure of that.

In order to do this, we used the **Compute** function to create a variable that is the change in approach motivation from before to after the induction (*app_diff*). Our manipulation check will test whether this variable is different from zero. Specifically, because we computed the score as [postinduction − preinduction], we hope that this difference will be positive, indicating that approach motivation following the induction was *greater* than before. To run this one-sample *t*-test, click on **Analyze** → **Compare Means** → **One-Sample T Test**. This brings up the following window.

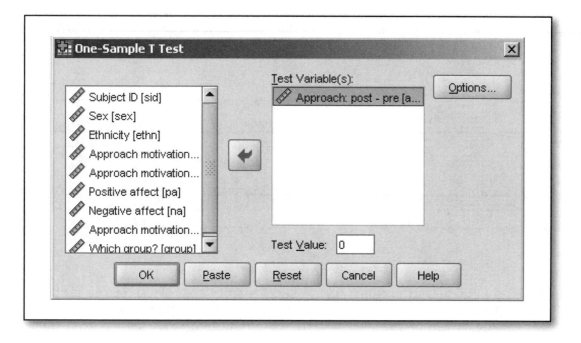

As the name indicates, you need to put only one variable in the "Test Variable(s)" window. If you put more than one, SPSS will perform a separate one-sample *t*-test for each variable. Also, note the "Test Value" box at the bottom. This defaults to "0," but if you wanted to test a different value (e.g., that induction creates an increase of 2 on the 7-point scale), you can specify that value here. The resulting syntax begins with "T-TEST" and contains several tags, but if you are using an alpha level of .05, then it reduces to just one line, where the test variables are listed after the "VARIABLE" tag and the value (defaulting to zero) is listed after the "TESTVAL" tag:

```
T-TEST /VARIABLE=app_diff /TESTVAL=0  .
```

When run, this statement will produce some descriptives:

One-Sample Statistics

	N	Mean	Std. Deviation	Std. Error Mean
Approach: post - pre	132	1.0473	1.28041	.11145

and the actual t value and its associated p value (evaluated on Student's t distribution with $df = N - 1$ degrees of freedom):

One-Sample Test

	Test Value = 0				95% Confidence Interval of the Difference	
	t	df	Sig. (2-tailed)	Mean Difference	Lower	Upper
Approach: post - pre	9.398	131	.000	1.04735	.8269	1.2678

Notice that we didn't really need a fancy statistics program to compute the t value for us. Based on the mean (1.05) and standard error (0.11) given in the descriptives, we can calculate the t value ourselves using the following equation:

$$t = \frac{M}{SE} = \frac{1.047}{0.111} = 9.4.$$

which yields the same result as SPSS (plus or minus some rounding error). Based on the significance value, ".000," which really means "$p < .001$," we can conclude that the change in approach motivation was greater than zero.

Next, we might want to know whether the change was different from +1. We can do this by changing the "/TESTVAL" tag in the syntax:

```
T-TEST /VARIABLE=app_diff /TESTVAL=1 .
```

The resulting output is as follows:

One-Sample Test

	Test Value = 1				95% Confidence Interval of the Difference	
	t	df	Sig. (2-tailed)	Mean Difference	Lower	Upper
Approach: post - pre	.425	131	.672	.04735	-.1731	.2678

Because the significance level is greater than our threshold of .05, we cannot reject the null that the mean change in approach motivation is not different from 1.

Finally, note that the "Mean Difference" listed in the output for this last test is ".0473," even though we learned from the descriptives that the actual mean of *app_diff* is 1.0473. This is because the "signal" that the one-sample *t*-test actually tests is the difference between the mean and the test value. Because the test value is usually zero, this part of the formula typically gets neglected. However, in this case, because we're testing whether the mean is different from a nonzero value, the numerator of the *t*-test equation is "1.0473 − 1," that is, the mean minus the test value. Conveniently, SPSS will always remind us of the value of the numerator of this equation in the "Mean Difference" column.

Computing the Paired-Samples *t*-Test Using SPSS

Another way to check whether the manipulation increased motivation is to run a paired-samples *t*-test on the before- and after-manipulation variables. A paired-samples test is appropriate because both measure approach motivation from the same individuals at two time points (i.e., we have reason to believe that those two variables would be correlated). In SPSS, click **Analyze** → **Compare Means** → **Paired-Samples T Test**. Click the first variable; then hold down the Control key (or Command-Control on a Mac) and select the second variable. Once both variables are highlighted, click the arrow button to move them to the right side of the window.

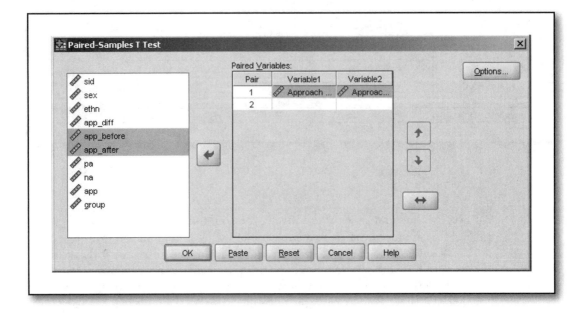

If you click Paste, you will see the syntax function is called "T-TEST," and the pairs are denoted as "V1 WITH V2." Multiple paired-sample tests can be run simultaneously by putting one variable from each pair on either side of the "WITH." If you do this, remember that SPSS will pair the variables by the order they appear before or after the "WITH." For example, "V1 VA WITH V2 VB" will compute t-tests for the pairs [V1-V2] and [VA-VB]. The full syntax to check our induction is the following:

```
T-TEST PAIRS=app_after WITH app_before (PAIRED)

/CRITERIA=CI(.9500)

/MISSING=ANALYSIS.
```

The "CRITERIA" and "MISSING" tags will default to the values shown and are not necessary if you don't want to change those defaults.

As with the one-sample test, SPSS will output some descriptives before the actual test. This includes not only the mean, N, standard deviation, and standard error for each variable (as with the one-sample test) but also the correlation between the two variables. We asked only for the t-test, so why would SPSS also include the correlation? It does this because the correlation is an important part of the calculation of the paired-samples t value—indeed, it represents the main advantage of the paired- over the independent-samples test. Recall that the *t* value is the ratio of the "signal," which in this case is the difference between two variables, to the "noise," which is the standard error of that signal. Part of the calculation of the noise is the variance of the difference between two variables, which is given by the variance sum law

$$VAR(X - Y) = VAR(X) + VAR(Y) - 2 * COV(X, Y).$$

In other words, the variance of the difference of two variables is *reduced* as the covariance between them increases. And, because the variance contributes to the denominator of the *t* value, the *t* value increases as the variance decreases. Thus, all else being equal, as the correlation between two variables increases, the *t* value of the difference between them also increases. Using the paired-samples *t*-test in SPSS allows you to capitalize on this fact when your variables are correlated. Conversely, when two variables are completely uncorrelated [i.e., $COV(X, Y) = 0$], then the paired- and independent-samples *t*-tests are equivalent.

Paired Samples Correlations

		N	Correlation	Sig.
Pair 1	Approach motivation after induction & Approach motivation before induction	132	.356	.000

Because *app_before* and *app_after* are significantly positively correlated, we will gain power in this case by using the paired-samples *t*-test.

Following the descriptives is a table that includes the mean difference (the "signal"), the standard deviation and standard error of that mean (the "noise"), and the 95% confidence interval around it. Based on these things, SPSS calculates the *t* value and its corresponding *p* value. As always, when SPSS gives a significance value of ".000," it really means "$p < .001$." (To find the actual *p* value, double-click on the table to open it in a new window; then double-click on the ".000" to reveal the value in scientific notation. Here, this value is 2.38E-16, indicating that this difference would have occurred by chance 238 times out of a quintillion if there were no real difference among scores in the population).

Paired Samples Test

		Paired Differences							
					95% Confidence Interval of the Difference				
		Mean	Std. Deviation	Std. Error Mean	Lower	Upper	t	df	Sig. (2-tailed)
Pair 1	Approach motivation after induction - Approach motivation before induction	1.04735	1.28041	.11145	.82688	1.26781	9.398	131	.000

Before we go any further, we should highlight one more thing. You may have noticed that the one-sample *t*-test on the difference between two variables and the paired-samples test between the same two variables is *identical*. When examining the difference between two variables (such as pre/post change), the one- and two-samples tests are statistically equivalent. Why is this? There are many ways to think about it, but one intuitive reason is that creating a difference score discards only the *absolute* scores, not the *relative* scores, and the relative scores are all that matter in terms of testing whether two variables are different.

Computing the Independent-Samples *t*-Test Using SPSS

What about when you want to compare a variable between two groups that are *not* related? For instance, suppose you measured approach motivation only once in two groups: one that completed the induction and another that completed a control task. This is an ideal job for the independent-samples *t*-test. The logic of this test is exactly the same as the one- and paired-samples *t*-tests; the only change is in the computation of the standard error.

The change from the other tests in SPSS is even more minor. In the same practice data set we've been using ("Motivation.sav"), you will find that the second-to-last variable contains a single approach motivation score for each of 264 participants (*app*) and that the last variable codes for the group membership of each participant (*group;* 0 = Control; 1 = Induction). To run the independent-samples *t*-test comparing the level of approach motivation between these two groups, click **Analyze → Compare Means → Independent-Samples T Test**. In the window that comes up, put your dependent variable or variables in the "Test Variable(s)" box and the independent variable into the "Grouping Variable" box. SPSS will compare the means of the two groups defined by the grouping variable on each of the dependent variables listed as a test variable. Once you add a grouping variable, you'll see that your independent variable has two question marks next to it.

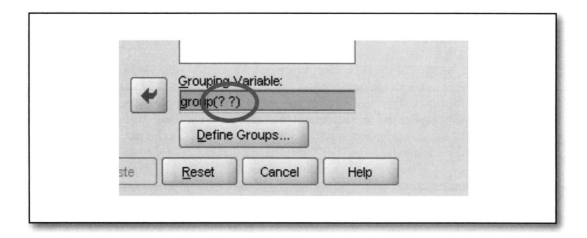

Those marks represent the values in the variable itself that code for the group membership. Click on "Define Groups . . ." and enter the code values that correspond to the two groups; here, we used "0" and "1" for the Control and Induction groups, respectively. SPSS will compute the "signal" part of the *t*-test as the first group minus the second group. Thus, we put the induction group (coded as "1") first and the control group ("0") second to make sure the "signal" is positive.

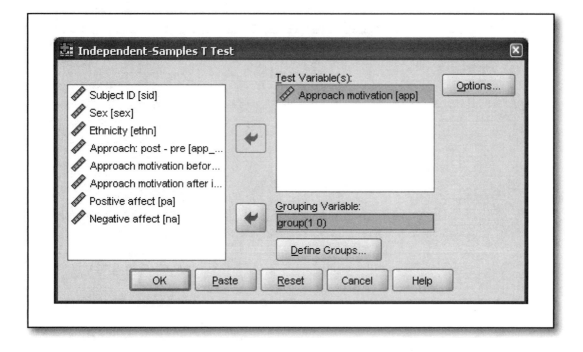

As is often the case, most of the options in the syntax are unnecessary unless you want to change the defaults. The simplest form of the syntax is

```
T-TEST GROUPS=group(1 0) /VARIABLES=app .
```

You can compare the two groups on several independent variables at once by adding them after the "/VARIABLES" list, separated by spaces.

The standard output for the independent-samples t-test includes the group means, sizes, standard deviations, and standard errors. The correlation between the two groups is not reported because it is assumed to be zero (by definition of the *independent*-samples test).

As with the other types of t-tests, the actual results are reported following the descriptives. The first piece of information shown is Levene's test, a check of the equality of variance assumption (*homoscedasticity* assumption). We'll discuss that test in more detail in the section on checking the assumptions. For now, focus on the top line of the right side of the table.

Independent Samples Test

	t	df	Sig. (2-tailed)	Mean Difference	Std. Error Difference	95% Confidence Interval of the Difference Lower	95% Confidence Interval of the Difference Upper
)0	7.629	262	.000	1.04735	.13728	.77703	1.31767
	7.629	241.626	.000	1.04735	.13728	.77693	1.31777

t-test for Equality of Means

As always, the t value (7.63) is derived from the ratio of the signal, or the mean difference of the induction minus the control group (1.047), to the noise, or the standard error (0.137). The significance value is calculated based on the degrees of freedom ($N_1 + N_2 - 2 = 132 + 132 - 2 = 262$) and the t value. SPSS also calculates the 95% confidence interval, which is essentially twice the standard error on each side of the mean difference. We say "essentially twice" the standard error, although the size of the confidence interval really depends on the degrees of freedom. It just happens that for sample sizes over about 25, "twice" is a convenient and memorable approximation.

CONNECTIONS: A COMPARISON OF
THE INDEPENDENT- AND PAIRED-SAMPLES *T*-TESTS
- -

The astute reader might have noticed that the mean difference in the independent-samples test that we just computed is identical to that of the paired-samples test. This was no accident. In reality, we never collected data from a control group. Instead, we pretended that the preinduction approach motivation scores (*app_before*) were from a fictional control group, and the postinduction scores (*app_after*) were from a fictional experimental group. Thus, the mean differences in the paired-samples test (between pre- and postinduction scores) and the independent-samples test (between the control and experimental groups) were identical.

But the *t*-tests were not. There was a stronger signal-to-noise ratio in the paired test (9.4) than in the independent test (7.6). Why? We have already established that the signal (numerator) part of the *t*-value ratio was identical. However, the noise, measured by the standard error, was larger in the independent (0.14) compared to the paired (0.11) test. As we discussed previously, the reason for the reduced standard error in the paired- but not independent-samples test is that only the paired-samples test can capitalize on the correlation between the samples to increase power. By using the same data with both tests, this example illustrates how a relatively small correlation (0.36) alone can increase the *t* value for the paired- compared to the independent-samples tests. Indeed, the paired-samples test was more powerful, even with half of the total sample size! The lesson to take away here is to try to choose paradigms that allow you to use the paired-samples test when you are designing your own experiments.

- -

Visualizing the Results From the *t*-Test

The most common way to present the *t*-test is the good old-fashioned bar graph. In SPSS, specifying the bar graph depends on how your data are organized in the spreadsheet. If the bars to be plotted along the *x*-axis (i.e., the levels of your independent variable) are defined by a coding variable, SPSS calls that "summaries for groups of cases." This is typically the case for independent-samples *t*-tests. However, if each bar is defined by a separate variable, such as in paired-samples *t*-tests, SPSS calls that "summaries for separate variables."

In both cases, you start by clicking on **Graphs → Legacy Dialogs → Bar** (the "Legacy Dialogs" step is not necessary for versions of SPSS before 15). In the window that appears, select "Simple," then choose "Summaries for groups of cases" if you used an independent-samples test, or "Summaries of separate variables" if you used a paired-samples test. We discuss how to plot results from the one-sample test that follows.

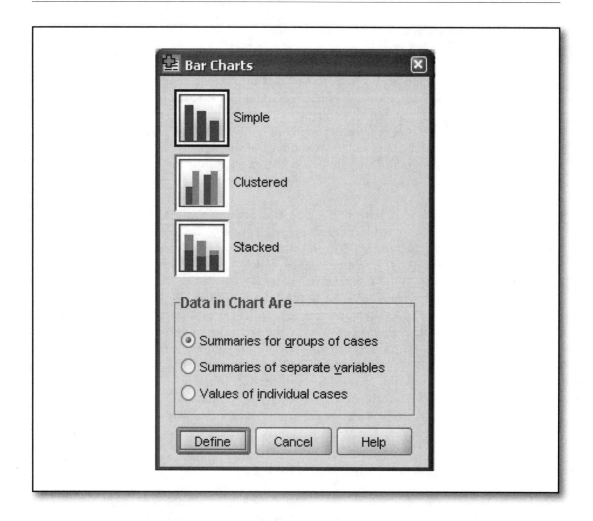

Let's begin with the paired-samples *t*-test. In the window titled "Summaries for separate variables," add both of your dependent variables into the "Bars represent" box. By default, SPSS will plot the mean of the bars. If you want to change that to something else (e.g., if you have some outliers and want to plot the median instead), you can click "Change Statistic" and select another summary statistic.

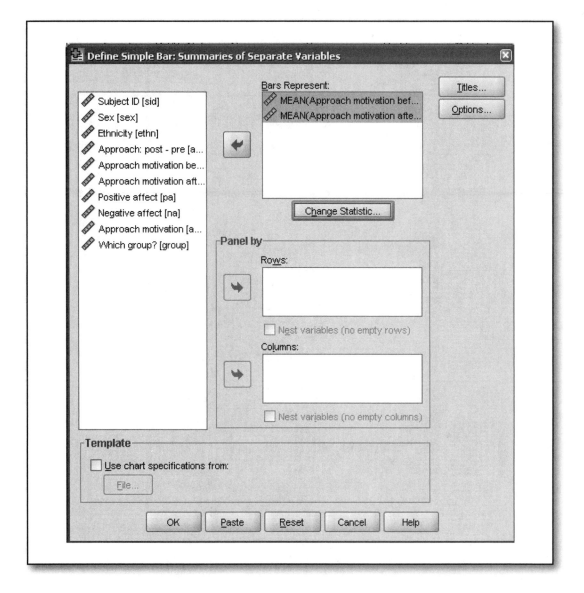

Next, click on "Options." There, you'll see that the default is to exclude cases "listwise," meaning it will exclude a participant from all variables if that person has missing data on *any* variable. You'll probably want to check the "Display error bars" button, and select either "Confidence intervals" (default) or "Standard error." As we mentioned earlier, the 95% confidence interval will look quite similar to two standard errors.

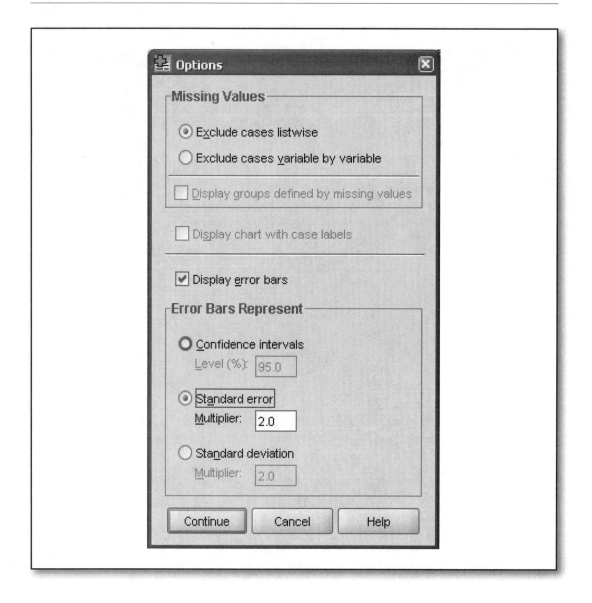

The corresponding syntax for this chart with these options is quite simple:

```
GRAPH
/BAR(SIMPLE) = MEAN(app_before) MEAN(app_after)
/INTERVAL SE(2.0).
```

And the output is exactly what we asked for:

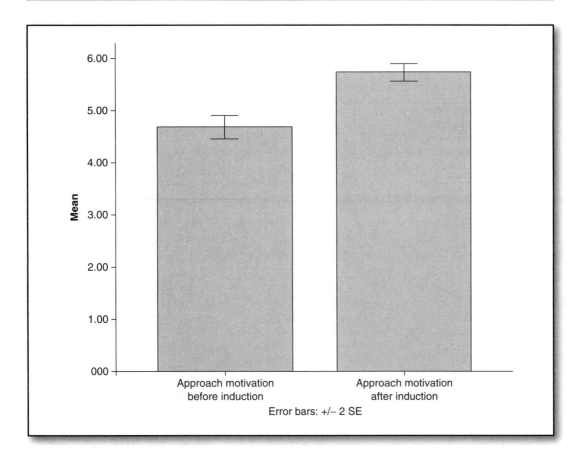

The bar chart box for the independent-samples *t*-test case is called "Summaries for groups of cases." Here, we need to put only one dependent variable (*app*) in the "Bars represent" box. We want to check "Other statistic" to plot the mean of that variable. The two bars along the *x*-axis are distinguished by the coding variable; put that into the "Category Axis" box.

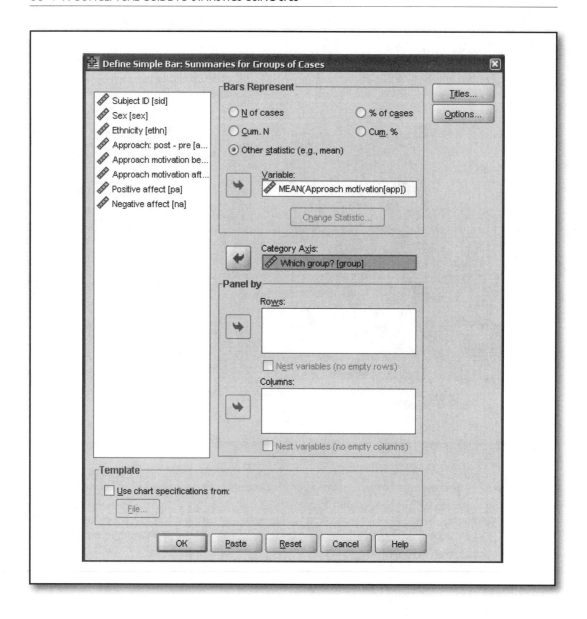

As before, click on "Options" and check "Display error bars" to put these into your chart.

The syntax for this is quite similar to the paired-samples case. The only difference is in the "/BAR(SIMPLE)" tag. Instead of listing the variables separated by spaces, the dependent variable and the independent variable are separated by the word "BY":

```
GRAPH /BAR(SIMPLE)=MEAN(app) BY group /INTERVAL SE(2.0) .
```

And, because the data were exactly the same as with the paired-samples example, the chart looks the same too (makes sense, huh?).

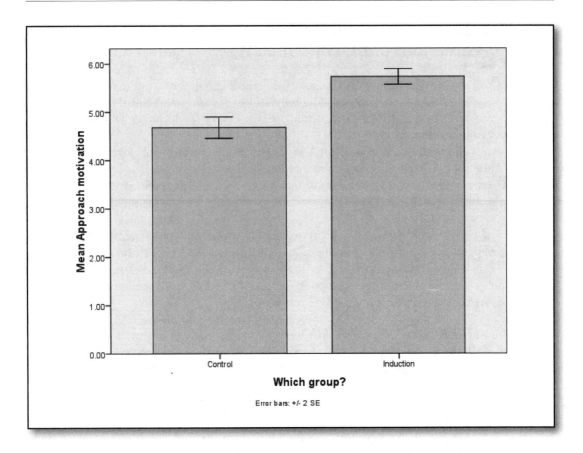

Error bars: +/- 2 SE

When you have independent samples, it's good practice to plot the error bars as two standard errors or the 95% confidence interval (whichever is wider). That way, informed readers could always tell which means are significantly different from each other. Ignoring the fact that we already know the *t* values are huge, it's clear that these two means are different because the error bars don't even come close to touching.

Incidentally, there is no way in SPSS to plot the results of a one-sample *t*-test from the point-and-click menu. Instead, you must use the "interactive chart" feature that is predominantly accessible using syntax. For example, the syntax

```
IGRAPH /Y=VAR(app_diff)

/BAR(MEAN) /ERRORBAR SE(2) CAPWIDTH(20) .
```

will produce a bar chart of our one-sample variable, *app_diff*, with ±2 standard error bars. As with all of these charts, you can tweak the figure to fit your needs by double-clicking on the chart to open the "Chart Editor" window, then clicking on each element and adjusting as desired.

A CLOSER LOOK: TESTING THE ASSUMPTIONS UNDERLYING THE *T*-TEST

You may have learned in your statistics class about the three main assumptions underlying the *t*-test: independent observations, normally distributed residuals (which is equivalent to normally distributed dependent variables in the *t*-test), and equality of variance across groups.

The assumption of independent observations is typically not formally examined, but instead trusted to hold by random sampling. However, in reality, very few experiments use true random sampling from a clearly defined population. For example, participants in most psychology experiments self-select into psychology courses and thus likely have more in common with each other than a random sample of university students. Another example of how nonrandom sampling can introduce dependence among observations is that participants might tell their friends about an experiment, causing clusters of similarly minded individuals in a sample. SPSS offers no direct way to test this assumption, so it is worthwhile to think about how your data might be affected by nonrandom sampling.

It is worth noting here that the independent observations assumption refers to the samples *between subjects* and does not apply to the pairs of observations within each participant in the paired-samples *t*-test. Indeed, we discussed previously how that test gains power from the nonindependence of the two samples. One way to think about this exception is that, although the two variables that make up the pair may be non-independent from one another, the data that actually get analyzed—the *difference between the two variables*—are still independent between subjects.

The normality assumption can be tested using the statistics and plotting tools that we described in Chapter 2 on descriptive statistics. These include the histogram overlaid with the normal curve, the P-P plot, and measures of skewness and kurtosis. Remember that the assumption of normality of the dependent measures applies to each group separately. For example, although it is acceptable for the distribution of the approach motivation variable with both groups together (*app*) to be nonnormal because the means of the two groups are different, it is not acceptable for the distribution of each group on its own (*app_before, app_after*) to be nonnormal.

The equality of variance assumption applies only to the independent-samples *t*-test. Even though there are technically two "groups" of data in the paired-samples *t*-test, we've already shown how that test is equivalent to the one-sample test on the difference between those pairs. Thus, in the paired-samples and one-sample tests, there is really only one measure of variance. But the independent-samples *t*-test does assume that the variance—essentially the amount of spread around the mean—is equal in the two groups. One formal test of this assumption is called "Levene's Test," and it is reported by default in the output of the independent-samples *t*-test. (Another one is called "Bartlett's Test," which we'll encounter later.)

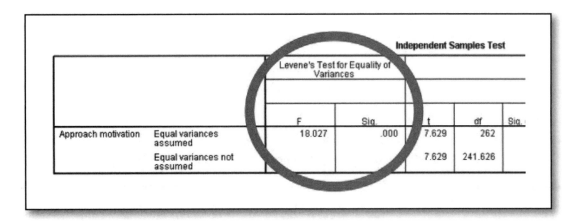

The null hypothesis of these tests is that the variances are equal across groups. Thus, a significance level of less than .05 suggests that we reject the null of equal variance. This is the case in the present sample.

What can be done if the variances are not equal? There are a few things. First, SPSS conveniently includes a sort of compensation for a violation of the homoscedasticity. SPSS automatically reports two rows of values in the independent-samples t-test; the first is for cases when the assumption is met, and the second is for cases when it is not.

Independent Samples Test

		Levene's Test for Equality of Variances		t-test for Equality of Means				
		F	Sig.	t	df	Sig. (2-tailed)	Mean Difference	Std. Error Difference
Approach motivation	Equal variances assumed	18.027	.000	7.629	262	.000	1.04735	.13728
	Equal variances not assumed			7.629	241.626	.000	1.04735	.13728

In these cases, the mean difference, standard error, and the t value itself are all exactly the same, but the degrees of freedom are "penalized" in an attempt to account for the violation of homoscedasticity. The significance level (p value) is also affected because it is based on the t value and the degrees of freedom.

Using the adjusted degrees of freedom is a perfectly acceptable solution to the violation. Another option is to try to identify the source of the unequal variances and

address it if possible. One way to do this is to examine the two distributions side by side and look for outliers using boxplots. You can tell SPSS to generate boxplots by clicking **Graphs → Legacy Dialogs → Boxplot**, then selecting "Simple" and either "Summaries for groups of cases" (for independent) or "Summaries for separate variables" (for paired).

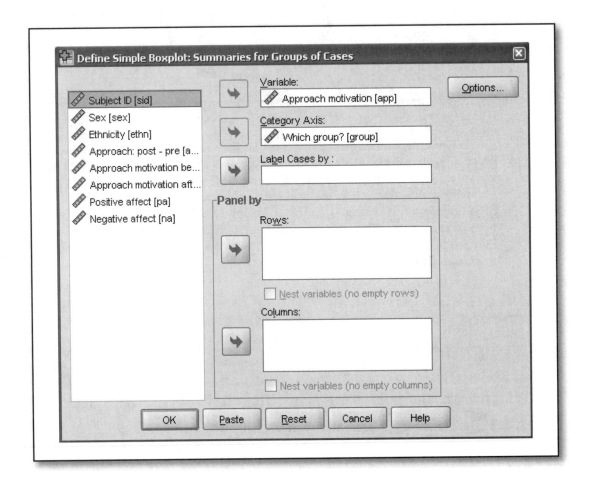

Put your dependent variable into the "Variable" box and your independent variable coding variable into the "Category Axis" box in the window that appears. The syntax is

```
EXAMINE VARIABLES=app_before app_after
/PLOT=BOXPLOT /STATISTICS=NONE /NOTOTAL.
```

If you omit the "/STATISTICS=NONE" tag, then the program will give detailed descriptives of the dependent variable; if you omit "/NOTOTAL," it will provide boxplots and descriptives for both the sample as a whole and separately by groups. We recommend omitting the first tag but leaving the second.

You do not need to specify any further options (e.g., error bars) because the boxplot by definition contains information about the variance. Specifically, the boxplot will show the mean, the first and third quartiles, the distance between the first and third quartiles (the "interquartile range"), and the distance from the boundaries of the range to the points closest to 1.5 times the interquartile range. Observations outside of *that* range (1.5 times above the upper boundary or 1.5 times below the lower boundary of the interquartile range) can be considered outliers and are labeled separately in the boxplot.

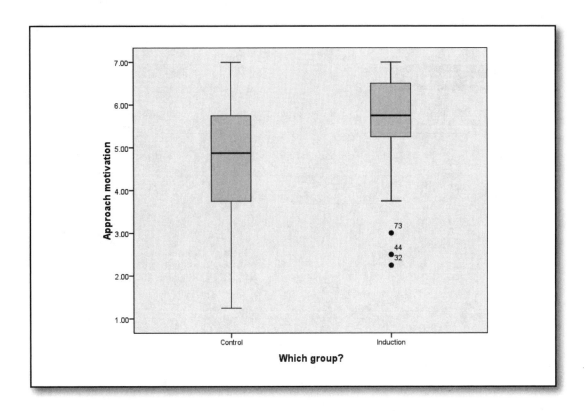

What the figure shows is that the mean approach motivation in the control group is about 5, and that the first and third quartiles are around 3.9 and 5.9, respectively (depicted by the box). The interquartile range, depicted by the total height of the box, is about 2. The stems extending above and below the box range to the points nearest 1.5 times the interquartile range (~3) above (5.9 + 3) and below (3.9 − 3). There are no points beyond this range in the control group, but there are three outliers in the induction group.

Knowing that the entire range of the variable is from 1 to 7, we can see the source of the unequal variances. Individuals in the control group were distributed all along the scale, whereas individuals in the induction group were mostly clustered around the top half. In this sense, the induction was successful. The variance is restricted in the induction group because we were trying to make everyone in that group have a high score. And we can be reassured that the unequal variances are not due to outliers—if anything, removing the outliers from the induction group would only make the problem worse.

What we were searching for in the boxplots is evidence that one of the groups had inflated variance due to outliers. Because this doesn't seem to be the case, we can only conclude that the induction succeeded, which consequently reduced the variance in one but not the other group. Thus, we are left to accept that the groups have unequal variance for which we must correct using the adjusted degrees of freedom in the *t*-test.

KEYWORDS

signal-to-noise ratio (SNR)

one-sample *t*-test

paired-samples *t*-test

independent-samples
t-test

bar chart

homoscedasticity
assumption

normality assumption

One-Way ANOVA

BEHIND THE SCENES: CONCEPTUAL BACKGROUND OF THE ANALYSIS OF VARIANCE (ANOVA)

Analysis of variance (known as "ANOVA") is nearly identical to the *t*-test. Just like the *t*-test, the heart of the analysis of variance is a signal-to-noise ratio. The ANOVA produces a single number, *F*, akin to *t*, which indicates how much "signal" relative to how much "noise" there is in the data. Also like the *t*-test, the signal measured by

ANOVA is the difference between means, and the noise is the amount of variability left after accounting for that difference. Indeed, ANOVA can be used anywhere that a t-test can be used, and their results are equivalent. When used on the same data, the F value is exactly the square of the t value, $F = t^2$, and, for a given sample size and significance level, the cutoff value for t^2 and F are the same. When you have only two groups or two within-subjects conditions, the t-test and ANOVA will lead you to the same conclusion.

However, ANOVA and the t-test differ in one critical way, which is also the reason for ANOVA's enormous popularity among scientists. Unlike the t-test, which is limited to examining the difference between two means, ANOVA can examine differences between any number of means. This small change not only enables researchers to examine designs with three or more groups but also allows them to make conceptual leaps, such as from comparing group means defined by one independent variable (IV) to comparing the effects of several IVs at once (e.g., two- and three-way ANOVAs), and from testing only a linear trend in the data to testing higher-order trends. We will discuss each of these uses of ANOVA in this and subsequent chapters.

The important conceptual change from the t-test to ANOVA is the definition of "signal" in the numerator of the F value. In the t-test, the signal is simply the mean or the difference between means. In ANOVA, the signal is instead *the amount of variance among the group means.* Because we know how to compute variance for samples of more than two, we can calculate the variance between more than two group means. Thus,

$$F = \frac{signal}{noise} = \frac{VAR(means)}{VAR(error)},$$

where the signal is the variance between the group means, and the noise is the average variance within each group (i.e., the variability that is left over after the differences between groups have been accounted for). The variance of the error is conceptually similar to the standard error.

Hence, the name "analysis of variance" is appropriate because the ANOVA literally tests the size of the signal in the data by parsing the total variance into two parts: that explained by the group means and everything else. If the amount of variability explained by the group means is large relative to what's left over, we declare that there is a significant difference between at least some of the group means—that there is a significant "signal" in the data.

The concept of dividing the variance into two parts comes from a model of the data called the General Linear Model (GLM). The GLM posits that each observation can be explained by two factors: its score (or group) on the IV(s) and random noise. You may be familiar with the matrix algebra formulation of the GLM:

$$Y = X\beta + \varepsilon,$$

where Y is the vector of observed data; X is the matrix of IVs; β is the vector of "parameters," or weights associated with each predictor or group; and ε is the "residual" vector, or what is left of the data after accounting for $X\beta$. Making this assumption—that two independent sources of variance contribute to each observation—allows us to compute the variance of each source and hence compute the F-test for significance of the group variability.

One of the reasons the GLM is so useful is that, as the name suggests, it is extremely general. The equation above can take on many different shapes depending on how you set up your experiment. For example, in the case of one categorical predictor (as in one-way ANOVA), the GLM can be written in informal equation form as

$$Obs_{ij} = Group_j + e_{ij},$$

where Obs_{ij} refers to observation i within group j, $Group_j$ is the mean of the jth group, and e_{ij} is the residual (i.e., the difference between the observed score and the group mean). In this case, $X\beta$ reduces to a vector of group means, which allows the one-way ANOVA to examine the differences among them. (See Chapter 16 to see exactly how this works and how $X\beta$ can be computed in SPSS.)

Any statistics book can show you how to calculate the F ratio by hand based on your data using the GLM. We're including the formula here because SPSS also uses the GLM to compute F, and this fact is reflected in the point-and-click menus, the syntax, and the output. In this and the following chapters, we explain how to compute the ANOVA and related tests using SPSS and SPSS syntax, and how your knowledge of the GLM can help you to better use the software and interpret the output.

Computing the One-Way ANOVA Using SPSS

For the next few chapters, we'll be practicing using the "Wedding.sav" data file on the website. This file contains data collected by one of the authors (we won't say which) before his wedding on the guests he planned to invite. For each guest, he recorded how many dances that guest was expected to participate in (*dances*), the type of relationship between the guest and the couple (*relation*; 1 = Friend, 2 = Family, 3 = Family friend, 4 = Co-worker), and whose side the guest was on (*side*; 0 = Bride, 1 = Groom). The first question he wanted to answer using these data was whether the relationship groups were expected to dance different amounts. A one-way ANOVA is perfect for this question because it can compare groups defined by an IV with more than two levels (e.g., *relation*) on their mean level of a continuous dependent variable (DV) (e.g., *dances*).

Click on **Analyze → General Linear Model → Univariate**. It is good to familiarize yourself with the window that appears ("Univariate") because it is one of the main ways to access the GLM in SPSS, which entails not only the one-way ANOVA but also two- and higher-way ANOVAs, ANCOVAs, and even regression, correlation, and *t*-tests.

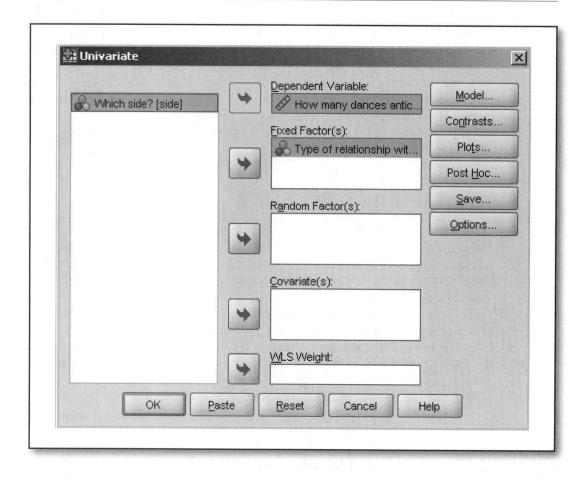

In this "Univariate" window, put the dependent measure, *dances*, in the "Dependent Variable" box, and the IV, *relation*, into the "Fixed Factor" box. In SPSS lingo, a categorical IV is called a "factor" and a continuous IV is called a "covariate." Although these are described with different terms and get put into different boxes, there is no mathematical distinction between them in the matrix algebra behind the GLM. Later, we will demonstrate that correlation and ANOVA are both based on the GLM by computing a correlation using this window by placing the continuous IV into the "Covariate" box.

Additionally, click the "Plots" button in order to plot means of the relationship groups. Put *relation* in the "Horizontal axis" box; then click the "Add" button to add it to the list of plots on the bottom half of the screen. The extra step to click "Add" is important (though annoying) because, as we will see later, it is how SPSS keeps track of several different plots generated within the same analysis when there is more than one IV. Finally, click "Continue" to return to the "Univariate" window.

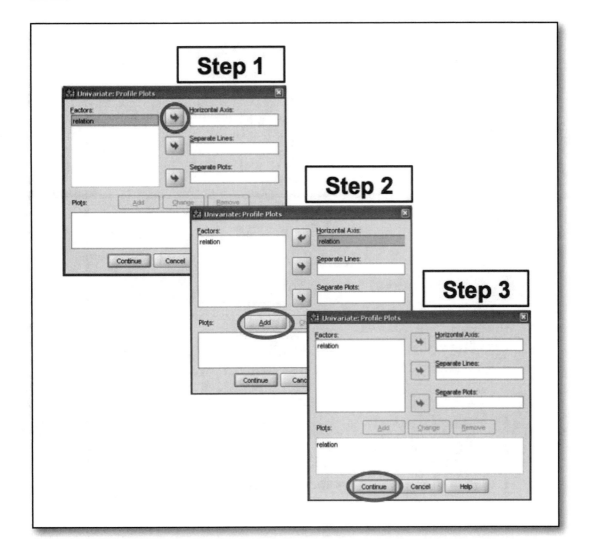

It's often useful to examine some descriptive statistics about your DV for each group defined by the IV. To do this, click on "Options," and then check "Descriptive Statistics" in the bottom half of the window ("Display").

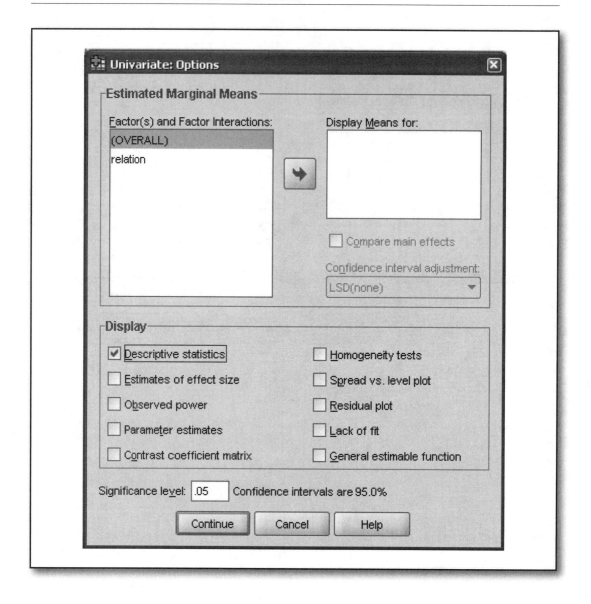

The full syntax for this one-way ANOVA is

```
GLM dances BY relation
/METHOD=SSTYPE(3)
/INTERCEPT=INCLUDE
```

```
/PLOT=PROFILE(relation)

/PRINT=DESCRIPTIVE

/CRITERIA=ALPHA(.05)

/DESIGN=relation.
```

We can reduce this syntax because what we usually want in the social sciences are the default values of the "METHOD," "INTERCEPT," and "CRITERIA" tags (i.e., Type III sum-of-squares, grand mean included, and .05 significance level, 2-tailed). After excluding those three lines, the syntax simplifies to

```
GLM dances BY relation

/PLOT=PROFILE(relation) /PRINT=DESCRIPTIVE

/DESIGN=relation .
```

You might be starting to see the underlying logic of the syntax for the GLM based on this simple example. Specifically, the syntax begins with the letters "GLM" to invoke the general linear model function, followed by each of the variables to be included in the model:

```
GLM [DV] BY [IV(s)] WITH [Covariate(s)],
```

where "DV" is the one dependent measure, "IV(s)" is (are) the list of *categorical* independent variable(s) (separated by spaces), and "Covariate(s)" is (are) the list of *continuous* independent variable(s) (separated by spaces). Next, you can specify any optional arguments with tags such as "/PLOT" and "/PRINT." Finally, the last line indicates which predictors to use in the model:

```
/DESIGN = IV(s) .
```

This last line will be more useful later when we have more than one IV because it allows the user to specify which variables and interactions to include and which to exclude.

Interpreting the ANOVA Output

Running this syntax will produce several tables and plots; we'll walk through them one by one. The first is a summary of the groups defined by the levels of your IV. In this case, we have four groups, each with 50 subjects. This table is included with all ANOVAs in SPSS.

Between-Subjects Factors

		Value Label	N
Type of relationship with the bride/groom	1	Friend	50
	2	Family	50
	3	Family friend	50
	4	Co-worker	50

Next is the (optional) descriptives table giving means, standard deviations, and Ns for each of the four groups listed in the first table. Note that although the standard error is not included here, it can easily be calculated for each group by dividing the standard deviation by the square root of N (e.g., the SE of the first group is $1.76/\sqrt{50} = 0.25$).

Descriptive Statistics

Dependent Variable:How many dances anticipated?

Type of relationship with the bride/groom	Mean	Std. Deviation	N
Friend	3.40	1.761	50
Family	4.38	2.717	50
Family friend	2.14	1.818	50
Co-worker	4.56	1.728	50
Total	3.62	2.250	200

The final table displays the actual ANOVA results. Proceeding left to right, SPSS lists the predictors (e.g., IVs) and the associated sum-of-squares, degrees of freedom, mean square, the F value, and significance value for each predictor. Not all of the predictors that SPSS reports are useful, and in fact, SPSS reports several redundant predictors that add confusion. The rows we want to focus on are the "Corrected Model," "relation," "Error," and "Corrected Total."

Test

Dependent Variable:How many

Source	Type III Sum of Squares
Corrected Model	185.0
Intercept	2620.
relation	185.
Error	822.
Total	3628.
Corrected Total	1007.

a. R Squared = .184 (Adjust

The "Corrected Model" refers to all of the included predictors ($X\beta$), "relation" refers to just that predictor, "Error" refers to the residuals (ε), and "Corrected Total" is the total variance to be explained ($X\beta + \varepsilon$). (In case you were wondering, the "Intercept" refers to the grand mean across all observations, and the "Total" is the same as the "Corrected Total" adding the "Intercept.")

The next column shows the sum-of-squares (SS), which can be thought of as the total variance in the data that is explained by each predictor. As such, the formula for the GLM applies in the most literal sense to the sum-of-squares terms. Specifically, notice that

1. SS-Corrected Total = SS-Corrected Model + SS-Error

2. SS-Corrected Model = SS-relation (because *relation* is the only predictor)

We noted above parenthetically that the "Intercept" is the grand mean across all observations. The sum-of-squares for the intercept is the squared difference between the grand mean and zero, summed across all observations. If your DV were to be mean-centered, SS-Intercept would be zero.

Dependent Variable:How many dances

Source	Type III Sum of Squares
Corrected Model	185.000[a]
Intercept	2620.880
relation	185.000
Error	822.120
Total	3628.000
Corrected Total	1007.120

a. R Squared = .184 (Adjusted R Sc

The next column contains the degrees of freedom, or *df*. The *df* eludes simple intuitive definition, but it can be loosely interpreted as the number of independent sources of variance that contribute to each term in the model, minus one. For example, the *df* of the "relation" term is 3 because there are 4 sources of variance in *relation*—the group means—and $4 - 1 = 3$. Likewise, the *df* for "Corrected Total" is 199 because there are 200 independent observations in the whole sample. As with the sum-of-squares, the degrees of freedom sum according to the GLM equation:

1. *df*-Corrected Total = *df*-Corrected Model + *df*-Error

2. *df*-Corrected Model = *df*-relation (because *relation* is the only predictor)

Dependent Variable:How many dances anticipated?

Source	Type III Sum of Squares	df	M
Corrected Model	185.000[a]	3	
Intercept	2620.880	1	
relation	185.000	3	
Error	822.120	196	
Total	3628.000	200	
Corrected Total	1007.120	199	

a. R Squared = .184 (Adjusted R Squared = .171

The fourth column of the ANOVA lists the mean square (MS) for each term in the model. Just as the sum-of-squares can be thought of as the *total* variance accounted for by each term, the mean square can be thought of as the *average* variance accounted for by each term. You can see this by the general formula for mean square: MS = SS/*df*. Specifically,

1. MS-Corrected model = SS-Corrected model/*df*-Corrected model

2. MS-relation = SS-relation/*df*-relation

3. MS-error = SS-error/*df*-error

People don't typically calculate the MS-Corrected total because it is not used as part of the *F* ratio (though you could do so using the equation given).

Dependent Variable:How many dances anticipated?

Source	Type III Sum of Squares	df	Mean Square
Corrected Model	185.000[a]	3	61.667
Intercept	2620.880	1	2620.880
relation	185.000	3	61.667
Error	822.120	196	4.194
Total	3628.000	200	
Corrected Total	1007.120	199	

a. R Squared = .184 (Adjusted R Squared = .171)

At long last, we arrive at the end result F ratios and their significance levels in the last two columns. Each F value is a signal-to-noise ratio where the signal is the mean square associated with that term, and the noise is the mean square error. For example, the F ratio for the "relation" term is MS-relation/MS-error. As with t values, larger F values indicate a greater signal-to-noise ratio. With two groups and a decent sample size, an F value of around 4 is the threshold for significance at $\alpha = .05$. As the number of groups increases, this threshold goes down. For example, with the same sample size, the threshold with four groups is around 3.

Tests of Between-Subjects Effects

Dependent Variable:How many dances anticipated?

Source	Type III Sum of Squares	df	Mean Square	F	Sig.
Corrected Model	185.000[a]	3	61.667	14.702	.000
Intercept	2620.880	1	2620.880	624.839	.000
relation	185.000	3	61.667	14.702	.000
Error	822.120	196	4.194		
Total	3628.000	200			
Corrected Total	1007.120	199			

a. R Squared = .184 (Adjusted R Squared = .171)

One way of describing the present result would be to say that there is 14 times as much variability between the "relation" group means as there is within them. Another way would be to say that the "signal" of group mean variation is more than 14 times the "noise" of error variation.

As luck would have it, the F value comes from a known sampling distribution, assuming that certain assumptions are met (which we discuss in the next "A Closer Look" section). Because the F value is a ratio of two random variables, this distribution is defined by two parameters: the *df* of the numerator "signal" and the *df* of the denominator "noise," which are, in this case, 3 and 196. As with the t value, SPSS will look up the cumulative probability of the obtained F value in the appropriate table and display the associated p value. As always, when SPSS says ".000," it really means "$p < .001$." Hence, we can conclude that the obtained F value of 14.7 was unlikely to have arisen by chance.

Perhaps the largest shortcoming of the F ratio as a test is that it sometimes can be nonspecific and thus difficult to interpret. To take the present case as an example, all we know from the ANOVA table is that there is significant variability among the relationship groups in how many times people in those groups are expected to dance during the wedding. But we do not know which group or groups are driving that effect or even which group has the largest mean. So it's a good thing we asked for the profile plot!

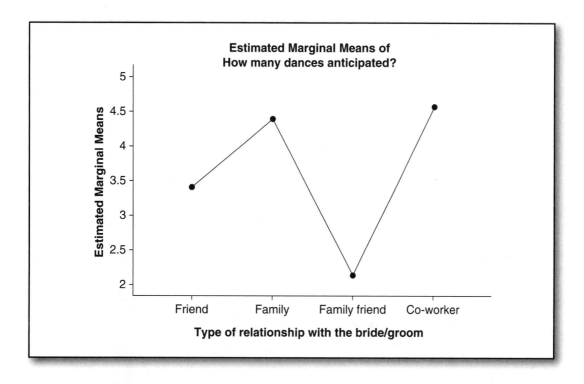

Later on, we'll show you how to produce more polished-looking figures for data presentation. But for now, you can use the profile plot that we generated as part of the one-way ANOVA syntax to give you a quick and dirty way of examining the group means, as well as some insight into the source of your significant effect (or lack thereof!). Based on the plot here, we can see that co-workers and family members are expected to dance the most, family friends will dance the least, and friends are somewhere in between.

A CLOSER LOOK: CUSTOM CONTRASTS IN ONE-WAY ANOVA

Perhaps you had a priori hypotheses about which group means would be greater than others, or perhaps you noticed a potentially interesting pattern in the data. Regardless, the usual first step to follow up on a significant one-way ANOVA result is to compare among the means, either by comparing them one-to-one as with *t*-tests, or by flexibly combining groups of means with *custom contrasts*. Both can be done easily in the context of one-way ANOVA. The trick is to figure out how to translate your psychological question into a form that SPSS can understand. And what SPSS understands takes the following form:

$$C_1 {}^*Group_1 + C_2 {}^*Group_2 + \ldots + C_n {}^*Group_n = Constant,$$

where the C_is are coefficients for each of the group means ($Group_i$), and *Constant* is a constant that is usually zero. SPSS can compute any contrast given a list of the coefficients for each group (C_is) and the constant. This can be done in two steps. First, figure out what the coefficients for each group mean are, and second, rearrange the terms so all the group means are on one side of the equation and constants are on the other.

For example, suppose we wanted to compare the expected number of dances that co-workers and family would enjoy, on one hand, to friends, on the other. Because we are comparing two groups (co-workers and family) to one group (friends), we want to weight the means accordingly. Specifically, what we'd want to do is compare the *average* of the first two to the third, essentially testing whether the means (co-workers + family)/2 = friends. Rearranging, we can test the equivalent question [(co-workers + family)/2] − friends = 0? You can see from this equation that the coefficients for co-workers, family, and friends are 0.5, 0.5, and −1, respectively. The other group, family friends, is not included in this equation, so its coefficient will be 0. Thus, our final vector of coefficients *in the order they are coded in the data* is [−1 .5 0 .5]. (You can look at the very first table in the ANOVA output to see the order of the groups in the coding of the IV).

These types of contrasts can be computed for one-way ANOVAs either using the point-and-click menu or in syntax. We'll show you how to use the point-and-click menu here, but we strongly recommend learning the syntax because it is the only way to compute contrasts in two- and higher-way ANOVAs.

Click on **Analyze → Compare Means → One-way ANOVA**. This window is a dumbed-down version of the GLM window that we used earlier, showing boxes only for the IV ("Factor") and the DVs.

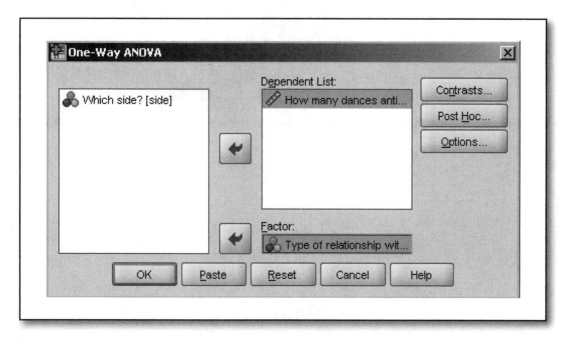

Click on the "Contrasts" button; then add the coefficients one at a time, clicking the "Next" button after each. In the end, you should see the list that we came up with earlier written top to bottom.

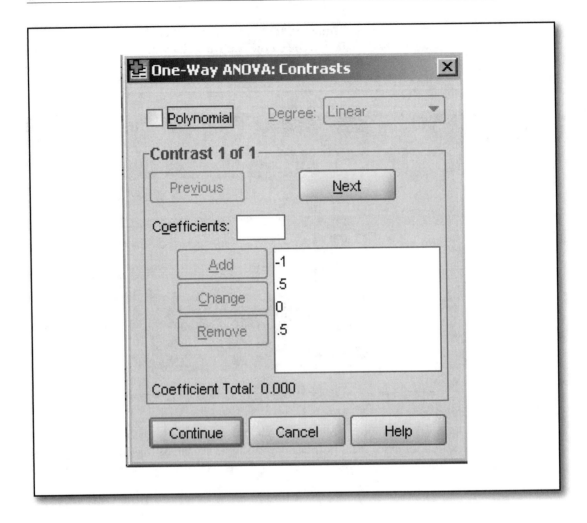

The output depicts a helpful summary table that is useful for checking your coefficients, and a report on the t-test between your two "groups" with and without violations of the homoscedasticity assumption.

Contrast Coefficients

Contrast	Type of relationship with the bride/groom			
	Friend	Family	Family friend	Co-worker
1	-1	.5	0	.5

Contrast Tests

		Contrast	Value of Contrast	Std. Error	t	df	Sig. (2-tailed)
How many dances anticipated?	Assume equal variances	1	1.07	.355	3.016	196	.003
	Does not assume equal variances	1	1.07	.337	3.171	116.941	.002

MAKING THE MOST OF SYNTAX:
CUSTOM CONTRASTS USING SYNTAX

We prefer instead to use the syntax for several reasons. We mentioned the first earlier—the syntax is the only way to compute contrasts like these in all other analyses, so you might as well learn it now. Another reason is that the command to compute custom contrasts is built right into the "GLM" syntax function and can easily be added to our existing syntax with just a line or two. The tag is called "LMATRIX," and follows the form

```
/LMATRIX = [IV] [C_1 C_2 . . . C_n]

/KMATRIX = [constant],
```

Where "IV" is the name of the independent variable, "C_1," and so on, are the coefficients for each level of the IV, and "constant" is the constant on the right side of the equation. If the "KMATRIX" line is omitted, SPSS will assume that the constant is 0 (which it usually is). Thus, to compare friends with family and co-workers, we can use

```
GLM dances BY relation

/LMATRIX = relation -1 .5 0 .5

/DESIGN = relation .
```

This syntax conveniently produces the full ANOVA table that we examined above and two tables called "Custom Hypothesis Tests."

Contrast Results (K Matrix)[a]

Contrast		Dependent... How many dances anticipated?
L1	Contrast Estimate	1.070
	Hypothesized Value	0
	Difference (Estimate - Hypothesized)	1.070
	Std. Error	.355
	Sig.	.003
	95% Confidence Interval Lower Bound	.370
	for Difference Upper Bound	1.770

a. Based on the user-specified contrast coefficients (L') matrix number 1

Test Results

Dependent Variable:How many dances anticipated?

Source	Sum of Squares	df	Mean Square	F	Sig.
Contrast	38.163	1	38.163	9.098	.003
Error	822.120	196	4.194		

The upper table shows the "contrast estimate," which is the sum of the coefficient-weighted group means. The contrast estimate here is the mean of the family and co-workers groups minus the friends group. The "hypothesized value" is the constant. The difference between these two quantities (i.e., contrast estimate − hypothesized value) composes the basis of the "signal" numerator of the t-test. The "noise" denominator is the standard error (.355).

The lower table shows the actual F-test. As always, the F value is calculated as MS-contrast/MS-error, and the MS values are calculated as SS/df. We can conclude based on this that friends are expected to dance less than the average of family and co-workers.

This lower table also demonstrates the power advantage of using custom contrasts over a simple t-test. To make this comparison using a t-test, we could have created a new group that was the average of co-workers and family, and compared the mean of that group to the expected number of dances of friends. This comparison would have had $50 + 50 - 2 = 98$ df. However, custom contrasts will always have $(1, N - k)$ degrees of freedom, where N is the total sample size and k is the number of levels of the IV (here it would be 1, 196). Furthermore, notice that the mean square error used in the contrast is identical to the mean square error used in the full ANOVA table (4.194). What is great about using custom contrasts is that these df and MS-e values will be used regardless of what your contrast coefficients are. In other words, even when you're comparing subsets of the sample (as we are here, essentially excluding the "family friends" group), you get to use the larger df based on the whole sample and consequently the smaller MS-e.

CONNECTIONS: ON THE EQUIVALENCE OF ONE-WAY ANOVA AND *T*-TESTS

In the last section, we noted the advantage of using custom contrasts within an ANOVA to using a *t*-test. This advantage stems from the fact that custom contrasts in ANOVA will always use the df and MS-e derived from the entire sample, whereas selecting only part of your sample to be included in a *t*-test will not. With that said, in cases where ANOVA and *t*-tests are based on *equal sample sizes,* the two statistics are equivalent.

To demonstrate this, compute a *t*-test comparing how much the bride's side is expected to dance to the groom's side (the IV here is *side*, where 0 = Bride's and 1 = Groom's):

```
T-TEST GROUPS=side(0 1) /VARIABLES = dances .
```

Then compute the same comparison using ANOVA:

```
GLM dances BY side /DESIGN = side .
```

The *t*-value is 2.947 with 198 df, yielding $p < .004$, and the F value is 8.685 with (1, 198) df, yielding the identical p value. If you look up the cutoff t and F values for 198 df, you'll find that they are 1.97 and 3.89, respectively. Using the rule that $F = t^2$, you can verify that these two tests are actually identical. The deeper insight into why this rule is true is that the F-test is based on sum-of-squares and variances, which are in squared units compared to the *t*-test, which is based on raw means and standard errors.

Plotting the Results of the One-Way ANOVA

We remarked earlier that the profile plots provided with the one-way ANOVA are useful but ugly. This remains true, but fortunately there is another way of plotting the group means. Click on **Graphs → Legacy Dialogs → Bar**; then select "Simple" and "Summaries for groups of cases," and click "Define."

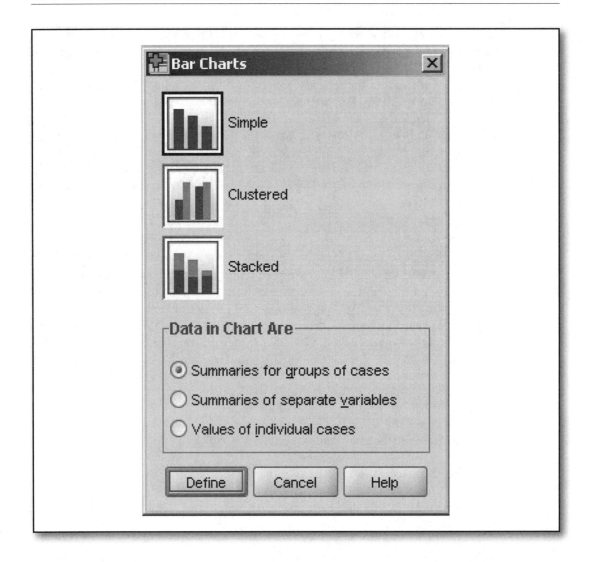

In the next window, put the DV in the "Variable" box, check "Other statistic (e.g., mean)" in the "Bars Represent" area, and put the categorical IV into the "Category Axis" box.

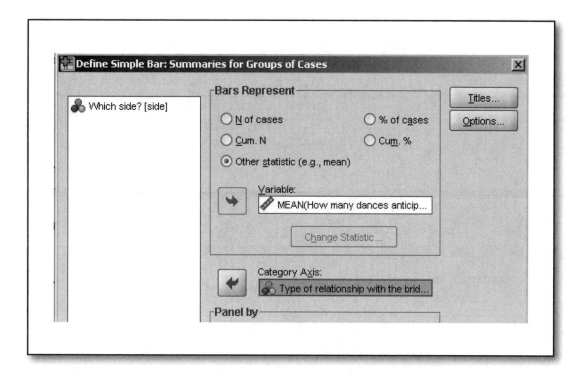

Finally, click on "Options" and add error bars to your liking. We recommend either 2 standard errors or 95% confidence intervals. When you have a relatively large sample size as we have here, 2 standard errors will be larger than the 95% CI.

The syntax is

```
GRAPH

/BAR(SIMPLE)=MEAN(dances) BY relation

/INTERVAL SE(2.0) [OR /INTERVAL CI(95.0)] .
```

Once the chart appears in SPSS, you can double-click on it to edit each of the elements. In this figure, we changed the color to be more print-friendly (remember that many of your readers will be viewing your chart in black-and-white), increased the font size for clarity, and arranged the groups in order of ascending group means.

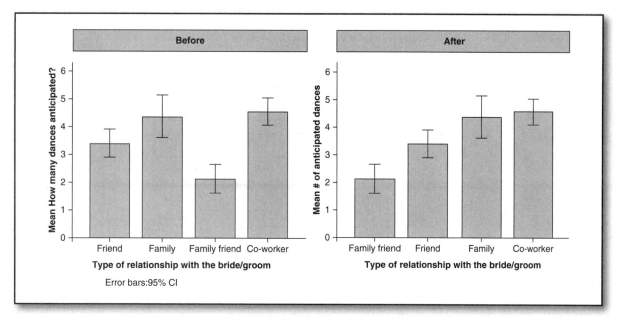

Error bars:95% CI

If you wanted to get really fancy, you could use PowerPoint or another graphical editing program to add horizontal lines or brackets above to bars to show that the mean number of expected dances by family and co-workers together is greater than that for friends.

A CLOSER LOOK: TESTING ASSUMPTIONS IN ONE-WAY ANOVA

If you are going to be using the GLM much, you should learn to recite the "assumptions mantra": independence of observations, homogeneity of variances, and normality of residuals. We discussed each of these in some detail in the chapter on *t*-tests (especially in the section on independent samples), so we won't reiterate them too much again here. But briefly observations are assumed to be independent of one another, and this is largely a function of your design and sampling procedure; variances are assumed to be equal across groups, and there are formal tests of this such as Levene's test; and the residuals are assumed to be normally distributed, and you can examine this using histograms of each group.

To formally check equality of variances, simply add the line "/PRINT= HOMOGENEITY" to your syntax, or just add "HOMOGENEITY" if you already have a "/PRINT" tag in your syntax (e.g., "/PRINT=DESCRIPTIVE HOMOGENEITY"). As with the independent-samples *t*-test, this will produce Levene's test, which tests the null hypothesis that the variances *are* equal.

Levene's Test of Equality of Error Variances[a]

Dependent Variable:How many dances anticipated?

F	df1	df2	Sig.
8.332	3	196	.000

Tests the null hypothesis that the error variance of the dependent variable is equal across groups.

a. Design: Intercept + relation

Because we see that homogeneity is violated, we can use boxplots or "spread-vs.-level" plots to identify the source. The spread-vs.-level plot shows the standard deviation and variance for each group in a plot and makes it easy to find outliers. Add the line "/PLOT=SPREADLEVEL" to the GLM function see the plot. It appears the source of the heterogeneity of variance is the group with the second-highest mean: family (fitting, isn't it?).

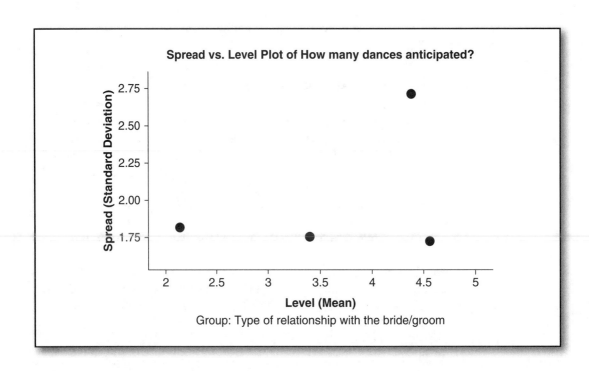

Fortunately for us, the ANOVA is relatively robust to violations of the assumption as long as the groups have approximately equal sample size.

Next, we can use histograms to examine the normality assumption. Click on **Graphs → Legacy Dialogs → Histogram**, and put your DV into the "Variable" box and your IV into the "Panel by Rows" box. The syntax is

```
GRAPH

/HISTOGRAM(NORMAL)=dances

/PANEL ROWVAR=relation ROWOP=CROSS.
```

It looks from the graph like the Friend and Co-worker groups are relatively normal, but Family is fairly uniform, and Family friend has a surplus of nondances compared to a normal distribution.

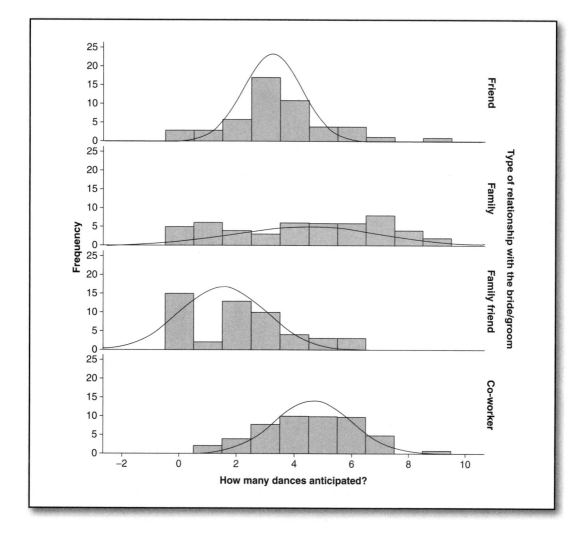

What you do from here is between you and your statistics book, but we hope that we have given you the tools to examine the assumptions, check if they are violated, and, if so, begin to make decisions about the source of the violations and how they might be addressed.

KEYWORDS

F ratio	factor	variance
general linear model (GLM)	sum-of-squares	custom contrast
group variance	degrees of freedom	Levene's test
error variance	mean square	histogram

7

Two- and Higher-Way ANOVA

Conceptual Background of the Higher-Order ANOVA

When talking about ANOVAs, people refer to several different types such as "one-way," "two-way," or "higher-way," which generally refers to two- or more-way ANOVAs. These numbers ("one-", "two-", etc.) refer to the number of *factors,* or independent variables, in the ANOVA. In Chapter 6, we discussed one-way ANOVAs in which means on the dependent variable varied as a function of a single factor (i.e., how number of dances varied according to the relation of the guests to the bride and groom). In this chapter, we discuss the concept behind and computation of higher-way ANOVAs using SPSS.

The logic of the two-, three-, or any-way ANOVA is identical to the one-way ANOVA (and the *t*-test for that matter): a signal-to-noise ratio represented by the *F* ratio. What is different in these cases is the way higher-order ANOVAs parse up the variability of the group means. In one-way ANOVA, the one factor is the only source of variability in the "signal" part of the *F* equation (the numerator). However, in higher-way ANOVAs, that "signal" in the numerator can come from any number of sources as well as the interactions among the sources.

Although it may seem trivial, the ability to look at multiple factors and their interactions is a huge advance for social scientists. An example will help illustrate why. Suppose you wanted to measure the happiness level of fans during a college basketball game as a function of the half (i.e., a one-way ANOVA with two levels of the IV: first half, second half). A random sample of the fans in the crowd revealed that, on average, there was no difference in happiness level between the two halves. This surprised you because the home team was losing in the first half and took a large lead in the second half. Then it occurred to you that you were looking at the wrong independent variable; perhaps dividing the crowd into two groups based on their team loyalty would detect difference in happiness. So you run another one-way ANOVA, this time with loyalty as the IV with two levels: home team and away team. Alas, again you find no difference between the groups. Why not? The problem is that happiness is not a function of loyalty or period alone, but instead varies by both factors together. Away team fans are happy in the first half and unhappy in the second half, and home team fans are unhappy in the first half and happy in the second half. In other words, there is a *two-way interaction* between period and loyalty.

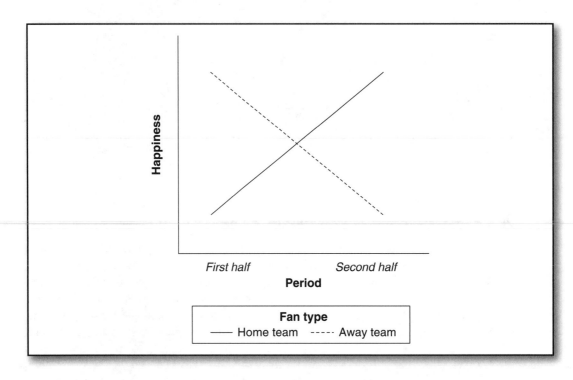

This simple example illustrates the essence of an interaction: a synergistic relationship between two or more variables that explains something that none of the variables can explain alone. Interactions have become the gold standard for social science research, and particularly experimental psychology, because adding additional factors has the potential to add nuance to the analysis by identifying boundary conditions of an effect (such as when groups differ in one situation but not in another).

> **BEHIND THE SCENES:** MODELING TWO- AND HIGHER-WAY ANOVA
> WITH THE GLM

As with the one-way ANOVA, this example too can be described in terms of the GLM. When we added the additional factor to the model, we not only added the main effect of that second factor, but we also added the effect of the interaction between the two factors into the model. This can be written schematically as

$$Obs_{ijk} = Loyalty_j + Half_k + Interaction_{jk} + e_{ijk},$$

where Obs_{ijk} refers to observation i within fan group j and during half k, $Loyalty_j$ is the mean happiness of the fans in the jth group, $Half_k$ is the mean of all the fans in half k, $Interaction_{jk}$ is the unique effect of being a fan in group j during half k, and e_{ijk} is the residual (i.e., the difference between the observed score and the predicted score based on the three means). An arbitrary number of additional factors can be added to the model, each adding a main effect term and an interaction term with each of the other factors. Conceptually, this equation represents that the variability among the individual observations in happiness can be broken down into an effect for half, an effect for loyalty, and an effect that is the unique combination of half and loyalty. In this case, very little of the variability can be explained by half and loyalty (i.e., there is no main effect of those variables) but much of the variance is explained by the unique combination of half and loyalty (i.e., there is an interaction).

This chapter describes how to compute these kinds of ANOVA models in SPSS, how to better understand the interactions using simple comparisons, and how to interpret the output.

Computing the Two-Way ANOVA Using SPSS

We will continue practicing with the data set "Wedding.sav" from the website. As a reminder, this file contains data about a wedding, and specifically the anticipated amount of dancing of the guests (*dances*) as a function of the type of relationship between the guest and the couple (*relation;* 1 = Friend, 2 = Family, 3 = Family friend, 4 = Co-worker) and whose side the guest was on (*side;* 0 = Bride, 1 = Groom). In Chapter 6, we established that there was a main effect of relationship on dancing, and specifically that friends are expected to dance less than family and co-workers. In this chapter, we examine the simultaneous effects of relationship and side on dancing, answering the question, "Does the effect of relationship on dancing change depending on guest side?" This is a perfect case for two-way ANOVA, which will allow us to examine the effects on dancing of relationship and side, and whether there is an interactive effect between them.

Click on **Analyze** → **General Linear Model** → **Univariate**. Note that this is exactly where we started when we computed the one-way ANOVA. In the window that opens, add *dances* as the "Dependent Variable" and add *relation* and *side* as "Fixed Factors." The analysis we're about to run is a *two-way* ANOVA because we selected two factors. If we had put a third factor in here, it would be a three-way ANOVA.

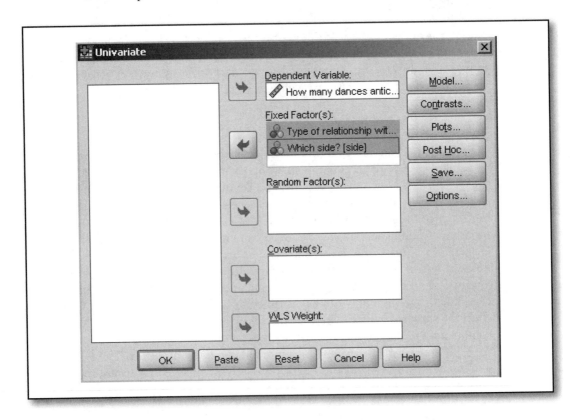

Next, click on "Model." By default, the "Full factorial" button is checked. This means that all main effects and all interactions will be represented in the model. In this case, there are two main effects (*relation* and *side*) and one interaction (*relation*-by-*side*). In three-way ANOVA, there are seven effects in the full factorial: three main effects (A, B, and C), three two-way interactions (A-by-B, A-by-C, and B-by-C), and one three-way interaction (A-by-B-by-C). The "Full Factorial" option is equivalent to selecting both main effects and the two-way interaction in two-way ANOVA. In general, you want to allow all of the effects that can be in the model to be in the model, but there are certain circumstances determined by your study design and theory when you may want to omit certain terms.

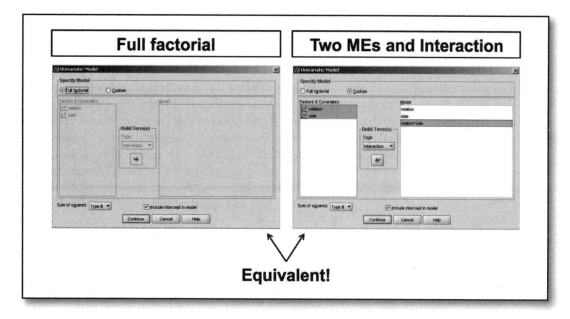

Back in the "Univariate" window (remember that "*uni*" refers to the one DV, not the multiple IVs), click on "Contrasts." The window that pops up allows us to specify contrasts among the levels of the IVs, but only one IV at a time. It doesn't allow for specific contrasts among the particular cells in the design (e.g., friends on the groom's side vs. family on the bride's side). In this case, we've requested "simple" tests among the levels of *relation* with reference to the last category, so this will produce simple *t*-tests of each level of *relation* in comparison to the last group, *co-workers*.

There are several other types of contrasts from which to choose. Perhaps the most useful one besides deviation is "Polynomial," which produces tests of the linear, the quadratic, the cubic, and so on effects among the levels of the IV. This is perfect in cases when the groups vary systematically along one dimension, as in drug dosage studies. In this case, the polynomial effect would be meaningless because the *relation* groups are qualitatively different kinds of relationships and do not vary along a single quantitative dimension. (In case you're curious about the other types of contrasts, "deviation" compares each relationship group to the grand mean, "difference" compares each group to the average of all the previous groups, "Helmert" compares each group to the average of all the following groups, and "repeated" compares each group to its nearest neighbor such as one to two, two to three, and three to four).

Next, click on "Plots" to open the plotting dialogue window. This allows us to design simple plots of the means of the factors levels. We can build plots of each of the factors alone (e.g., *relation* in the "Horizontal Axis" field and nothing else), which will plot the so-called marginal means averaged across the levels of *side*, or we can build plots of the factors together in order to visualize the interaction (e.g., *relation* in the "Horizontal Axis" field and *side* in the "Separate Lines" field). Several plots can be generated with each ANOVA run, but they must be specified one at a time by filling the desired fields and then clicking "Add" to enter them in the plots list at the bottom.

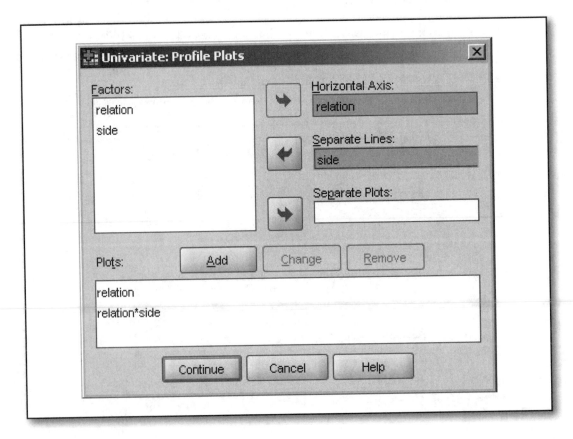

Finally, click on "Options" to bring up the miscellaneous options box for the GLM. Toward the bottom, check the optional output that you'd like for the analysis. In this case, we've requested descriptive statistics (means and standard deviations for each of the 8 cells in our 2 × 4 ANOVA), estimates of effect size (output in terms of eta-squared for each of the three effects), and homogeneity tests (indicating whether the variances of the group means are unequal).

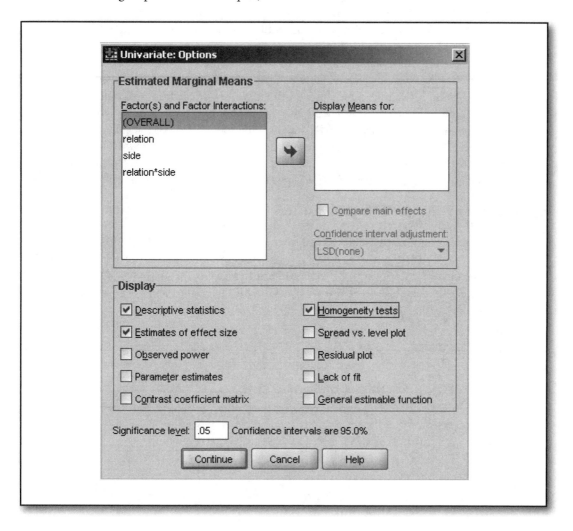

As always, click "Paste" to generate the syntax form of the requested command. Excluding some of the default and unnecessary options, the syntax is as follows:

```
GLM dances BY relation side
/CONTRAST(relation)=Simple
```

```
/PLOT=PROFILE(relation relation*side)

/PRINT=ETASQ HOMOGENEITY DESCRIPTIVE

/DESIGN=relation side relation*side.
```

The "CONTRAST" tag corresponds to the simple contrast (relative to the last group) that we requested; the "PLOT" tag corresponds to the "profile," or mean plots, of the *relation* marginal means plot and the *relation*-by-*side* interaction plot; and the "PRINT" tag corresponds to the output options we requested.

The "DESIGN" tag is where the model is specified. Because we used a full factorial, there are three terms there: two main effects and one interaction. If we wanted to change the model, for example, by removing the two-way interaction, we could simply delete "relation*side" from the syntax. Note that a common error for new syntax users is a mismatch between the "DESIGN" tag and the "GLM" line. Specifically, each IV that is specified in the GLM line (and remember the general syntax for the GLM function is GLM [DV] BY [IV1] [IV2] . . .) must be present somewhere in the "DESIGN" tag. Otherwise, SPSS will produce an error instead of running your ANOVA.

Interpreting the ANOVA Output

After running the syntax (or just clicking on "OK" in the "UNIVARIATE" window instead of "Paste"), the ANOVA results will appear in the output window. The first output item to appear will be the descriptives if you requested them. They do not appear by default, but we always recommend including them because you'll want to report them in your research write-up.

Descriptive Statistics

Dependent Variable:How many dances anticipated?

Type of relationship with the bride/groom	Which side?	Mean	Std. Deviation	N
Friend	Bride	2.88	1.563	25
	Groom	3.92	1.824	25
	Total	3.40	1.761	50
Family	Bride	6.56	1.387	25
	Groom	2.20	1.803	25
	Total	4.38	2.717	50
Family friend	Bride	2.04	1.513	25
	Groom	2.24	2.107	25
	Total	2.14	1.818	50
Co-worker	Bride	4.84	2.014	25
	Groom	4.28	1.370	25
	Total	4.56	1.728	50
Total	Bride	4.08	2.390	100
	Groom	3.16	2.009	100
	Total	3.62	2.250	200

One thing to note about the descriptives is that they are presented in an unusual format. The means, *SD*s, and *N*s of each of the eight cell means, as well as each of the six marginal means, are reported, but they are interleaved in a way that some people find to be confusing.

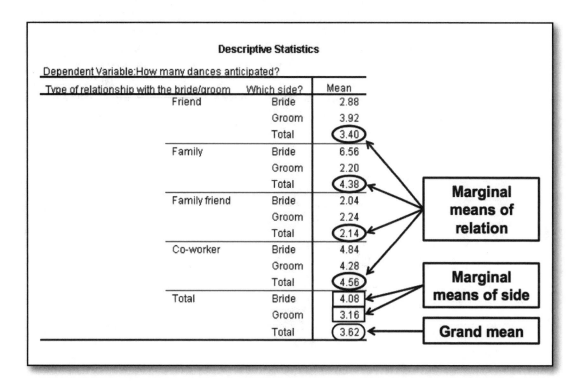

To specify exactly what we mean, we have redrawn the table in the more conventional way.

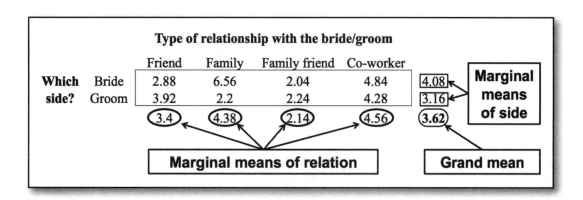

As you can see, in SPSS, the marginal means (and *SD*s and *N*s) are interleaved with the cell means. In case you get confused, the *N*s can be a good guide. In an equal-*N* design such as this one (where all the cells have the same number of subjects), the cell means will always have the smallest *N* (25 here), the grand mean will have the largest (200 here), and the marginals will be in between (50 or 100 here).

After the descriptives comes the test for equality of variances (i.e., homogeneity of variance). Note that the null hypothesis of this test is that the variances *are* equal, so a significant *p* value indicates a violation of the assumption of homogeneity. This test treats all the groups as levels of a single factor and ignores the multiple-factor structure of the data. Hence, the degrees of freedom correspond to a one-way ANOVA with one level for each cell in your design. Because we have a 2×4 ANOVA for 8 total cells, the degrees of freedom are 7 ($k - 1 = 8 - 1$) and 192 ($N - k = 200 - 8$). The result is not significant, indicating no violation of the assumption. Good!

Levene's Test of Equality of Error Variances[a]

Dependent Variable:How many dances anticipated?

F	df1	df2	Sig.
1.378	7	192	.217

Tests the null hypothesis that the error variance of the dependent variable is equal across groups.

a. Design: Intercept + relation + side + relation * side

The next piece of output is the ANOVA table with the details of the analysis.

Tests of Between-Subjects Effects

Dependent Variable:How many dances anticipated?

Source	Type III Sum of Squares	df	Mean Square	F	Sig.	Partial Eta Squared
Corrected Model	440.560[a]	7	62.937	21.329	.000	.437
Intercept	2620.880	1	2620.880	888.183	.000	.822
relation	185.000	3	61.667	20.898	.000	.246
side	42.320	1	42.320	14.342	.000	.070
relation * side	213.240	3	71.080	24.088	.000	.273
Error	566.560	192	2.951			
Total	3628.000	200				
Corrected Total	1007.120	199				

a. R Squared = .437 (Adjusted R Squared = .417)

Because both the one- and two-way ANOVAs are both based on the GLM, the interpretation of the output from these analyses is quite similar. The degrees of freedom for each of the effects sums to $N-1$: 3 (*relation*) + 1 (*side*) + 3 (*interaction*) + 192 (*error*) = 199 (total). For each effect, the sum-of-squares represents the total variance accountable to that factor, the mean square is the sum-of-squares divided by the degrees of freedom, and the *F* ratio is the mean square for each effect divided by the mean squared error. Because the *p* values of each effect are below our threshold of .05, we can declare that there are significant main effects of *relation* and *side* as well as a significant *relation*-by-*side* interaction on *dances*. In the sections that follow, we follow-up this analysis with pairwise and custom contrasts to better interpret these effects.

We should pause here to make a cautionary note about interpreting the "partial eta-squared" measure of effect size. This measure is calculated as SS-effect/(SS-effect + SS-error). As such, it can be interpreted loosely as the amount of variability explained by the effect relative to error, and it is useful for roughly comparing the size of several effects within the same analysis. For example, in this case, we can safely say that the effect of relation (eta-squared = .25) is greater than the effect of size (eta-squared = .07). But our inferences must end there. Partial eta-squared is *not* a percentage of variance explained, and the partial eta-squared values in the ANOVA table do not sum to one. Although SPSS does not report it, the proper estimate of eta-squared, which *is* interpreted as percentage of variance explained, is calculated as SS-effect/SS-Total. The eta-squared values for the effects in a given analysis sum to 1. These estimates can be derived easily from the ANOVA table (e.g., eta-squared for relation = 185/1007 = .18) and are preferable to the partial eta-squared values that SPSS reports. Nonetheless, any measure of effect size is preferable to no measure of effect size.

The next two pieces of output can help us begin to unpack the meaning of the three effects that we observed in the ANOVA table. First, the "simple" pairwise contrasts compare each group to our reference group of co-workers.

Contrast Results (K Matrix)

		Dependent... How many dances anticipated?
Type of relationship with the bride/groom Simple Contrast[a]		
Level 1 vs. Level 4	Contrast Estimate	-1.160
	Hypothesized Value	0
	Difference (Estimate - Hypothesized)	-1.160
	Std. Error	.344
	Sig.	.001
	95% Confidence Interval for Difference — Lower Bound	-1.838
	Upper Bound	-.482
Level 2 vs. Level 4	Contrast Estimate	-.180
	Hypothesized Value	0
	Difference (Estimate - Hypothesized)	-.180
	Std. Error	.344
	Sig.	.601
	95% Confidence Interval for Difference — Lower Bound	-.858
	Upper Bound	.498
Level 3 vs. Level 4	Contrast Estimate	-2.420
	Hypothesized Value	0
	Difference (Estimate - Hypothesized)	-2.420
	Std. Error	.344
	Sig.	.000
	95% Confidence Interval for Difference — Lower Bound	-3.098
	Upper Bound	-1.742

a. Reference category = 4

By examining the contrast estimates and their associated p values, we can see that Groups 1 (friends) and 3 (family friends) are different from Group 4 (co-workers), but Group 2 (family) is not. More specifically, because the contrast estimates are all negative, we can tell that friends and family friends are expected to dance less than co-workers. The profile plot of the marginal means of *relation* also helps to clarify this relationship.

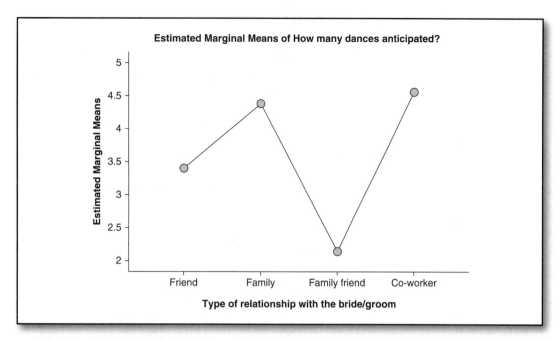

All of this we could have gotten from a one-way ANOVA. This plot, and the simple contrasts, can help us understand the main effects. But we still haven't unpacked the interaction. What does it mean that there is an interaction between *relation* and *side*? The profile plot of the interaction provides some clues.

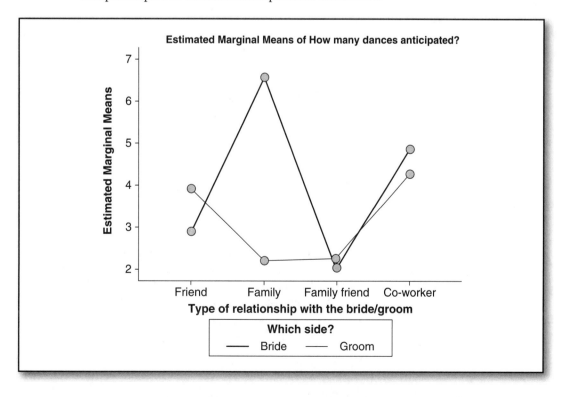

The essential interpretation of an interaction between two factors is that the effect of one factor on the DV differs across the levels of the other factor. In this case, we can see that the effect of relationship on dancing, especially for family, depends on the side of the guest. On the groom's side, family dances *less* than the other groups, but on the bride's side, family dances *more* than the other groups.

These profile plots can point us in the right direction, but formal statistical tests are needed to identify exactly which mean differences are driving the effect; in other words, which of the eight means is and is not different from the others. The next section describes how to use SPSS syntax to perform custom contrast tests between arbitrary groups of means.

MAKING THE MOST OF SYNTAX:
CUSTOM CONTRASTS IN TWO-WAY ANOVA

SPSS has the capability to formally test the differences between any combination of cell means, but this function is accessible only via the "LMATRIX" tag in syntax. As we pointed out earlier, the "Contrasts" menu in the univariate ANOVA window can test differences among *marginal* means of the factor levels, but not among *cell* means. For example, the "simple" contrasts can compare co-workers to family members but cannot compare co-workers on just the bride's side to family members on just the bride's side. To compute that comparison (bride's co-workers vs. bride's family), we would want to weigh the cell means in the following way:

		Type of relationship with the bride/groom				
		Friend	Family	Family friend	Co-worker	
Which	Bride	0	-1	0	1	0
side?	Groom	0	0	0	0	0
		0	-1	0	1	**0**

Weighing the means as indicated will test whether bride's co-workers dance *more* than bride's family (because co-workers are weighed with a +1 and family with a −1). Notice that the table also includes the marginal sums: [0 0] for *side* and [0 -1 0 1] for *relation*. The grand sum of the contrasts should always equal zero. We can use these marginal sums and cell values to translate our desired contrast—bride's co-workers versus bride's family—to an LMATRIX tag and a comparison that SPSS can run.

The general syntax for custom contrasts using LMATRIX is

```
/LMATRIX = [IV1] [marginal sums for IV1] [IV2]
[marginal sums for IV2] [IV1*IV2] [cell values for the
interaction]
```

Where the "marginal sums for IV1" are the two figures from the rightmost column of the table ([0 0]), the "marginal sums for IV2" are the four figures from the bottom row of the table ([0 -1 0 1], and the "cell values for the interaction" are the cell values read left to right for each row beginning at the top. In this case, this translates to

```
/LMATRIX side 0 0 relation 0 1 0 -1 side*relation 0 -1
0 1 0 0 0 0
```

However, there is one catch here. If you were to try to run the GLM command with this LMATRIX tag, SPSS would generate an error. The problem is that one of the marginal sums contains only "0"s. For reasons unbeknownst to us, SPSS does not accept these kinds of marginal sums. The program is able to compute contrasts with marginal sums with only zeros, but for it to work, *any marginal sums with "0"s only must be omitted.* Omitting the zeros and the factor name here, the contrast reduces to

```
/LMATRIX relation 0 1 0 -1 side*relation 0 1 0
-1 0 0 0 0 .
```

The full syntax for this command is thus

```
GLM dances BY side relation

/LMATRIX = relation 0 -1 0 1 side*relation 0 -1 0
1 0 0 0 0

/DESIGN=side relation side*relation .
```

Note that the order of the factors—*side* then *relation*—must be consistent throughout the command starting at the "GLM..." line and continue through the "DESIGN" tag.

Running this piece of syntax code will generate the custom contrast test(s) specified in the "LMATRIX" tag as well as the main ANOVA table that we reviewed earlier. The output associated with the contrast is broken into two pieces, the "contrast results" and the "test results":

Contrast Results (K Matrix)[a]

Contrast		Dependent... How many dances anticipated?
L1	Contrast Estimate	-1.720
	Hypothesized Value	0
	Difference (Estimate - Hypothesized)	-1.720
	Std. Error	.486
	Sig.	.001
	95% Confidence Interval for Difference Lower Bound	-2.678
	Upper Bound	-.762

a. Based on the user-specified contrast coefficients (L') matrix number 1

The most important piece of information to examine in the "contrast results" table is the "contrast estimate" value. This is the literal value of the contrast based on the formula that we described in the previous chapter:

$$Contrast\ estimate = C_1*Cell_1 + C_2*Cell_2 + \ldots + C_n*Cell_n$$

Where the C_is are coefficients for each of the (eight) cell means $(Cell_i)$, and n is the total number of cells (here, $2*4 = 8$). In this case, the estimate is

$$= (0)*2.88 + (-1)*6.56 + (0)*2.04 + (1)*4.84 + (0)*3.92 + (0)*2.2$$
$$+ (0)*2.24 + (0)*4.28$$

$$= (-1)*6.56 + (1)*4.84$$

$$= -1.72,$$

which is exactly what we wanted: the difference between co-workers and family on the bride's side. It is good practice to always check the "contrast estimate" to ensure that you're testing the difference that you intend.

The next piece of output is the actual statistical test of the contrast estimate, testing whether that difference is different from 0.

Test Results

Dependent Variable:How many dances anticipated?

Source	Sum of Squares	df	Mean Square	F	Sig.
Contrast	36.980	1	36.980	12.532	.001
Error	566.560	192	2.951		

Note that the contrast has only 1 degree of freedom (because there is only one line in this contrast) and that the error term has 192 degrees of freedom. This relatively large *df*-error represents a key advantage of using custom contrasts as opposed to merely running an independent-groups *t*-test between those two groups: Even though only 50 data points contribute to the cell means (25 co-workers and 25 family members), the *df*-error is based on the entire sample of 200 individuals. SPSS allows us to capitalize on the GLM assumption that the error variance is equal across groups, and hence the best estimate of the MS-error is based on all groups in the sample.

Based on 1 and 192 degrees of freedom, an *F* value of 12.532 is significant at traditional levels, suggesting that the bride's family is expected to dance significantly more than the bride's co-workers.

For details on creating any arbitrary contrast in two- and three-way ANOVA, see the appendix, "General Formulation of Contrasts Using LMATRIX."

A CLOSER LOOK: MULTIPLE-LINE CONTRASTS

Although many comparisons, including all that we have discussed so far, can be expressed in a single line, others cannot. This is most commonly the case for compound comparisons that test more than a single equivalency, such as the comparison $mean_1 = mean_2 = mean_3$. This comparison actually contains two pairwise comparisons: $mean_1 = mean_2$ and $mean_2 = mean_3$. (Under the null hypothesis, each of these equivalencies is true. Hence, the third pairwise comparison, $mean_1 = mean_3$, is redundant because it follows if the other two are true). Because it contains two pairwise contrasts, the comparison $mean_1 = mean_2 = mean_3$ can only be entirely expressed in two lines:

$mean_1 - mean_2 = 0$, and

$mean_2 - mean_3 = 0$

These lines would translate into two "LMATRIX" tags, "/LMATRIX = IV 1 −1 0" and "/LMATRIX = IV 0 1 −1."

Compound comparisons can be computed in SPSS syntax using the LMATRIX command by separating the lines with a semicolon:

```
/LMATRIX = IV 1 -1 0;

IV 0 1 -1
```

In the wedding data set that we've been using for this chapter, we can practice a compound contrast by testing whether there are any differences among any levels of *relation*. Specifically, the comparison *Friends = Family = Family friends = Co-workers* contains three pairwise comparisons and can thus be expressed in three lines:

Line 1

	Friend	Family	Family friend	Co-worker	
Bride	1	0	0	-1	0
Groom	1	0	0	-1	0
	2	0	0	-2	0

Line 2

	Friend	Family	Family friend	Co-worker	
Bride	0	1	0	-1	0
Groom	0	1	0	-1	0
	0	2	0	-2	0

Line 3

	Friend	Family	Family friend	Co-worker	
Bride	0	0	1	-1	0
Groom	0	0	1	-1	0
	0	0	2	-2	0

which translates to the syntax

```
GLM dances BY side relation

/LMATRIX = relation 2 0 0 -2 side*relation 1 0 0
-1 1 0 0 -1;
```

```
relation 0 2 0 -2 side*relation 0 1 0 -1 0 1 0 -1;
relation 0 0 2 -2 side*relation 0 0 1 -1 0 0 1 -1
/DESIGN=side relation side*relation .
```

The output gives a contrast estimate and significance value for each line separately:

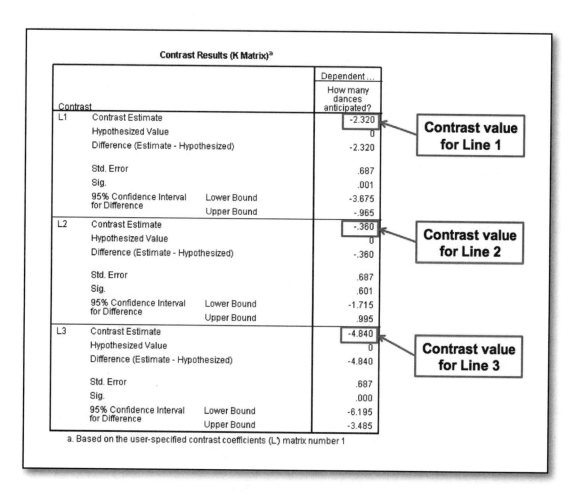

Contrast Results (K Matrix)[a]

Contrast		Dependent... How many dances anticipated?
L1	Contrast Estimate	-2.320
	Hypothesized Value	0
	Difference (Estimate - Hypothesized)	-2.320
	Std. Error	.687
	Sig.	.001
	95% Confidence Interval for Difference — Lower Bound	-3.675
	Upper Bound	-.965
L2	Contrast Estimate	-.360
	Hypothesized Value	0
	Difference (Estimate - Hypothesized)	-.360
	Std. Error	.687
	Sig.	.601
	95% Confidence Interval for Difference — Lower Bound	-1.715
	Upper Bound	.995
L3	Contrast Estimate	-4.840
	Hypothesized Value	0
	Difference (Estimate - Hypothesized)	-4.840
	Std. Error	.687
	Sig.	.000
	95% Confidence Interval for Difference — Lower Bound	-6.195
	Upper Bound	-3.485

a. Based on the user-specified contrast coefficients (L') matrix number 1

Contrast value for Line 1

Contrast value for Line 2

Contrast value for Line 3

and an estimate of the entire comparison together, which tests whether *any* of the pairwise null comparisons is rejected.

Test Results

Dependent Variable:How many dances anticipated?

Source	Sum of Squares	df	Mean Square	F	Sig.
Contrast	185.000	3	61.667	20.898	.000
Error	566.560	192	2.951		

Note that in this overall comparison, there are 3 degrees of freedom for the comparison, corresponding to the three lines in the contrast.

CONNECTIONS: EQUIVALENCE BETWEEN MAIN EFFECTS TESTS AND CUSTOM CONTRASTS

Like any other comparison, main effects can also be broken down into contrasts among means. For example, the main effects of *side* can be expressed as the sum of all relation types on the bride's side minus the sum of all relation types on the groom's side.

Type of relationship with the bride/groom

		Friend	Family	Family friend	Co-worker	
Which side?	Bride	1	1	1	1	4
	Groom	-1	-1	-1	-1	-4
		0	0	0	0	0

Using the steps written earlier, the syntax for this contrast is

```
GLM dances BY side relation
/LMATRIX = side 4 -4 side*relation 1 1 1 1 -1 -1 -1 -1
/DESIGN=side relation side*relation .
```

The output demonstrates that this contrast is equivalent to the main effect that SPSS generates with each GLM run.

Tests of Between-Subjects Effects

Dependent Variable:How many dances anticipated?

Source	Type III Sum of Squares	df	Mean Square	F	Sig.
Corrected Model	440.560ᵃ	7	62.937	21.329	.000
Intercept	2620.880	1	2620.880	888.183	.000
side	42.320	1	42.320	14.342	.000
relation	185.000	3	61.667	20.898	.000
side * relation	213.240	3	71.080	24.088	.000
Error	566.560	192	2.951		
Total	3628.000	200			
Corrected Total	1007.120	199			

a. R Squared = .437 (Adjusted R Squared = .417)

Results from main effect

Test Results

Dependent Variable:How many dances anticipated?

Source	Sum of Squares	df	Mean Square	F	Sig.
Contrast	42.320	1	42.320	14.342	.000
Error	566.560	192	2.951		

Results from contrast

Plotting the Results of the Two-Way ANOVA

As with the one-way ANOVA, SPSS can generate cell mean plots to illustrate the results of two- or higher-way ANOVAs. The key difference is that the group means are now clustered by factor level. To see this, click on **Graphs → Legacy Dialogs → Bar**; then select "Clustered," "Summaries for groups of cases"; then click "Define."

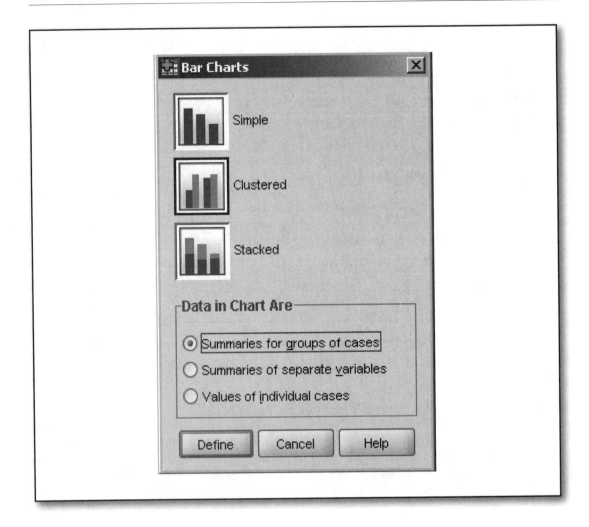

Specify that the "bars represent" the mean of your DV (e.g., *dances*); then specify the IVs in the boxes below. The levels of the IV in the "Category axis" box will be displayed across the horizontal axis, and the levels of the IV in the "define clusters by" box will be plotted in separate color-coded bars.

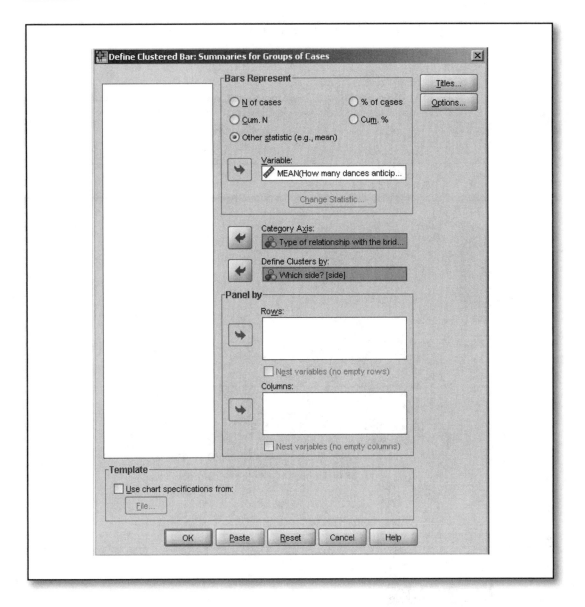

The syntax is quite simple:

```
GRAPH /BAR(GROUPED) = MEAN([DV]) BY [IV on horizontal
axis] BY [IV to be clustered] .
```

For the current example, this syntax is

```
GRAPH /BAR(GROUPED)=MEAN(dances) BY relation BY side.
```

To add 95% confidence intervals to each bar (recommended), add the line

```
/INTERVAL CI(95.0)
```

Editing the chart is similar to what was covered in Chapter 6 on one-way ANOVA. Here, as recommended, we've changed the chart to be friendly for black-and-white printing.

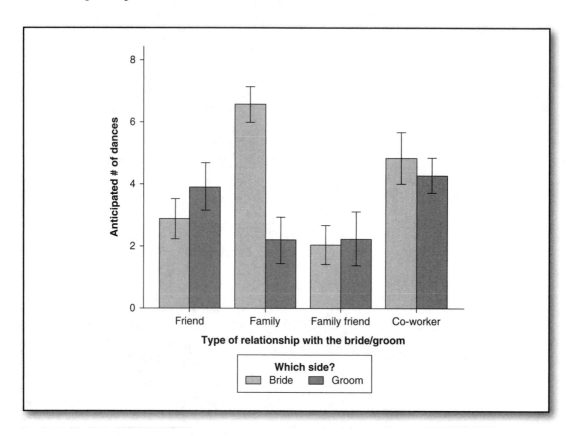

KEYWORDS

higher-order ANOVA	marginal means	contrast estimate
two-way interaction	LMATRIX	clustered bar chart

8

Within-Subjects ANOVA

❖

Conceptual Background of the Within-Subjects ANOVA

Just as there are two different forms of the *t*-test depending on whether your samples are drawn from the same or different individuals, there are also two different forms of the ANOVA model. Thus far, we've been describing the *independent samples* form of the ANOVA, often referred to as "factorial" ANOVA. In this chapter, we discuss the case when each participant in your study completes a task under each of several conditions known as *within-subjects* ANOVA.

Like its two-condition paired *t*-test cousin, the within-subjects ANOVA capitalizes on the covariance of scores across conditions to reduce error variance and thereby increase power. This form of ANOVA is most powerful when there is a relatively high degree of (between-subjects) correlation between the scores on the conditions; in other words, when people who score highly in one condition also score highly in the other conditions. The general amount of between-subjects variability is less important to the power of the test. The reason for this is that, as the name implies, the within-subjects ANOVA analyzes only within-subject variability, essentially equating for between-subject variability.

The figures that follow illustrate the core concept behind within-subjects ANOVA.

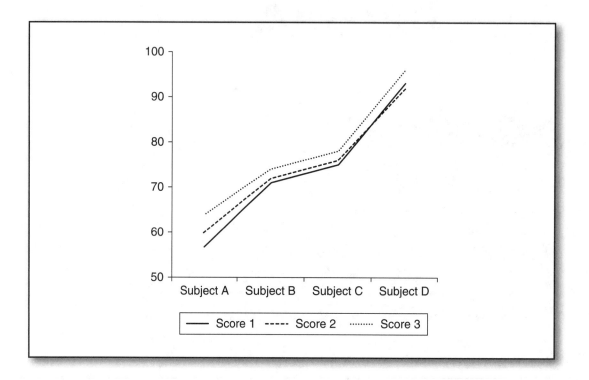

The scores on three tests (1 through 3) are shown for each of four subjects (A, B, C, and D). As you can see, most of the variability in the figure is between-subjects, and there is almost no difference between the tests. Because of this, it would seem to be difficult to draw any conclusions regarding which test scores higher or lower than the others.

However, in the next figure, the between-subject variability has been removed by subtracting each subject's mean from his or her score on each test.

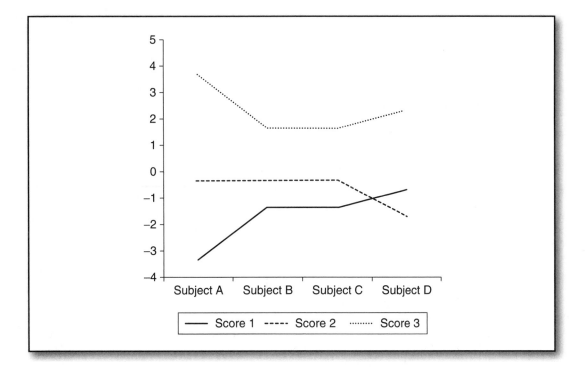

This figure captures the essence of within-subjects ANOVA: The effect of the within-subject manipulation (in this case, the different tests) is isolated by removing the between-subject variability.

BEHIND THE SCENES: MODELING THE WITHIN-SUBJECTS ANOVA

Recall that in the between-subjects ANOVAs discussed earlier, each observation is characterized as the sum of the group (or cell) mean plus error. The logic of the within-subjects ANOVA is similar, but there is one major conceptual difference. Instead of being a function of the group mean, each observation is broken down into the *individual* mean, a *deviation from that mean* for each within-subject treatment condition, and error.

$$Obs_{ij} = indiv_i + treatment_j + e_{ij}$$

This schematic equation reveals the two main advantages of within-subjects ANOVA. First, the variability of the middle term (*treatment*) across subjects reflects the effect of the treatment *around each subject's own mean,* and because each individual's mean (*indiv*) is included in the model, it controls for general differences between subjects (i.e., individual differences) on the dependent measure. This is the idea captured by comparing the first two figures in this chapter. Second, the very fact that the individual mean term (*indiv*) is explicitly included in the model means that it is not part of the error term. This reduces error variance and hence increases power to detect differences between the treatment conditions.

Computing the Within-Subjects ANOVA Using SPSS

We'll practice computing the within-subjects ANOVA using SPSS on the data file called "TestStrategy.sav" from the website. This file contains a data set of scores on a standardized achievement test. Each participant took each of the six modules of the test in one of six conditions (in counterbalanced order, of course). In the first two conditions, the participants were told to answer with their "gut response" either quickly (first condition) or slowly (second condition); in the next two conditions, the participants were told to reason through each problem, narrow the multiple choices down to the top two, then choose between those either quickly (third condition) or slowly (fourth condition); in the final two conditions, the participants always chose "a" either quickly (fifth condition) or slowly (sixth condition). The scores on the dependent measure reflect percent correct answers.

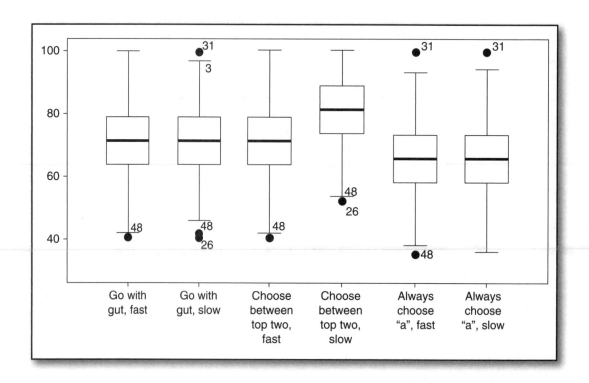

The figure displays boxplots for each of the six test scores. You can see that there is quite a bit of variation within each test (indexing between-subject variability). Because of this within-group variability, it might be difficult to find significant differences using between-subjects ANOVA. A within-subjects approach is justified to address person-to-person variation in general intelligence or test-taking ability. Before we begin, briefly notice the way the data are structured for within-subjects ANOVA.

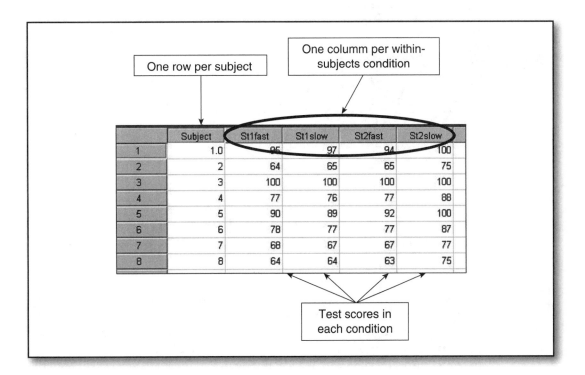

Instead of having all of the scores in a single variable and the condition codes in a second variable (as in between-subjects ANOVA), here each participant has his or her own row with all six scores entered as columns. There is no indicator variable with the condition codes (e.g. "1," "2," etc.), as that information is contained in the variable names.

To begin, click on **Analyze → General Linear Model → Repeated Measures**. This will bring up the initial "Define Factors" box.

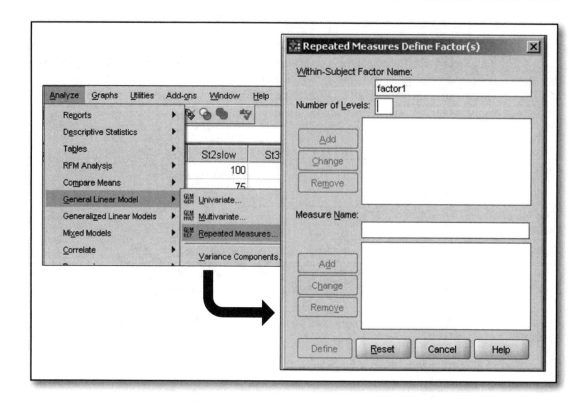

As we noted previously, each condition has its own data column, and there is no indicator variable that tells SPSS which column of data goes with which condition. The purpose of this dialogue box is to specify which variables correspond to which factor levels. In this case, there are two factors: *strategy,* with three levels (gut response, choose between top two, and choose "a"), and *speed,* with two levels (fast and slow). Add the names into the "Within-Subject Factor Name" field, indicate the number of levels, and then click "Add" for each. Click "Define" to proceed to the next step.

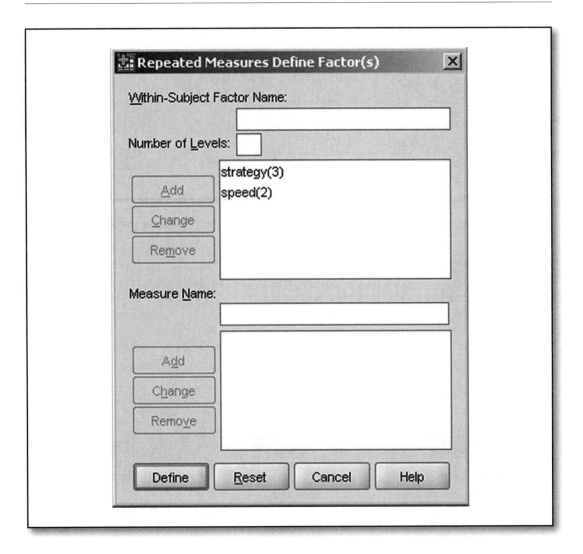

Next, SPSS needs to know which of the columns in the data file correspond to each of the cells in our 3 × 2 design. Each cell is given a designation using two numbers: The first is the level of the first factor (*strategy*), and the second is the level of the second factor (*speed*). In case you forget which one is which (I always do!), SPSS reminds you of the order at the top of the box (*strategy, speed*). For example, cell "3,1" refers to the third strategy level ("choose 'a'") and the first speed level ("fast").

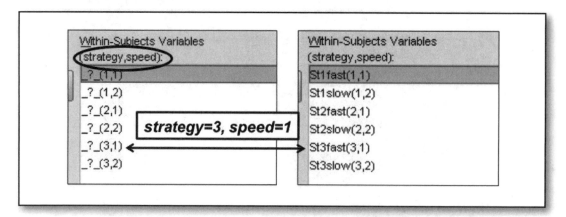

As with the between-subjects ANOVA (and with all GLM functions), the "Model" button allows you to specify which terms go into the model (e.g., interactions). The full factorial—with all interactions and all main effects—is the default selection.

The "Contrasts" button allows you to specify a restricted set of contrasts *only among the levels of each factor on its own*. More sophisticated contrasts require syntax and are covered the following text.

Specify the line graphs you'd like by clicking on the "Plots" button. This is identical to the boxes we've encountered in previous chapters. We tend to plot the factor with more levels on the horizontal axis, so we've put *strategy* there. Don't forget to click "Add" when you're done.

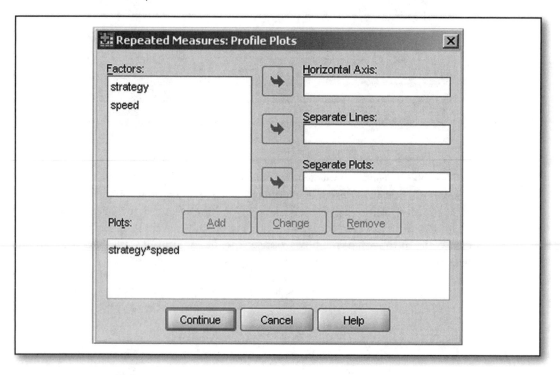

The "Options" button allows you to specify a number of miscellaneous and sometimes useful outputs. Here, we've selected to display descriptive statistics (means and standard deviations) for each cell. The "Homogeneity tests" option refers only to *between-group* equality of variance and will not produce output in this context. A slightly different (though analogous) type of equality of variance, sphericity, will be tested automatically in all within-subjects ANOVAs.

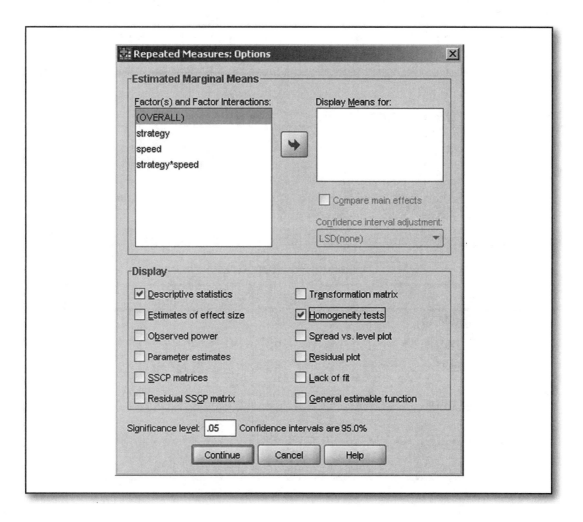

In the end, the full syntax for this maneuver is

```
GLM St1fast St1slow St2fast St2slow St3fast St3slow
/WSFACTOR=strategy 3 Polynomial speed 2 Polynomial
/PLOT=PROFILE(strategy*speed)
```

```
/PRINT=DESCRIPTIVE

/WSDESIGN=strategy speed strategy*speed.
```

An important point to note is that the conceptual factor names, *strategy* and *speed,* are not actually listed on the first line as variables because there are no variables called "strategy" and "speed." Those two conceptual factors are defined by the variables that comprise them, which is specified in the "/WSFACTOR" tag. That tag links the six variables listed in the "GLM" line with the conceptual 3 × 2 structure. As such, the order of the variables in the "/WSFACTOR" tag matters: *Strategy 3 speed 2* will produce different results than *speed 2 strategy 3* because it maps the factor levels to different variables.

Interpreting the ANOVA Output

The within-subjects output largely mirrors the output we've already seen from between-subjects ANOVA. The core pieces are conceptually similar—descriptives, tests of homogeneity of variance, ANOVA tables, and means plots—but the details are slightly different in some cases. The descriptives are first. Note that the means are fairly close considering the standard deviations.

Descriptive Statistics

	Mean	Std. Deviation	N
Go with gut, fast	71.53	11.822	100
Go with gut, slow	71.53	11.765	100
Choose between top two, fast	71.53	11.798	100
Choose between top two, slow	81.28	11.286	100
Always choose "a", fast	66.07	12.142	100
Always choose "a", slow	66.26	12.106	100

As an important aside, remember that in within-subjects ANOVAs, the standard deviations don't contain much useful information for hypothesis testing (unlike in between-subjects ANOVA) because the tests also depend on the extent of covariation among the conditions.

The next piece of output is one of the most confusing tables that SPSS produces. It's titled "Multivariate Tests" and contains what looks like tests of our two main effects and their interaction.

Multivariate Tests[b]

Effect		Value	F	Hypothesis df	Error df	Sig.
strategy	Pillai's Trace	.951	944.985[a]	2.000	98.000	.000
	Wilks' Lambda	.049	944.985[a]	2.000	98.000	.000
	Hotelling's Trace	19.285	944.985[a]	2.000	98.000	.000
	Roy's Largest Root	19.285	944.985[a]	2.000	98.000	.000
speed	Pillai's Trace	.918	1111.995[a]	1.000	99.000	.000
	Wilks' Lambda	.082	1111.995[a]	1.000	99.000	.000
	Hotelling's Trace	11.232	1111.995[a]	1.000	99.000	.000
	Roy's Largest Root	11.232	1111.995[a]	1.000	99.000	.000
strategy * speed	Pillai's Trace	.945	835.167[a]	2.000	98.000	.000
	Wilks' Lambda	.055	835.167[a]	2.000	98.000	.000
	Hotelling's Trace	17.044	835.167[a]	2.000	98.000	.000
	Roy's Largest Root	17.044	835.167[a]	2.000	98.000	.000

This is NOT what you want to look at for within-subjects tests!

This actually reports the results of a *multivariate* ANOVA (or MANOVA) testing the effect of the manipulations on all of the dependent measures simultaneously. There will be more discussion of this kind of ANOVA in Chapter 10, but for now, simply be warned that *this output is not interpretable in the context of within-subjects ANOVAs.*

The next piece of output is the test of equality of variance. Not equality between groups, but equality of variances across different factor levels. Mauchly's test actually compares the *differences* in the error covariance between the levels, for example, the difference between [cov(Strategy 1) – cov(Strategy 2)] and [cov(Strategy 2) – cov(Strategy 3)]. As such, it will be computed only for factors with three or more levels. This explains why it was not computed for *speed*, which has only two levels.

Mauchly's Test of Sphericity[b]

Measure:MEASURE_1

Within Subjects Effect	Mauchly's W	Approx. Chi-Square	df	Sig.	Epsilon[a]		
					Greenhouse-Geisser	Huynh-Feldt	Lower-bound
strategy	.609	48.594	2	.000	.719	.727	.500
speed	1.000	.000	0	.	1.000	1.000	1.000
strategy * speed	.900	10.362	2	.006	.909	.925	.500

Tests the null hypothesis that the error covariance matrix of the orthonormalized transformed dependent variables is proportional to an identity matrix.

a. May be used to adjust the degrees of freedom for the averaged tests of significance. Corrected tests are displayed in the Tests of Within-Subjects Effects table.

b. Design: Intercept
Within Subjects Design: strategy + speed + strategy * speed

By selecting "Residual SSCP" matrix in the "Options" button, or equivalently by adding "/PRINT = RSSCP" to the syntax, SPSS will (a) print out the error variance-covariance matrix for all six factors, showing the 6 variances along the diagonal and the 15 covariances in the off-diagonal, and (b) test the somewhat conservative assumption (compared to sphericity) that all the variances are equal to each other and that all the covariances are equal to zero. This second piece of output is called Bartlett's test. This is a nice feature because it gives us some information about the sphericity assumption even when there is a factor with only two levels. See Chapter 9 for more detailed information about the various tests of homogeneity of variance.

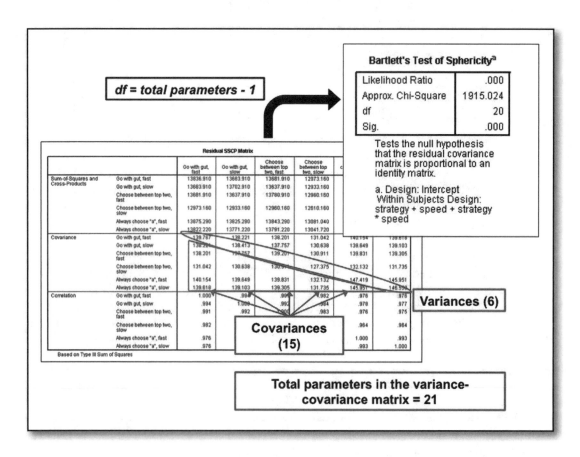

As with all of the homogeneity tests in SPSS, the null hypothesis is that equality of variance is *met,* so a significant test (as is the case here) indicates a violation of the homogeneity of variance assumption. A violation of this assumption can be addressed by using one of the corrected tests that follow, in which the degrees of freedom are adjusted according to the parameter *epsilon,* which indicates the degree of the violation. Smaller values indicate a larger violation.

Finally, the "Tests of Within-Subjects Effects" ANOVA table displays the actual hypothesis tests.

Tests of Within-Subjects Effects

Measure:MEASURE_1

Source		Type III Sum of Squares	df	Mean Square	F	Sig.
strategy	Sphericity Assumed	10493.763	2	5246.882	1058.748	.000
	Greenhouse-Geisser	10493.763	1.438	7298.164	1058.748	.000
	Huynh-Feldt	10493.763	1.453	7220.681	1058.748	.000
	Lower-bound	10493.763	1.000	10493.763	1058.748	.000
Error(strategy)	Sphericity Assumed	981.237	198	4.956		
	Greenhouse-Geisser	981.237	142.348	6.893		
	Huynh-Feldt	981.237	143.876	6.820		
	Lower-bound	981.237	99.000	9.911		
speed	Sphericity Assumed	1646.727	1	1646.727	1111.995	.000
	Greenhouse-Geisser	1646.727	1.000	1646.727	1111.995	.000
	Huynh-Feldt	1646.727	1.000	1646.727	1111.995	.000
	Lower-bound	1646.727	1.000	1646.727	1111.995	.000
Error(speed)	Sphericity Assumed	146.607	99	1.481		
	Greenhouse-Geisser	146.607	99.000	1.481		
	Huynh-Feldt	146.607	99.000	1.481		
	Lower-bound	146.607	99.000	1.481		
strategy * speed	Sphericity Assumed	3108.203	2	1554.102	1109.019	.000
	Greenhouse-Geisser	3108.203	1.818	1710.031	1109.019	.000
	Huynh-Feldt	3108.203	1.850	1680.338	1109.019	.000
	Lower-bound	3108.203	1.000	3108.203	1109.019	.000
Error(strategy*speed)	Sphericity Assumed	277.463	198	1.401		
	Greenhouse-Geisser	277.463	179.945	1.542		
	Huynh-Feldt	277.463	183.125	1.515		
	Lower-bound	277.463	99.000	2.803		

Each test is offered in several variations, the first of which should be used if sphericity is met ("Sphericity assumed"), and one of the others if it is not. The sum-of-squares is identical for all versions of the test, but the degrees of freedom is adjusted to account for nonindependence of error variances. For example, we learned from Mauchly's test that sphericity was not met for the *strategy* factor with a Greenhouse-Geisser epsilon of 0.719. The degrees of freedom for the "sphericity assumed" test is 2 (number of levels minus one), and the degrees of freedom for the Greenhouse-Geisser corrected test of the *strategy* effect is 2 * 0.719 = 1.438. Note that this correction is also applied to the degrees of freedom of the error term.

As always, the mean squares are computed by dividing the sum-of-squares by the degrees of freedom, and the *F* ratio is computed by dividing the mean square value by the mean square error. The *F* ratios are identical for all the versions of the tests (violation-corrected or not), but the *p* values differ slightly because the *F* values are drawn from distributions with different degrees of freedom (e.g., an *F* value with 2, 30 degrees of freedom produces a different *p* value than the same *F* value with 1, 15 degrees of freedom). In this case, there is a significant effect of *strategy*, a significant effect of *speed*, and a significant interaction between the two. An examination of the means plot will be required to understand these effects.

Plotting the Results of Within-Subjects ANOVA

The means plot shows the average test score in each of the six conditions.

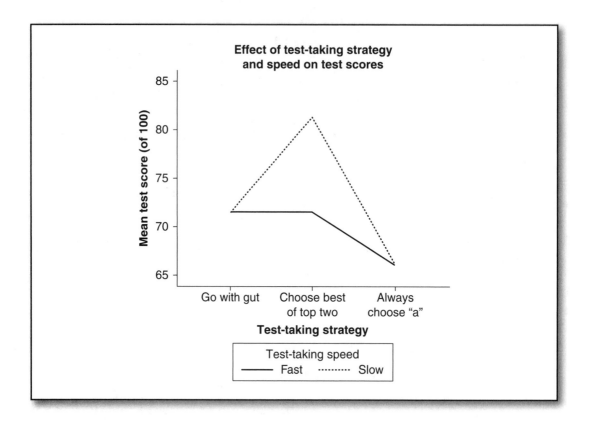

We can clearly see that the source of the interaction is the combination of the lack of differences between fast and slow test-taking for the first and third strategies ("go with gut" and "always choose 'a'"), but the large difference between fast and slow test-taking for the second strategy ("reason through and choose the best of the top two"). The main effect of *strategy* (qualified by the interaction) is that scores were higher overall during the second strategy compared to the other two, and the main effect of *speed* (also qualified by the interaction) is that scores were higher overall during slow rather than fast test-taking.

Notice that we have intentionally omitted error bars from this figure. The usual error bars (e.g., standard errors) are based on the standard deviation of the scores within each category *across subjects* and are thus misleading when paired with *within-subjects* tests. The proper error bars for within-subjects tests must be adjusted for covariation between the means. SPSS is currently not capable of producing those, so we recommend plotting error bars based on the mean *difference* between the conditions (e.g., standard error of *fast – slow*) in other software such as Microsoft Excel.

MAKING THE MOST OF SYNTAX:
CUSTOM CONTRASTS IN WITHIN-SUBJECTS ANOVA

After you've run the full factorial, you may want to follow it up with planned comparisons. Like in the between-subjects ANOVA, these can be computed to a limited degree from the point-and-click menus, and far more flexibly using syntax. Add the tag "/MMATRIX" followed by a list of factor levels and coefficients to your GLM syntax to compute custom contrasts for within-subjects ANOVAs. The general syntax is

```
GLM [FL₁₁] [FL₁₂] . . . [FL₁ⱼ] [FL₂₁] [FL₂₂] . . .
[FL₂ⱼ] . . . [FLᵢ₁] [FLᵢ₂] . . . [FLᵢⱼ]

/WSFACTOR = [F1] i [F2] j

/MMATRIX = [FL₁₁] c₁ [FL₁₂] c₂ . . . [FLᵢⱼ] cᵢ*ⱼ

/WSDESIGN = F1 F2 F1*F2 .
```

Where "FL_{ij}" is the variable corresponding to the ith level of the first factor and the jth level of the second factor, "F1" is the first factor, "F2" is the second factor, and c_k is the custom contrast coefficient for the kth within-subjects variable (where $k = i*j$).

For example, suppose we wanted to test whether fast gut responses (Factor 1 level 1 / Factor 2 level 1) produce higher test scores than choosing "a" quickly (Factor 1 level 3 / Factor 2 level 1). We could add the line

```
/MMATRIX = St1fast 1 St1slow 0 St2fast 0 St2slow 0
St3fast -1 St3slow 0
```

to our syntax. Alternatively, SPSS will automatically assume that any factor levels not listed on the "/MMATRIX" tag have zero coefficients, so we can omit those entirely. The final syntax is

```
GLM St1fast St1slow St2fast St2slow St3fast St3slow

/WSFACTOR= strategy 3 Polynomial speed 2 Polynomial

/MMATRIX = St1fast 1 St3fast -1

/WSDESIGN=strategy speed strategy*speed
```

which produces the output that we've seen before and additionally the custom contrast test seen next.

Custom Hypothesis Tests

Contrast Results (K Matrix)

Contrast[a]		Transfor... T1
L1	Contrast Estimate	5.460
	Hypothesized Value	0
	Difference (Estimate - Hypothesized)	5.460
	Std. Error	.262
	Sig.	.000
	95% Confidence Interval for Difference Lower Bound	4.940
	Upper Bound	5.980

a. Estimable Function for Intercept

Test Results

Transformed Variable:T1

Source	Sum of Squares	df	Mean Square	F	Sig.
Contrast	2981.160	1	2981.160	433.486	.000
Error	680.840	99	6.877		

It's always good to check the "contrast estimate" value (here, 5.46) against the descriptive statistics to make sure that you're testing the comparison you intend. The mean score for fast gut responses is 71.53, and the mean for fast "a" choices is 66.07, and the difference between them is indeed 5.46. The ANOVA table is given in the "Test Results" output that follows. This test has 1, 99 degrees of freedom: 1 because there is only one line in the contrast ([1 0 0 0 –1 0]) and 99 because there are 100 total independent observations, and $df\text{-}error = N - 1$. The significant p value indicates that gut responses—even rapidly produced ones—generate higher test scores than does quickly choosing the first option on a multiple-choice test. How much higher? The 95% confidence interval (in the bottom of the "Contrast Results" table) suggests about 5% to 6% higher.

The "/MMATRIX" command can be used in conjunction with "/KMATRIX" to test arbitrary differences. For example, to test whether fast responses decreased test scores by at least 10% compared to slow responses for the second strategy, add the following two lines to your GLM syntax:

```
/MMATRIX = S2fast -1 S2slow 1
/KMATRIX = 10
```

CONNECTIONS: EQUIVALENCE BETWEEN WITHIN-SUBJECTS ANOVA AND PAIRED-SAMPLES *T*-TESTS

The within-subjects ANOVA is conceptually and computationally identical to paired-samples *t*-tests when examining a single factor with two levels. Each capitalizes on the (presumed) correlation between the two variables to reduce error variance related to between-subjects differences. In other words, they both correct for person-to-person variability by examining difference scores rather than raw values. For instance, the custom contrast computed on the previous page (between fast gut responses and fast "a" choices) is the test of the difference between only two variables. It can be computed as a paired-samples *t*-test using the following syntax:

```
T-TEST PAIRS=St1fast WITH St3fast (PAIRED) .
```

The output automatically includes descriptives (means, *N*s, standard deviations, and standard errors) for both variables, as well as the correlation between the pair to remind you that SPSS is using that information in the paired-sample test.

Paired Samples Statistics

		Mean	N	Std. Deviation	Std. Error Mean
Pair 1	Go with gut, fast	71.53	100	11.822	1.182
	Always choose "a", fast	66.07	100	12.142	1.214

Paired Samples Correlations

		N	Correlation	Sig.
Pair 1	Go with gut, fast & Always choose "a", fast	100	.976	.000

Paired Samples Test

		Paired Differences					t	df	Sig. (2-tailed)
		Mean	Std. Deviation	Std. Error Mean	95% Confidence Interval of the Difference				
					Lower	Upper			
Pair 1	Go with gut, fast - Always choose "a", fast	5.460	2.622	.262	4.940	5.980	20.820	99	.000

Notice that the standard errors of the variables individually are roughly 1.2, but that the standard error of the difference is only 0.26; this is due to the high correlation between the variables.

The mean difference is 5.46 as on the previous page, and the *t* value is 20.82. Recall that $F = t^2$, suggesting that the *F* value for this comparison is $20.82^2 = 433.47$. This is identical to the value from the planned comparison test computed earlier (with rounding error).

The main effect of speed can also be replicated using a paired *t*-test between the average score of the three fast conditions and the average score of the three slow conditions:

```
COMPUTE fast = mean(St1fast, St2fast, St3fast) .
COMPUTE slow = mean(St1slow, St2slow, St3slow) .
EXE .
T-TEST PAIRS=slow WITH fast (PAIRED) .
```

This produces the following output:

Paired Samples Test

		Paired Differences							
					95% Confidence Interval of the Difference				
		Mean	Std. Deviation	Std. Error Mean	Lower	Upper	t	df	Sig. (2-tailed)
Pair 1	slow - fast	3.31333	.99360	.09936	3.11618	3.51049	33.347	99	.000

You can confirm for yourself that this *t*-test result is identical to the main effect of *speed* computed earlier using the GLM function.

KEYWORDS

treatment effect	sphericity	MMATRIX
repeated measures	Mauchly's test	

Mixed-Model ANOVA

Conceptual Background of the Mixed-Model ANOVA

So far, we've discussed experiments with only within- or between-subjects data. The mixed-model ANOVA is for special cases with at least one of each in the data. In these cases, two or more *independent* groups of subjects each complete some experimental task in two or more *within-subjects* (and thus correlated) conditions. Continuing with the example from Chapter 8, suppose two separate groups of students at different *ages* (first graders/third graders) each took a multiple-choice test using three different *strategies* (gut response/choose best of two answers/always pick "a"). In this case, *age* is a between-subjects factor because it consists of two (assumed to be) independent levels with zero correlation between them, and *strategy* is a within-subjects factor because it consists of three correlated levels. Just as with the within-subjects ANOVA, the mixed-model ANOVA can capitalize on the correlation between the levels of the within-subjects factor(s) to reduce error variance and increase power for those effects.

In a general sense, including more experimental factors (within- or between-subjects) in your model will often increase power because variance associated with those factors will be accounted for and excluded from the error variance. But beyond this general rule, tests of between-subjects effects in the context of a mixed-model design are not necessarily more powerful than simply running a between-subjects ANOVA separately on each of the within-subjects factors. For example, the test of the effect of age on test scores in the "gut response" condition will be identical whether the other test-taking strategies are included or not. Including the additional correlated data does not change the power to detect between-subjects effects.

So if there is not an increase in power, why use the mixed-model ANOVA? The main advantage is the ability to test interesting theoretical questions (e.g., interactions between factors of interest) using relatively fewer subjects than would be required by a pure between-subjects ANOVA. In other words, mixed-model ANOVAs are *efficient*. For instance, in the context of the present example, a researcher might want to know whether the effect of test-taking strategy (i.e., the difference among the levels of *strategy*) was different for first and third graders (i.e., whether there is an interaction between *strategy* and *age*). The researcher has at least three options: (a) a two-way between-subjects ANOVA using six different groups of participants (three third grade and three first grade) to take a single test each; (b) a mixed-model ANOVA using two different groups of participants (one first grade and one third grade) to take three tests each; or (c) a within-subjects ANOVA using one group of participants taking three tests when they are in first grade and then again when they are in third grade.

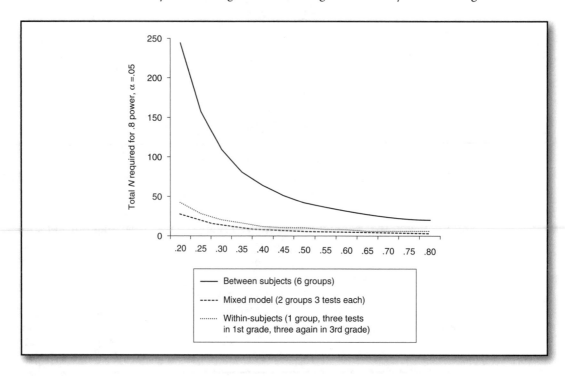

Assuming the interaction effect was about 0.2 in size and a researcher wanted 0.8 power with an alpha of .05, power analyses indicate that the first option would require 158 total subjects, the second option would require 28 total subjects, and the third option would require 19 subjects. Considering that the third option is the most efficient but would take 2 years to run, the second option—the mixed-model ANOVA—seems like a good compromise between efficiency and timeliness. For this reason, the mixed-model ANOVA is a popular choice among researchers when some variables can be measured within-subjects but where it is impractical or impossible for others to be.

Computing the Mixed-Model ANOVA Using SPSS

Continuing with the example test strategy data from Chapter 9, the data set "TestStrategyGrades.sav" on the website contains scores on a standardized multiple-choice test from two groups of subjects—first graders and third graders—each taking the same test using one of three strategies—answer with your "gut response," narrow down to the top two and choose the best one, or always choose option "a." The raw data are displayed in the figure.

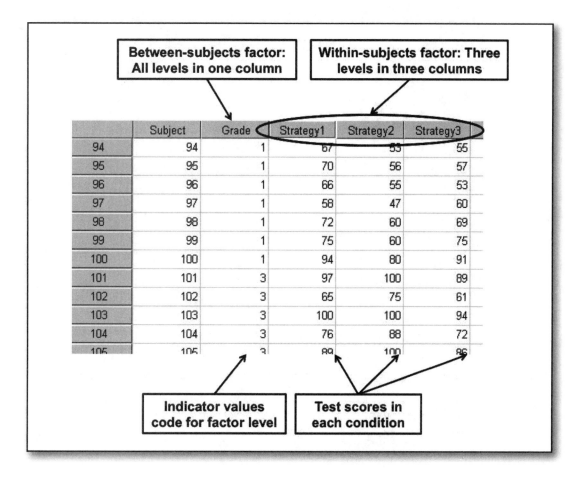

Notice that the scores on each of the three different strategies—the *within-subjects* variable—are stored in separate columns in the data file. The three columns together form a single conceptual factor, *strategy,* with each factor level represented by one column. In contrast, the entire *between-subjects* variable, *grade,* is stored as a single column containing values that indicate the factor level (i.e., condition) for each participant.

As far as SPSS is concerned, the mixed-model ANOVA is a special case of the within-subjects ANOVA. With that in mind, it makes sense that you begin your computation by clicking **Analyze → General Linear Model → Repeated Measures.** Next, define the *within-subjects factor only* in the dialogue box. In this case, *strategy* has three levels. Then click "Define."

In the next window, specify the three levels of strategy (imaginatively named "Strategy1," "Strategy2," and "Strategy3"):

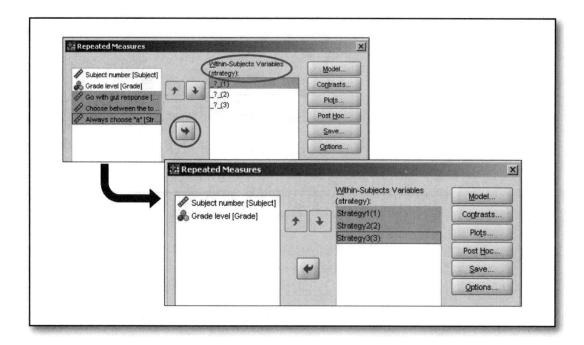

Then specify the one between-subjects factor, *grade,* in the following box:

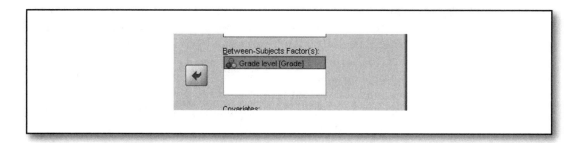

As with the previous forms of the GLM we've seen, a number of options can be customized for the mixed-model ANOVA. The "Model" button allows you to customize the terms to include in the model; by default, it will include all main effects and interactions, including the "mixed" interaction of the between- and within-subjects variables. The "Contrasts" button allows you to perform specific comparisons among the levels of each of the IVs but not between the IVs. The options offered in this menu are somewhat restricted, so we recommend using syntax to specify custom contrasts as an alternative. The "Plots" menu allows you to specify plots of the means to better understand the main effects and interaction. These can be generated in the usual way (for example, see Chapters 6 and 7).

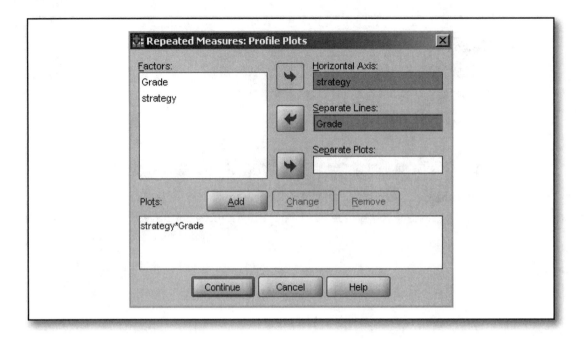

The "Post Hoc" menu contains options for post hoc tests of pairwise comparisons *among the levels of the between-subjects factor only.* These tests can be used to correct for the inflated experiment-wise Type 1 error that follows from running all of the multiple tests required to compare each cell mean to every other (see Chapter 6 and your statistics textbook for more information on these tests). This feature is generally useful only when there are a large number of factor levels in the between-subjects factor (e.g., more than 4). As there are only two levels of the between-subjects factor in the present example and the difference between them is tested as the main effect of that factor, we will omit post hoc tests for now.

As we've seen before, the "Options" menu contains a number of useful miscellaneous options that produce some useful output.

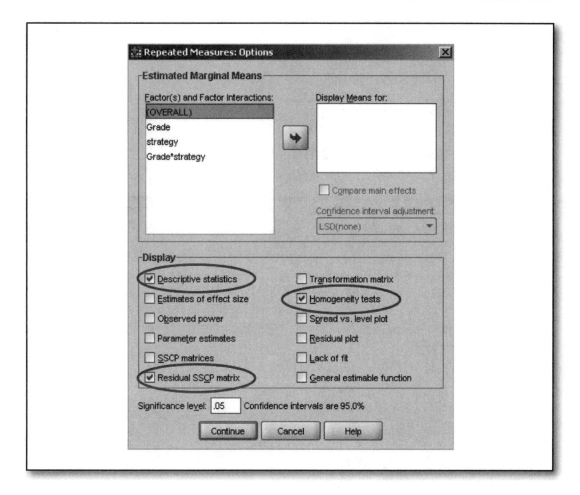

Notably, we've requested "Descriptive statistics" to see *N*s, *M*s, and *SD*s for each of the cells, as well as "Residual SSCP matrix" and "Homogeneity tests," in order to see several tests to check for homogeneity of variance among the levels of the within- and between-subjects factors, respectively.

The syntax for this function is

```
GLM Strategy1 Strategy2 Strategy3 BY Grade

/WSFACTOR=strategy 3 Polynomial

/PLOT=PROFILE(strategy*Grade)

/PRINT=DESCRIPTIVE RSSCP HOMOGENEITY

/WSDESIGN=strategy

/DESIGN=Grade.
```

Note that there are two separate designs: one for the *within-subjects* effect ("/WSDESIGN") and another for the *between-subjects* effect ("/DESIGN"). Any and all interactions between within- and between-subjects variables are automatically tested even though they are not included explicitly in the syntax. As we will learn later, there is also a division between the two types of factors when specifying custom contrasts in mixed-model ANOVA.

A CLOSER LOOK: TESTING THE ASSUMPTIONS OF THE MIXED-MODEL ANOVA

We want to briefly discuss the various and at times confusing tests of homogeneity before we begin to parse the rest of the output. In mixed-model ANOVA, there are actually *two* assumptions regarding equality of error variances. The first relates to the *within-subject* variance-covariance matrix of the residuals. The assumption is that the variances of the levels of the within-subject factors are equal to one another and the covariances among the levels are equal to one another (but not necessarily the same as the variances). This assumption is called *sphericity* or sometimes *compound symmetry.* It is assumed that all subjects have the same compound symmetric variance-covariance matrix.

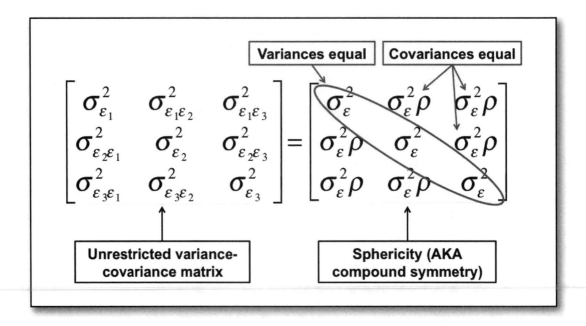

In the case of the test-taking strategy example, each subject took three different tests. Hence, there is a 3 × 3 matrix describing the structure of the *within-subject* variances of those scores. The assumption of sphericity tests whether the error variance of each test-taking strategy is equal to the variance of the others *and* whether the covariances among them are equal. This assumption is tested primarily with Mauchly's test, which is generated automatically when you run any within-subjects or repeated-measures model.

Mauchly's Test of Sphericity[b]

Measure:MEASURE_1

Within Subjects Effect	Mauchly's W	Approx. Chi-Square	df	Sig.	Epsilon[a]		
					Greenhouse-Geisser	Huynh-Feldt	Lower-bound
strategy	.828	37.159	2	.000	.853	.864	.500

Tests the null hypothesis that the error covariance matrix of the orthonormalized transformed dependent variables is proportional to an identity matrix.

a. May be used to adjust the degrees of freedom for the averaged tests of significance. Corrected tests are displayed in the Tests of Within-Subjects Effects table.

b. Design: Intercept + Grade
Within Subjects Design: strategy

Note that Mauchly's test produces output in SPSS only when the within-subjects factor has three or more levels. When there are only two within-subject levels, the assumption of sphericity is not necessary because the statistical tests used in the two cases (sphericity met vs. sphericity not met) produce identical output.

The actual within-subject variance-covariance matrix being tested for sphericity is called the "SSCP Matrix" (from "sum-of-squares cross-product") and can be requested from the "Options" menu or "/PRINT = RSSCP" in syntax.

Residual SSCP Matrix

		Go with gut response	Choose between the top two	Always choose "a"
Sum-of-Squares and Cross-Products	Go with gut response	27489.020	26702.970	27602.530
	Choose between the top two	26702.970	26722.670	27044.730
	Always choose "a"	27602.530	27044.730	29103.750
Covariance	Go with gut response	138.833	134.863	139.407
	Choose between the top two	134.863	134.963	136.590
	Always choose "a"	139.407	136.590	146.989
Correlation	Go with gut response	1.000	.985	.976
	Choose between the top two	.985	1.000	.970
	Always choose "a"	.976	.970	1.000

Based on Type III Sum of Squares

$$? = \begin{bmatrix} \sigma_\varepsilon^2 & \sigma_\varepsilon^2 \rho & \sigma_\varepsilon^2 \rho \\ \sigma_\varepsilon^2 \rho & \sigma_\varepsilon^2 & \sigma_\varepsilon^2 \rho \\ \sigma_\varepsilon^2 \rho & \sigma_\varepsilon^2 \rho & \sigma_\varepsilon^2 \end{bmatrix}$$

Mauchly's test:
Does this covariance matrix meet
sphericity (AKA compound symmetry)?

The second assumption is that the within-subject variance-covariance matrix—the one that we just tested for sphericity—is equal across the two *between-subjects* groups. This assumption can be examined using Box's test, which answers the question, "Are the error variances among the within-subjects factor levels the same for all groups of subjects?"

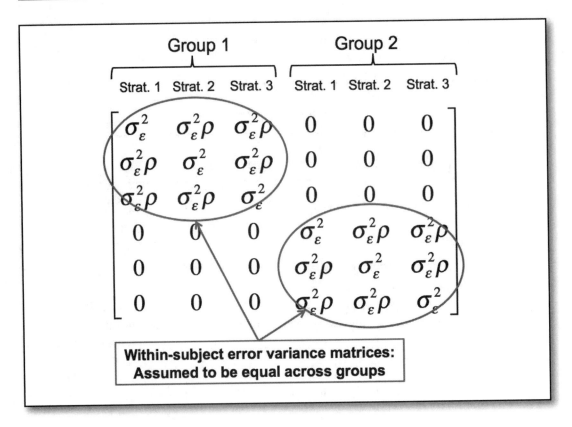

In the case of the present example, this simply tests whether the error variance matrix for first graders is the same as that for third graders. According to Box's test, it is (just barely—phew!).

Box's Test of Equality of Covariance Matrices[a]

Box's M	11.101
F	1.820
df1	6
df2	284044.075
Sig.	.091

Tests the null hypothesis that the observed covariance
matrices of the dependent variables are equal across groups.

a. Design: Intercept + Grade
Within Subjects Design: strategy

If there is a violation of this second assumption, it may be helpful to inspect Levene's test for each of the three within-subjects factor levels. This test compares the variance of the two groups for each test-taking strategy independently.

Levene's Test of Equality of Error Variances[a]

	F	df1	df2	Sig.
Go with gut response	.002	1	198	.967
Choose between the top two	.076	1	198	.784
Always choose "a"	.004	1	198	.947

Tests the null hypothesis that the error variance of the dependent variable is equal across groups.

a. Design: Intercept + Grade
Within Subjects Design: strategy

Given that the F values for all of the strategies are very low (indicating no between-group heteroscedasticity), the near-significant result of Box's test is likely driven by between-group differences in the *covariances* among the strategies.

Both tests of between-group equality of variance—Box's test and Levene's test—will be generated by checking "Homogeneity tests" in the Options menu or by adding "/PRINT=HOMOGENEITY" to the syntax.

People are often confused by the third test of "sphericity" presented here, Bartlett's test. SPSS generates this test as part of the output when you request "Residual RSSCP matrix" from the Options menu or add "/PRINT=RSSCP" to the syntax. Bartlett's test evaluates a more restrictive condition than sphericity or equality of variance-covariance matrices across groups as discussed earlier. It tests whether the variances of all the variances (i.e., each within-subjects factor level from each group) are equal to each other (which is part of sphericity) *and* whether all the covariances, including within-subjects covariances, are equal to zero (which is not part of sphericity).

$$
\begin{array}{c}
\overbrace{\qquad\text{Group 1}\qquad}\;\overbrace{\qquad\text{Group 2}\qquad}\\[2pt]
\text{Strat. 1 Strat. 2 Strat. 3} \quad \text{Strat. 1 Strat. 2 Strat. 3}\\[2pt]
\begin{bmatrix}
\sigma^2_\varepsilon & \sigma^2_\varepsilon\rho & \sigma^2_\varepsilon\rho & 0 & 0 & 0\\
\sigma^2_\varepsilon\rho & \sigma^2_\varepsilon & \sigma^2_\varepsilon\rho & 0 & 0 & 0\\
\sigma^2_\varepsilon\rho & \sigma^2_\varepsilon\rho & \sigma^2_\varepsilon & 0 & 0 & 0\\
0 & 0 & 0 & \sigma^2_\varepsilon & \sigma^2_\varepsilon\rho & \sigma^2_\varepsilon\rho\\
0 & 0 & 0 & \sigma^2_\varepsilon\rho & \sigma^2_\varepsilon & \sigma^2_\varepsilon\rho\\
0 & 0 & 0 & \sigma^2_\varepsilon\rho & \sigma^2_\varepsilon\rho & \sigma^2_\varepsilon
\end{bmatrix}
\end{array}
\qquad
\begin{array}{c}
\overbrace{\qquad\text{Group 1}\qquad}\;\overbrace{\qquad\text{Group 2}\qquad}\\[2pt]
\text{Strat. 1 Strat. 2 Strat. 3} \quad \text{Strat. 1 Strat. 2 Strat. 3}\\[2pt]
\begin{bmatrix}
\sigma^2_\varepsilon & 0 & 0 & 0 & 0 & 0\\
0 & \sigma^2_\varepsilon & 0 & 0 & 0 & 0\\
0 & 0 & \sigma^2_\varepsilon & 0 & 0 & 0\\
0 & 0 & 0 & \sigma^2_\varepsilon & 0 & 0\\
0 & 0 & 0 & 0 & \sigma^2_\varepsilon & 0\\
0 & 0 & 0 & 0 & 0 & \sigma^2_\varepsilon
\end{bmatrix}
\end{array}
$$

Sphericity _and_ equality of covariance matrices (Mauchly's _and_ Box's tests)	**Homoscedasticity and independence (Bartlett's test)**

Because Bartlett's test is partly checking whether the within-subject covariances are zero, and we assume that they are not, the null hypothesis of Bartlett's test will nearly always be rejected in repeated-measures or mixed-model ANOVAs. This test is most useful in evaluating whether to use within-subjects or repeated-measures, or whether there is any correlation between your within-subjects factor levels at all.

Bartlett's Test of Sphericity[a]

Likelihood Ratio	.000
Approx. Chi-Square	1303.445
df	5
Sig.	.000

Tests the null hypothesis that the residual covariance matrix is proportional to an identity matrix.

a. Design: Intercept + Grade
Within Subjects Design: strategy

Interpreting the Output of the Mixed-Model ANOVA

As with other forms of the GLM, the first few pieces of output from the mixed-model ANOVA contain descriptive information about the cells. The only different thing to note here is the different sample sizes in the between-subject cells (100) and within-subject cells (200).

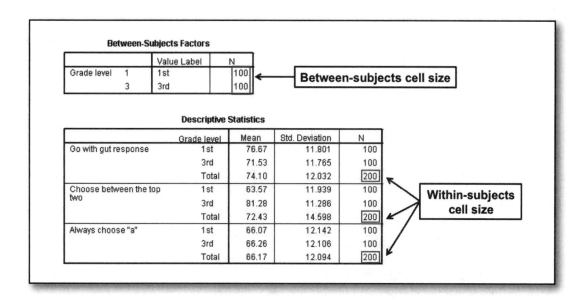

If requested, Box's test (of equality of variance-covariance matrices between groups) and Bartlett's test (of homoscedasticity and independence of error variances) are presented next. See the section in this chapter on assumption testing for more information about those.

As before, you can ignore the "Multivariate Tests" section (containing test statistics for Pillai's Trace, Wilks's Lambda, Hotelling's Trace, and Roy's Largest Root). These tests are primarily for testing the effect of a manipulation or condition on multiple qualitatively different dependent measures simultaneously (MANOVA), but can be used in within-subjects or mixed-model ANOVAs when sphericity is violated. Consult your statistics text for a more detailed discussion of when to use these versus the within-subjects tests reviewed later.

Mauchly's test appears next and is discussed further in the section on assumption testing.

The main effect of the within-subjects factor and the within-between interaction are found in the "Tests of Within-Subjects Effects" table. Use the "Sphericity Assumed" test (Wald F) if sphericity is met, and use one of the others if it is not.

Tests of Within-Subjects Effects

Measure:MEASURE_1

Source		Type III Sum of Squares	df	Mean Square	F	Sig.
strategy	Sphericity Assumed	6997.163	2	3498.582	1057.474	.000
	Greenhouse-Geisser	6997.163	1.707	4100.002	1057.474	.000
	Huynh-Feldt	6997.163	1.729	4047.734	1057.474	.000
	Lower-bound	6997.163	1.000	6997.163	1057.474	.000
strategy * Grade	Sphericity Assumed	14291.363	2	7145.682	2159.838	.000
	Greenhouse-Geisser	14291.363	1.707	8374.054	2159.838	.000
	Huynh-Feldt	14291.363	1.729	8267.299	2159.838	.000
	Lower-bound	14291.363	1.000	14291.363	2159.838	.000
Error(strategy)	Sphericity Assumed	1310.140	396	3.308		
	Greenhouse-Geisser	1310.140	337.912	3.877		
	Huynh-Feldt	1310.140	342.275	3.828		
	Lower-bound	1310.140	198.000	6.617		

In this case, Mauchly's test indicates a violation of sphericity, so we would report one of the other (*df*-adjusted) test statistics. Whichever one we choose, we conclude that there is a main effect of test-taking strategy on test scores and that this effect is qualified by a strategy-by-grade-level interaction. We must examine the means plots and custom contrasts to further understand these effects.

The next table presents tests of polynomial effects among the levels of the within-subject factor. SPSS will automatically test polynomial trends up to order $k - 1$ when your within-subject factor has k levels (>2).

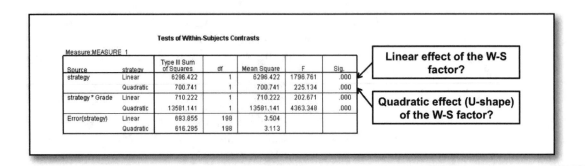

Tests of Within-Subjects Contrasts

Measure:MEASURE_1

Source	strategy	Type III Sum of Squares	df	Mean Square	F	Sig.
strategy	Linear	6296.422	1	6296.422	1796.761	.000
	Quadratic	700.741	1	700.741	225.134	.000
strategy * Grade	Linear	710.222	1	710.222	202.671	.000
	Quadratic	13581.141	1	13581.141	4363.348	.000
Error(strategy)	Linear	693.855	198	3.504		
	Quadratic	616.285	198	3.113		

Linear effect of the W-S factor?

Quadratic effect (U-shape) of the W-S factor?

The current example has three factor levels, so SPSS tested the second-order (quadratic) and first-order (linear) trends. However, notice that *these tests are meaningless for factor levels that are qualitative instead of quantitative in nature,* because the order of the levels is arbitrary for qualitative factors. Be sure to interpret these *only* when you have a meaningful order to your within-subject factor levels (e.g., test-taking after 1, 3, or 5 hours of studying).

Next is the "Tests of Between-Subjects Effects" table, which displays the ANOVA for the between-subjects effect(s) *summing across the levels of the within-subjects factor.*

Tests of Between-Subjects Effects

Measure:MEASURE_1
Transformed Variable:Average

Source	Type III Sum of Squares	df	Mean Square	F	Sig.
Intercept	3015802.407	1	3015802.407	7281.589	.000
Grade	2713.627	1	2713.627	6.552	.011
Error	82005.300	198	414.168		

The significant result here indicates that there is a difference between first-grade and third-grade test scores on average across all the tests. This ANOVA tests essentially the same question as MANOVA (see Chapter 10)—is there an effect of the between-subjects factor on all of the within-subjects factor levels simultaneously?—but it is significantly less powerful because it averages across the levels instead of combining the power of two separate tests.

Plotting the Results of the Mixed-Model ANOVA in SPSS

The final piece of output is the profile plot of the cell means. Here, we've used the syntax "/PLOT=PROFILE(strategy*grade)" to put strategy along the *x*-axis and plot grade levels as separate lines. We double-clicked on the plot in the SPSS output window to bring up the Chart Editor, then double-clicked on each of the elements in the chart (e.g., the line representing scores for 3rd graders) to bring up the Properties window for that element, and finally adjusted the properties.

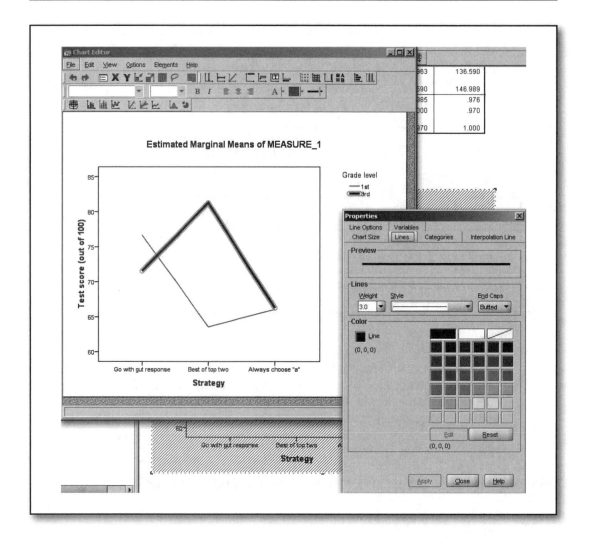

We added labels for each of the axes and factor levels, changed the font and font size, and converted the chart to black-and-white to make it more print-friendly.

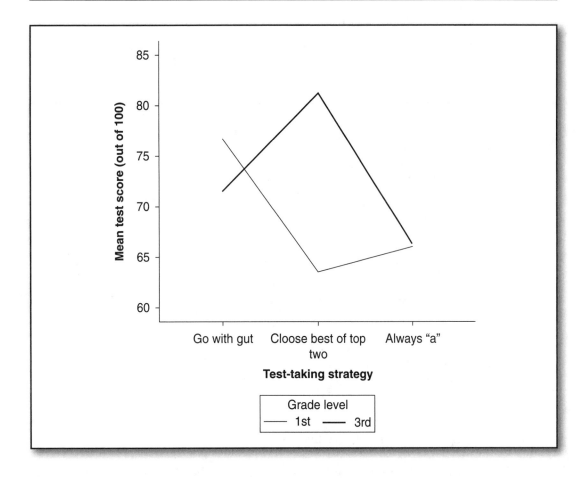

It is always good practice to add standard errors (SEs) or confidence intervals (CIs) to your charts. However, keep in mind what we learned in Chapter 8 about within-subjects variables: Error bars based on the standard deviation of the observations in the group (e.g., CI or SE) only contain information about *between-subject* factors and *do not* pertain to comparisons across within-subject factor levels. Unless you use standard deviations based on difference scores, you can use error bars only to make inferences about the between-subject factors. In this case, error bars could help you see significant differences between the two lines, but not among the three points along the lines.

MAKING THE MOST OF SYNTAX:
CUSTOM CONTRAST TESTS IN MIXED-MODEL ANOVA

We noticed earlier that the point-and-click menus offer only a limited range of specific contrast testing. Syntax offers a far more robust mechanism for testing custom contrasts by combining the LMATRIX command for between-subjects contrasts with the MMATRIX command for within-subjects contrasts. Each command follows the rules described in Chapters 7 (for LMATRIX) and 8 (for MMATRIX).

Type of test	LMATRIX	MMATRIX	Example
Main effect or simple effect of *within-subjects* factor	1s and 0s only Sum > 0	1s, 0s, -1s Sum = 0	/LMATRIX = all 2 1 0 1 /MMATRIX = [FL1] 1 [FL2] -1
Main effect or simple effect of *between-subjects* factor	1s, 0s, -1s Sum = 0	1s and 0s only Sum >0	/LMATRIX = all 0 1 -1 0 /MMATRIX = [FL3] 1
Interaction or simple interaction of *both* factors	1s, 0s, -1s Sum = 0	1s, 0s, -1s Sum = 0	/LMATRIX = all 0 1 0 -1 /MMATRIX = [FL2] 1 [FL3] -1

For example, suppose you had one between-subjects factor with 3 levels and one within-subjects factor with 3 levels. To compare Levels 1 and 2 of the within-subjects factor to each other *only* for Levels 1 and 3 of the between-subjects factor, use

```
/LMATRIX = all 2 1 0 1

/MMATRIX = [FL1] 1 [FL2] -1
```

This syntax is given on the first row of the table above. The second row compares Levels 1 and 2 of the *between-subjects* factor for only the third within-subjects factor level, and the third row of the table would test whether the difference between the second and third factor levels of the within-subjects factor is the same for the first and third group of the between-subjects factor (i.e., a "simple interaction").

We will give a few examples using the practice data set. We know there is an interaction between grade and test-taking strategy. We can break down this interaction into a simple interaction between grade and the middle strategy (choose between the top two) compared to the other two strategies combined (gut response + always "a"):

		Strategy			
		Strat. 1	Strat. 2	Strat. 3	
Which	1st	0.5	-1	0.5	0
grade?	3rd	-0.5	1	-0.5	0
		0	0	0	**0**

```
/LMATRIX = grade -1 1

/MMATRIX = Strategy1 -0.5 Strategy2 1 Strategy3 -0.5
```

This syntax produces the following output:

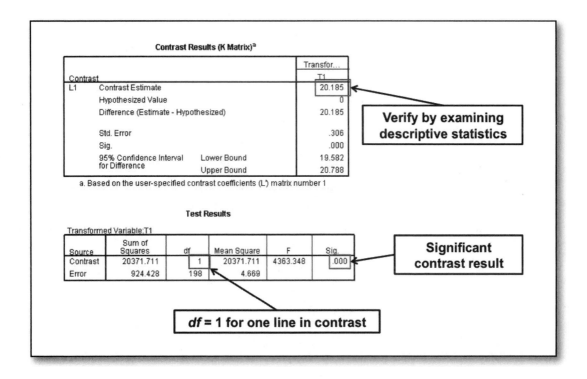

which indicates that the simple interaction is significant. We can further explore this simple interaction by testing the second strategy versus the other two combined for only first graders (the "simple effect of strategy among first graders"):

```
/LMATRIX = all 1 1 0

/MMATRIX = Strategy1 -0.5 Strategy2 1 Strategy3 -0.5
```

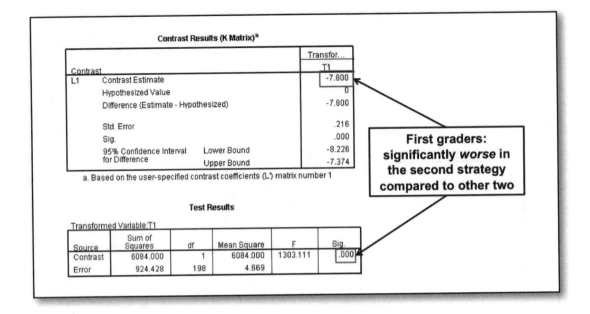

and the same for only third graders (the "simple effect of strategy among third graders"):

```
/LMATRIX = all 1 0 1

/MMATRIX = Strategy1 -0.5 Strategy2 1 Strategy3 -0.5
```

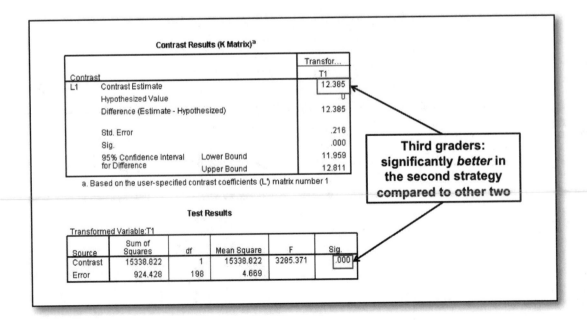

Taken together, we can say that the significant interaction between strategy type and grade is due to the fact that using the "pick the best of the top two" strategy compared to the other two strategies significantly reduces test scores for first graders, but significantly enhances test scores for third graders. Of course, there were several other ways we could have gone about unpacking that interaction; the exact simple effects that you examine will be determined by your research question. The overall goal is to reduce the result into smaller pieces that can be reduced to pairwise comparisons among scientifically meaningful groups.

KEYWORDS

design efficiency

compound symmetry

residual sum-of-squares and cross-product (RSSCP) matrix

Box's test

10

Multivariate ANOVA

Conceptual Background of the Multivariate ANOVA

All of the tests we've described to this point have a single dependent measure. Two-way ANOVA tests the separate and additive effects of two independent factors on one dependent measure. Within-subjects ANOVA compares several measures for each participant, but each measure reflects the same conceptual variable; the ANOVA examines how that single variable is altered in different conditions. In contrast, the multivariate ANOVA, also known as MANOVA, tests the effect of a between-groups factor on two or more dependent measures simultaneously. Those multiple DVs are not compared to each other (as they would be in within-subjects ANOVA); instead, they are compared in parallel as they change across between-subjects groups.

Multivariate ANOVA is the perfect test when you have several *qualitatively different dependent variables* (QDDVs) that are all distinct indicators of the same underlying construct. For example, in education, it is common to assess achievement using a variety of means (e.g., test scores, behavioral measures, self-report questionnaires) that together form a more complex and nuanced measure of the construct "achievement" than any would represent on its own. It wouldn't make sense to compare them to each other because they measure different variables—what would it mean that response times on a cognitive task are greater than scores on a standardized test?—but it would be informative to see whether they change together in response to a manipulation.

Multivariate ANOVA can be more powerful than running several univariate ANOVAs. First, for rhetorical purposes, it can be more convincing to show your effect in a single statistical test rather than as a piecemeal series of tests that is essentially testing the same conceptual hypothesis. Second, in some cases, multivariate ANOVA is statistically more powerful than any univariate ANOVA on its own. This is especially the case when the QDDVs are negatively correlated with each other. Depending on the data, it is possible to find a statistically significant group difference using MANOVA when none of the individual variables shows a difference in an ANOVA.

In some ways, the MANOVA approach is similar to latent variable approaches such as structural equation modeling. Both techniques assume that the measured variables each relate to an unobserved (or latent) construct that is the target of the group-based manipulation, and both techniques capitalize on the increased power of using several different measures as indicators of that latent construct. One key difference is that MANOVA is intended to be used for *categorical* independent measures (like all members of the ANOVA family), whereas structural equation modeling is based on a regression model and is more appropriate for *continuous* independent measures (see Chapter 11). Although structural equation modeling can be used to test MANOVA-like effects, it is beyond the scope of this book.

Computing MANOVA Using SPSS

The file on the website "Baseball.sav" contains two indicators of offensive performance for 20 games from two baseball teams. The dependent variables are *BA* (batting average) and *PPAB* (pitches per at bat), and the independent variable is *team* with two levels: the Giants and the Dodgers. We want to see if one team's offense is superior to the other based on these two variables together. Multivariate ANOVA is appropriate here because we want to test the difference between the teams on these two qualitatively different dependent measures simultaneously, and we don't care about the differences between the two variables.

Before we compute any statistical tests, let's plot the raw data to get a sense of whether there are differences at all between the teams. Click on **Graphs → Legacy Dialogues → Box Plot**.

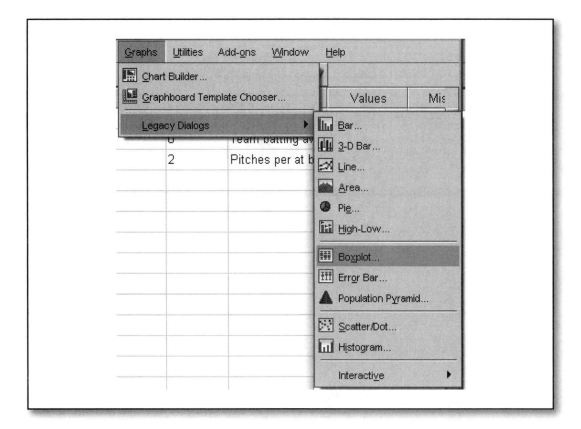

Then specify that we want a "simple boxplot" for "summaries of groups of cases."

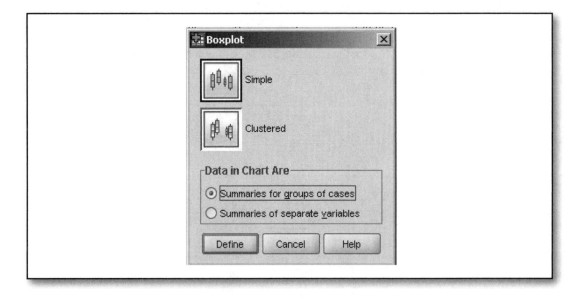

Finally, specify which of the DVs to plot, and specify *team* to be on the category (*x*) axis.

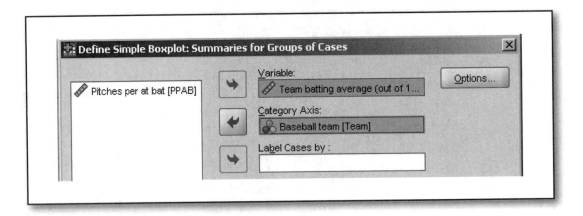

The syntax (for future reference) is

```
EXAMINE VARIABLES=BA PPAB BY Team
/PLOT=BOXPLOT
/STATISTICS =NONE
/NOTOTAL .
```

If you omit the "/STATISTICS=NONE" tag, SPSS will generate a rather useful and almost overly thorough table of descriptive statistics for each variable divided by groups. Omitting the "/NOTOTAL" tag will print a boxplot for each variable collapsed across the groups. Adding the tag "/COMPARE VARIABLES" will print all of the DVs on the same chart, but that can be difficult to read when the units of the variables are as disparate as they are in this case.

The resulting graphs compare the two teams on the two QDDVs.

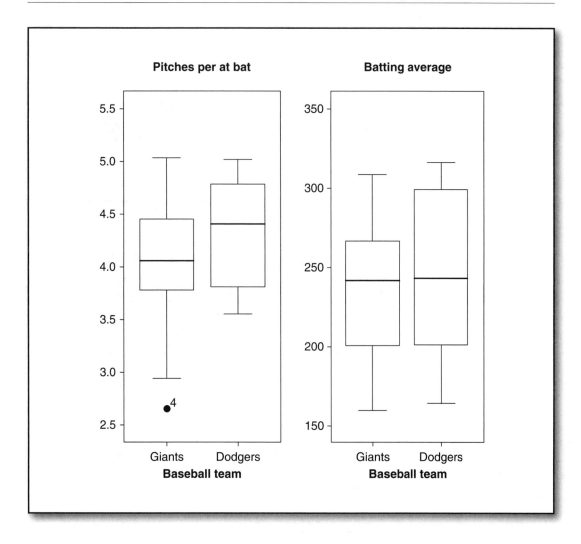

The means appear quite close in both cases. The Dodgers have a higher mean PPAB, but the distributions for that variable overlap substantially. It seems unlikely that there would be any significant difference in a one-way ANOVA comparing the teams on either of the two dependent measures. What about if we use MANOVA?

To start, click on **Analyze → General Linear Model → Multivariate.**

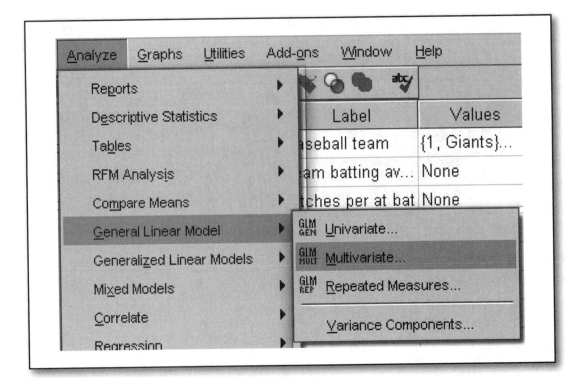

The window that appears is exactly like the one that would have come up for the univariate GLM except it allows for more than one dependent variable. Put the two dependent measures in the appropriate box on the top and *team* into the "fixed factor" independent measure box.

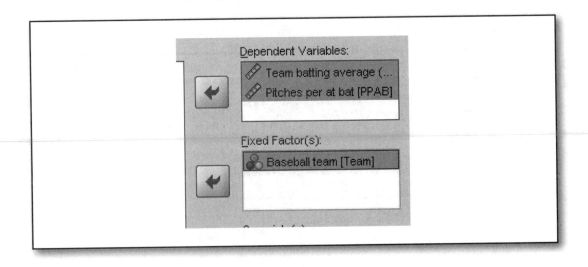

The "Model" menu allows you to specify the terms in the model. Although there are several DVs, there is only a single IV in this case—*team*—so the only possible term to include in the model is the main effect of *team*. More complicated designs such as two- or higher-way MANOVAs are possible and specified exactly as two- or-higher way ANOVAs. See Chapter 7 for more details on advanced model specification.

The "Contrasts" menu presents options for computing contrasts among the levels of the IV(s). These are limited to a handful of options and do not allow arbitrary (custom) contrasts among the groups; use LMATRIX to specify those (see Chapter 7). For now, there is only one IV with two levels, so the only contrast possible is [1 –1], the main effect, which will be automatically included in the MANOVA table.

The "Plots" and "Post Hoc" menus allows you to specify means plots and post hoc tests in the same way as with univariate GLMs.

In the "Options" menu, it's good practice to always request descriptive statistics. In this case, we have also requested to see the residual sum-of-squares and cross-products (RSSCP) matrix and homogeneity tests.

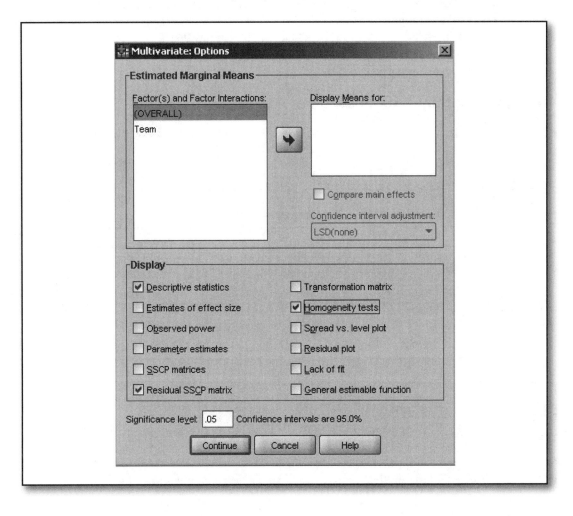

The RSSCP matrix contains the variances of the two DVs and the covariance between them, and requesting this matrix also generates the test of sphericity of that matrix. The homogeneity tests include Levene's (for univariate) and Box's (for multivariate) tests of equality of variances across groups.

The syntax for the MANOVA, including all of these options, is

```
GLM BA PPAB BY Team

/PLOT=PROFILE(Team)

/PRINT = DESCRIPTIVE RSSCP HOMOGENEITY

/DESIGN = Team.
```

Notice how this syntax is similar to and different from the syntax for univariate and within-subjects ANOVAs. Like univariate ANOVA, there is only one "/DESIGN" tag; like within-subjects ANOVA, there are several DVs specified before "BY" in the "GLM" function (i.e., GLM [DV1] [DV2] . . . BY [IV]). Because there is no "/WSDESIGN" or "/WSFACTOR" tag, SPSS assumes that the IV is between subjects and treats the multiple DVs specified in the GLM line as qualitatively different dependent variables.

Interpreting the SPSS Output

The first few output tables contain descriptives including cell Ns, Ms, and SDs.

Descriptive Statistics

	Baseball team	Mean	Std. Deviation	N
Team batting average (out of 1000)	Giants	235.80	43.148	20
	Dodgers	246.85	54.469	20
	Total	241.33	48.823	40
Pitches per at bat	Giants	4.0615	.57576	20
	Dodgers	4.3103	.51796	20
	Total	4.1859	.55504	40

This between-group MANOVA has 20 observations per team (i.e., 20 games of data) for *both* of the dependent measures.

Next, because we requested the RSSCP matrix, SPSS automatically computed Bartlett's test on that matrix. We include it here only to highlight the fact that

MANOVA does *not* require the variances of the DVs to be equal and their covariances to be zero. In other words, *MANOVA assumes sphericity to be violated,* so the results of this test are inconsequential.

Bartlett's Test of Sphericity[a]

Likelihood Ratio	.000
Approx. Chi-Square	314.522
df	2
Sig.	.000

Tests the null hypothesis that the residual covariance matrix is proportional to an identity matrix.

a. Design: Intercept + Team

In fact, as we learned earlier, MANOVA is more powerful when there is a negative correlation between the DVs, so as a researcher, you may hope for a violation of sphericity due to a negative correlation.

The RSSCP matrix (found slightly below in the output) displays the unequal variances and nonzero covariances between the DVs.

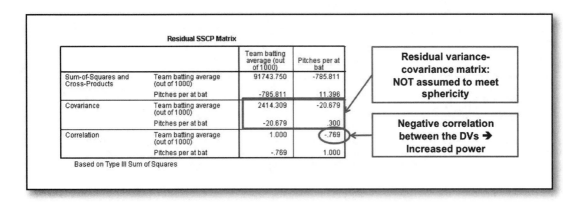

Residual SSCP Matrix

		Team batting average (out of 1000)	Pitches per at bat
Sum-of-Squares and Cross-Products	Team batting average (out of 1000)	91743.750	-785.811
	Pitches per at bat	-785.811	11.396
Covariance	Team batting average (out of 1000)	2414.309	-20.679
	Pitches per at bat	-20.679	.300
Correlation	Team batting average (out of 1000)	1.000	-.769
	Pitches per at bat	-.769	1.000

Based on Type III Sum of Squares

Residual variance-covariance matrix: NOT assumed to meet sphericity

Negative correlation between the DVs ➔ Increased power

We can see that the correlation (and covariance) are negative, suggesting that this particular MANOVA might be better able to detect a group difference compared to if there were a zero or positive correlation between the DVs.

Below Bartlett's test in the output is Box's test. This test appears because we requested between-group homogeneity tests ("/PRINT=HOMOGENEITY") in the syntax.

Box's Test of Equality of Covariance Matrices[a]

Box's M	4.498
F	1.414
df1	3
df2	259920.000
Sig.	.237

Tests the null hypothesis that the observed covariance matrices of the dependent variables are equal across groups.

a. Design: Intercept + Team

In contrast to Bartlett's test of sphericity of the residual variance-covariance matrix, MANOVA still *does* assume that the condition tested here—equality of variance-covariance matrices across groups—is met. You can think of this as the multivariate equivalent of the homoscedasticity test (Levene's test, which is also included along with Box's test for each dependent measure separately).

Levene's Test of Equality of Error Variances[a]

	F	df1	df2	Sig.
Team batting average (out of 1000)	2.206	1	38	.146
Pitches per at bat	.045	1	38	.834

Tests the null hypothesis that the error variance of the dependent variable is equal across groups.

a. Design: Intercept + Team

In the univariate case, we assume that the variances are equal across groups; in the multivariate case, we assume that the variance-covariance matrices are equal across groups. (See Chapter 9 for more details about assumption testing in ANOVA and MANOVA.) We can safely assume that the assumption is met because we do not reject the null hypothesis of Box's test.

Buried among all of these homogeneity tests is the actual multivariate ANOVA table, which tests the effect of *team* simultaneously on both DVs.

Multivariate Tests[b]

Effect		Value	F	Hypothesis df	Error df	Sig.
Intercept	Pillai's Trace	.997	6671.869[a]	2.000	37.000	.000
	Wilks' Lambda	.003	6671.869[a]	2.000	37.000	.000
	Hotelling's Trace	360.642	6671.869[a]	2.000	37.000	.000
	Roy's Largest Root	360.642	6671.869[a]	2.000	37.000	.000
Team	Pillai's Trace	.210	4.923[a]	2.000	37.000	.013
	Wilks' Lambda	.790	4.923[a]	2.000	37.000	.013
	Hotelling's Trace	.266	4.923[a]	2.000	37.000	.013
	Roy's Largest Root	.266	4.923[a]	2.000	37.000	.013

a. Exact statistic

b. Design: Intercept + Team

What hypothesis is being tested exactly? The degrees of freedom for the hypothesis contain a hint. There are *two* degrees of freedom, which indicates a two-line contrast. What are the two lines?

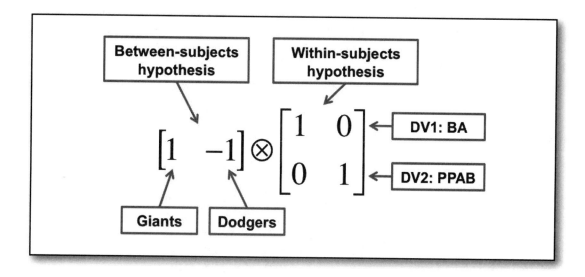

Formally, the hypothesis is the Kronecker product of the between-subjects main effect (i.e., Giants vs. Dodgers) and the DVs *one at a time* (i.e., each on its own row). The first line asks whether the Giants and Dodgers differ in batting average, and the second line asks whether the Giants and Dodgers differ in pitches per at bat. Together, the two lines ask whether the teams differ on both of these variables simultaneously. The result of the MANOVA indicates that the two teams do indeed differ on those measures of offensive ability.

Just below the MANOVA table are separate univariate ANOVA calculations for each of the two DVs.

Tests of Between-Subjects Effects

Source	Dependent Variable	Type III Sum of Squares	df	Mean Square	F	Sig.
Corrected Model	Team batting average (out of 1000)	1221.025[a]	1	1221.025	.506	.481
	Pitches per at bat	.619[b]	1	.619	2.064	.159
Intercept	Team batting average (out of 1000)	2329510.225	1	2329510.225	964.877	.000
	Pitches per at bat	700.883	1	700.883	2337.138	.000
Team	Team batting average (out of 1000)	1221.025	1	1221.025	.506	.481
	Pitches per at bat	.619	1	.619	2.064	.159
Error	Team batting average (out of 1000)	91743.750	38	2414.309		
	Pitches per at bat	11.396	38	.300		
Total	Team batting average (out of 1000)	2422475.000	40			
	Pitches per at bat	712.898	40			
Corrected Total	Team batting average (out of 1000)	92964.775	39			
	Pitches per at bat	12.015	39			

Main effect of *team* on the two DVs separately

a. R Squared = .013 (Adjusted R Squared = -.013)
b. R Squared = .052 (Adjusted R Squared = .027)

Neither is significant at traditional thresholds. But using MANOVA still allowed us to detect the difference between the teams *on both measures together* because of the negative correlation between them.

Finally, the means plots are presented to help interpret the significant main effect of *team*. Naturally, the Dodgers are a superior offensive team.

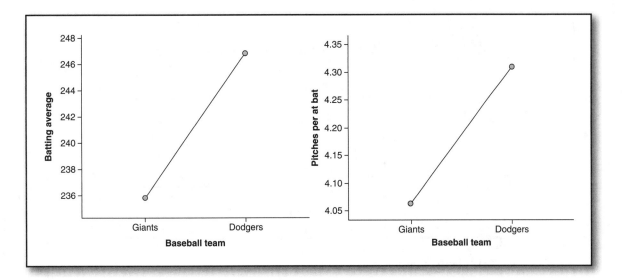

A *CLOSER LOOK:* WHICH MULTIVARIATE TEST TO REPORT?

Among the four options that SPSS presents, Pillai's Trace is the most conservative and most robust to violations of assumptions. Wilks's Lambda is less conservative but is less robust to violations, but still widely used. Wilks's Lambda is more powerful when all assumptions are met—particularly equality of error covariance matrices (Box's test) and equal cell sizes.

All four tests become equivalent when (a) sample sizes are extremely large, or, as in the case of the current example, (b) when there is only one line in the between-subjects hypothesis matrix (i.e., there are only two levels of the between-subjects factor).

We refer you to your statistics textbook for more thorough coverage of this topic.

MAKING THE MOST OF SYNTAX:
TESTING CUSTOM CONTRASTS IN MANOVA

We alluded earlier to the fact that the point-and-click menus offer limited options when it comes to testing custom hypotheses among cell means. As usual, syntax comes to the rescue. The "LMATRIX" command can be used for arbitrary custom contrasts because SPSS treats MANOVA the same way it would a between-groups ANOVA (just with more than one DV). In the present example with one 2-level IV, the command

```
/LMATRIX = team -1 1
```

will replicate the main effect of team that is produced as part of the MANOVA table.

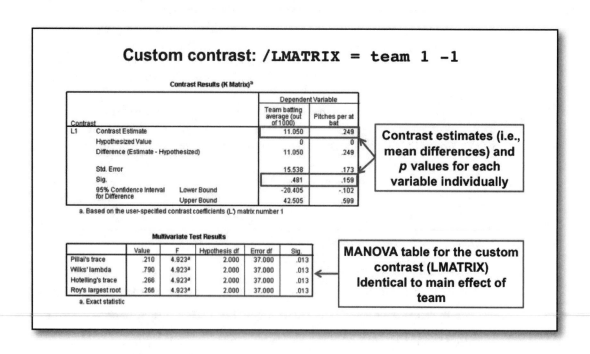

MANOVA table: Main effect of team

Multivariate Tests[b]

Effect		Value	F	Hypothesis df	Error df	Sig.
Intercept	Pillai's Trace	.997	6671.869[a]	2.000	37.000	.000
	Wilks' Lambda	.003	6671.869[a]	2.000	37.000	.000
	Hotelling's Trace	360.642	6671.869[a]	2.000	37.000	.000
	Roy's Largest Root	360.642	6671.869[a]	2.000	37.000	.000
Team	Pillai's Trace	.210	4.923[a]	2.000	37.000	.013
	Wilks' Lambda	.790	4.923[a]	2.000	37.000	.013
	Hotelling's Trace	.266	4.923[a]	2.000	37.000	.013
	Roy's Largest Root	.266	4.923[a]	2.000	37.000	.013

a. Exact statistic

b. Design: Intercept + Team

Custom contrast: /LMATRIX = team 1 -1

Contrast Results (K Matrix)[a]

Contrast		Dependent Variable	
		Team batting average (out of 1000)	Pitches per at bat
L1	Contrast Estimate	11.050	.249
	Hypothesized Value	0	0
	Difference (Estimate - Hypothesized)	11.050	.249
	Std. Error	15.538	.173
	Sig.	.481	.159
	95% Confidence Interval for Difference Lower Bound	-20.405	-.102
	Upper Bound	42.505	.599

a. Based on the user-specified contrast coefficients (L) matrix number 1

Contrast estimates (i.e., mean differences) and *p* values for each variable individually

Multivariate Test Results

	Value	F	Hypothesis df	Error df	Sig.
Pillai's trace	.210	4.923[a]	2.000	37.000	.013
Wilks' lambda	.790	4.923[a]	2.000	37.000	.013
Hotelling's trace	.266	4.923[a]	2.000	37.000	.013
Roy's largest root	.266	4.923[a]	2.000	37.000	.013

a. Exact statistic

MANOVA table for the custom contrast (LMATRIX) Identical to main effect of team

With only two levels of the IV, there are not many direct comparisons among means that we can make. However, we can use "LMATRIX" together with "KMATRIX" to test point predictions about the group means. For example, we can test whether the Giants have a batting average significantly greater than .220 and see more than 4 pitches per at bat:

```
/LMATRIX = all 1 1 0
/KMATRIX = 220 4
```

(We need to use "all 1 1 0" instead of "team 1 0" because the marginal sum of the two coefficients is greater than zero. See Chapter 7 for a more detailed discussion.)

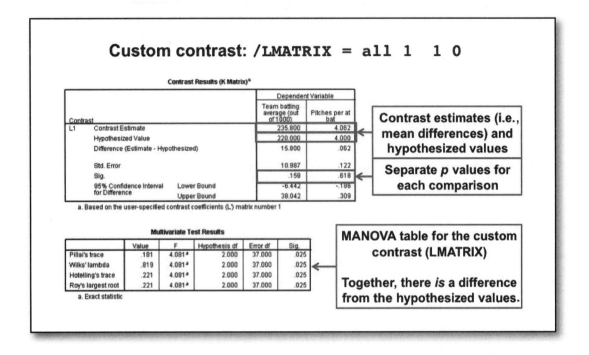

As with the main effect test, the custom contrast MANOVA table reveals a significant difference between the hypothesized and actual means even though neither of the DVs showed a significant difference on its own. We can conclude that the Giants do hit higher than .220 and see more than 4 pitches per at bat on average.

A CLOSER LOOK: WHEN TO USE MANOVA VERSUS WITHIN-SUBJECTS ANOVA

We discuss this important topic briefly here because SPSS has several tools that will aid in your decision, though you should consult your statistics book for a more detailed discussion.

The main consideration is theoretical: Does your research question involve several distinct dependent variables (i.e., qualitatively different dependent variables) or only a single dependent variable in a number of conditions? If the former is the case, the MANOVA is appropriate; if the latter, within-subjects ANOVA.

If you choose MANOVA, then your search is complete and you can begin analysis. But if you choose within-subjects ANOVA, then there is a second, statistical consideration. The within-subjects ANOVA makes the assumption of sphericity on the residual variance-covariance matrix (the "RSSCP Matrix" in SPSS), whereas MANOVA allows for an unrestricted RSSCP matrix. Thus, it may be appropriate to use MANOVA even to test a single-DV, within-subjects hypothesis when sphericity is violated according to Mauchly's test.

Finally, then, the assumption of sphericity does not apply when the within-subjects dependent measure(s) has only two levels (i.e., one degree of freedom). In fact, in these cases, all four multivariate tests as well as the "sphericity assumed" Wald test yield identical F values.

KEYWORDS

qualitatively different dependent variables (QDDVs)	Kronecker product	Wilks's Lambda
	Pillai's Trace	KMATRIX

11

Linear Regression

BEHIND THE SCENES: CONCEPTUAL BACKGROUND OF LINEAR REGRESSION

Linear regression is the hallmark technique in the social sciences for describing the relationship between two or more continuous variables (the technique is called *multiple regression* when used with more than one IV). Regression can test whether the relationship between an IV and a DV is nonzero, can produce a standardized estimate of the magnitude of that relationship, can parse overlapping and unique variance in a DV between several IVs, can compute the total amount of variance in the DV explained by the set of IVs, and much more. On its surface, linear regression seems to be entirely different from ANOVA, but it is not. Remarkably, regression is actually *identical* to ANOVA at a conceptual level as both techniques are based on the general linear model.

How are regression and ANOVA identical? Recall the conceptual model of ANOVA from Chapter 6:

$$Obs_{ij} = Group_j + e_{ij}.$$

In other words, any individual observation is divided into variability due to the group mean and residual (error) variance. The logic of regression is identical, except instead of categorizing subjects by groups, subjects are categorized by their scores on one or more continuous independent variables:

$$Obs_i = (IV_i * const) + e_i.$$

Each observation is broken down into its score on the IV times a constant factor that is equal for all subjects, plus noise. For example, a researcher could examine the relationship between height and weight using an ANOVA model by dividing people into three height groups (short, average, and tall) and comparing their mean differences in weight. According to the GLM, each participant's weight would be described as the mean of his or her height group plus noise. Alternatively, a researcher could examine the same question using a regression model by treating height as a continuous predictor. In this case, each participant's weight would be described as his or her height times a constant scaling factor plus noise. In this sense, in regression, each subject is treated as his or her own group, and the "group mean" is just a function of his or her score on the independent variable.

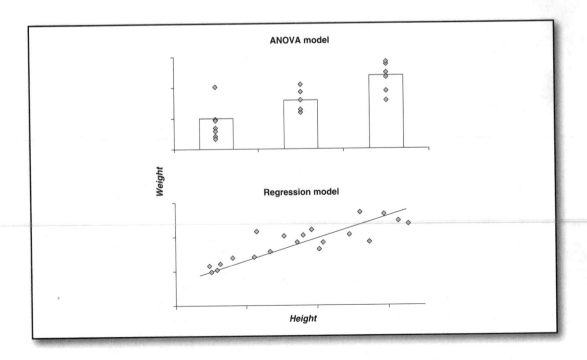

What about this constant scaling factor? Formally, it is called *beta,* and it is a single number that describes the relationship between the continuous IV and DV. In other words, *beta* is the *slope* of the line between the IV and the DV. When unstandardized, the slope can be multiplied by a subject's raw score on the IV to predict that subject's score on the DV with the smallest error (in the least-squares sense). When standardized, the slope ranges from –1 to +1 and can be thought of as an estimate of the strength of the relationship between the IV and the DV. When there is exactly one IV, the standardized slope is equivalent to the correlation between the IV and the DV.

The slope describes a line that summarizes the relationship between the two variables (hence, *linear* regression). This *regression* line is the equivalent to the group means in ANOVA; it is the "best guess" that the model can make about a score on the DV given the corresponding score on the IV. Without any IVs, the best guess that we can make about a subject's score on the DV is the mean of the DV itself. This is the null hypothesis in regression—that the variance of DV scores at each value of the IV is equal to the variance around the mean of the DV. Hence, the starting point of regression is a regression line with a flat (zero) slope and an intercept at the mean of the DV.

If the relationship between the IV and the DV is more than zero, the slope of the regression line will increase in absolute value from zero. For each observation, the distance from the mean of the DV—the "best guess" of a subject's score on the DV under the null—to the regression line can be thought of as the *amount of variance explained by the regression line* for that observation. The arrows in the figure depict this explained variance as distance from the null.

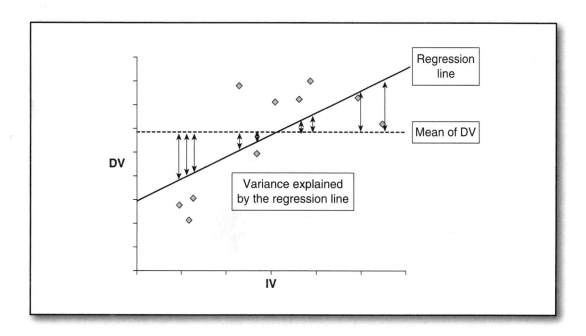

But not every point is exactly on the line, just as, in the ANOVA model, not every point was exactly at its group mean. There is *error* in our regression line, just as there was error in our group means. The distance between each point and the regression line captures this error, shown by the arrows in the next figure.

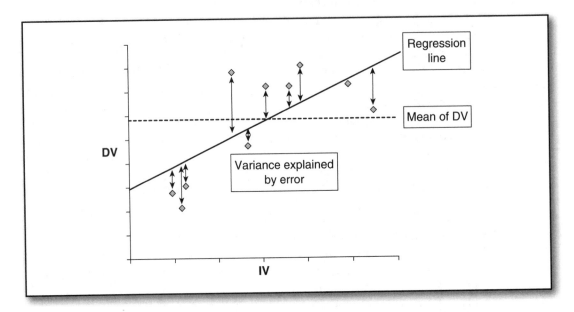

Together, the variability captured by the regression line and the variability due to error describe all of the variability around the mean of the DV. In terms of sum-of-squares (literally, the sum of the squared distances between each observation and the line, each observation and the mean, and the line and the mean), this is written as

$$SS\text{-total} = SS\text{-regression} + SS\text{-error}$$

From here, even the calculations are identical to ANOVA. Mean squares equal sum-of-squares divided by degrees of freedom, and the *F* test for the model is the mean squared for the model divided by the mean squared error.

Computing Linear Regression in SPSS

The file "FacultyImpact.sav" on the course webpage contains impact scores from 25 faculty members ranging from 0 to 100 (*impact*). This file also contains two predictor variables: average citations per paper (*cits*) and years on faculty (*years*). We can use this data set to practice multiple regression by predicting faculty impact based on citations and years on faculty. The linear model that we will be computing is

$$Impact = \beta_0 + \beta_1 * cits + \beta_2 * years + error$$

In this model, β_1 is the slope of citations on impact (holding years constant), β_2 is the slope of years on impact (holding citations constant), and β_0 is the impact score for someone who has 0 citations and 0 years on faculty (i.e., the intercept).

To compute this model, click on **Analyze → Regression → Linear**.

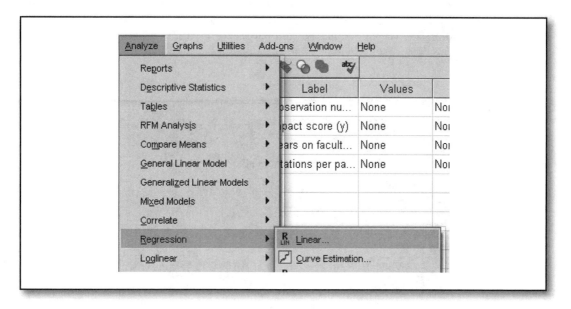

In the window that appears, place *impact* in the Dependent field, and *years* and *cits* in the Independent field.

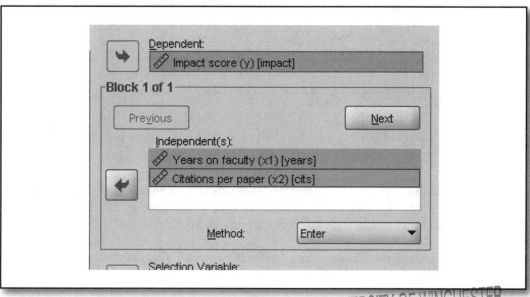

Next, click the "Statistics" button. This window contains various descriptive statistics that are useful for evaluating the model. The "estimates" option is checked by default—that will produce a table of standardized and unstandardized βs. We've also selected "model fit" to give some details about how well the model as a whole performs (i.e., all of the predictors together). Select "Descriptives" to get SPSS to produce *N*s, *M*s, and *SD*s of the variables and the correlations among them, and select "part and partial correlations" to see the semipartial and partial correlations, respectively, between each of the predictors and the DV.

Skip the "Plots" button for now. The "plots" window contains several tools that are useful for examining model assumptions, which are covered later in this chapter.

Next, click on the "Save" button. SPSS will produce a number of new variables as part of the regression. For example, once the betas are computed, a *predicted* score can be computed for each observation based on the regression line, and the *residual* score can be computed as the difference between the predicted score and the actual score. Other statistics that can be computed include the measures of influence each point has on the overall model parameters ("Influence statistics") and measures of outlier status ("Distances").

The "Save" window allows you to choose which of these scores (if any) to save into the data file along with the IVs and DV. For now, we've chosen to save only the unstandardized predicted value for each observation. This value will be calculated based on the βs (slopes) for each of the IVs:

$$Predicted\ impact = \beta_0 + \beta_1{*}cits + \beta_2{*}years.$$

The "Options" menu contains some parameters that can be adjusted to include more or fewer predictors in the model. Because we have only two predictors and we want them both in the model, we will ignore this menu for now.

The syntax for the regression as specified is

```
REGRESSION
/DESCRIPTIVES MEAN STDDEV CORR SIG N
/STATISTICS COEFF OUTS R ANOVA ZPP
/DEPENDENT impact
/METHOD=ENTER years cits
/SAVE PRED.
```

The "/STATISTICS" tag produces the slopes (standardized and unstandardized, each with its own standard error, *t*-test, and *p* value; "COEFF"), zero-order, and part and partial correlations for each IV ("ZPP"); a model summary table with information about the overall regression equation ("*R*"); and an ANOVA table with an *F* value for the overall model ("ANOVA"). Notice that the "/DESCRIPTIVES," "/STATISTICS," and "/SAVE" tags are optional, so an even more basic version would be

```
REGRESSION /DEPENDENT impact /METHOD=ENTER years cits.
```

Interpreting the Linear Regression Output

The descriptives are printed to the output first in two tables.

Descriptive Statistics

	Mean	Std. Deviation	N
Impact score (y)	49.9951	19.98843	25
Years on faculty (x1)	8.24	5.395	25
Citations per paper (x2)	3.3176	1.80304	25

Correlations

		Impact score (y)	Years on faculty (x1)	Citations per paper (x2)
Pearson Correlation	Impact score (y)	1.000	.982	.493
	Years on faculty (x1)	.982	1.000	.378
	Citations per paper (x2)	.493	.378	1.000
Sig. (1-tailed)	Impact score (y)	.	.000	.006
	Years on faculty (x1)	.000	.	.031
	Citations per paper (x2)	.006	.031	.
N	Impact score (y)	25	25	25
	Years on faculty (x1)	25	25	25
	Citations per paper (x2)	25	25	25

You may want to inspect the correlation matrix for high multicollinearity (intercorrelations) among the IVs, as that tends to decrease power in regression (see your statistics book for more details).

A summary of the variables that were included and excluded in the model comes next. In this case, all variables were included.

Variables Entered/Removed

Model	Variables Entered	Variables Removed	Method
1	Citations per paper (x2), Years on faculty (x1)[a]	.	Enter

a. All requested variables entered.

By default, SPSS includes variables with a *p* value of less than .05 and excludes variables with a *p* value of greater than .1. If you find that a variable that you would like to be included in the model for theoretical reasons is not being included, you can change those thresholds in the "Options" menu.

Next is the "model summary" table. This contains information about how well the model as a whole (i.e., all of the IVs together) predicts the DV.

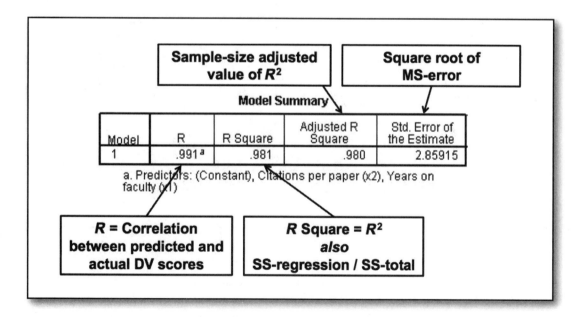

The first number, *R*, describes the correlation between the predicted score (based on the slopes of the predictors) and the actual score. Remember that we asked SPSS to save the unstandardized predicted score to the data set with the syntax "/SAVE=PRED." These now appear in the variable called "PRE_1."

3	years	Numeric	4	0	Years on faculty (x1)	None
4	cits	Numeric	8	2	Citations per paper (x2)	None
5	PRE_1	Numeric	11	5	Unstandardized Predicted Value	None
6						
7						

If you run a plain old Pearson correlation between the unstandardized predicted scores that were saved into the data window and the actual scores ("CORRELATIONS /VARIABLES=impact PRE_1 ."), you can see that the R value from the model summary table is exactly the same as the correlation between the predicted and actual scores.

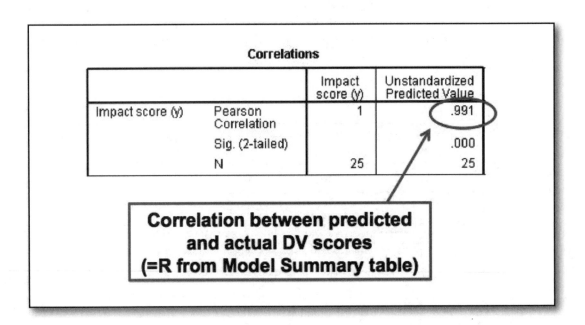

Correlations

		Impact score (y)	Unstandardized Predicted Value
Impact score (y)	Pearson Correlation	1	.991
	Sig. (2-tailed)		.000
	N	25	25

Correlation between predicted and actual DV scores (=R from Model Summary table)

The model summary also contains the R-square value for the model. This number can be calculated in two ways. First, literally as the square of the R value from above, .991*.991 = .981. Second, and perhaps more meaningfully, as the proportion of variance explained by the model compared to the total variance to be explained, SS-regression/SS-total (each presented in the ANOVA table immediately below the Model Summary table). This is the reason why R^2 is often referred to as the percentage of variance explained.

Next to R-square is the "adjusted R-square" value, which can be interpreted as the proportion of variance explained *accounting for the sample size and the number of predictors in the model.* The logic is that regression estimates are biased to be larger when there are few observations relative to the number of predictors. For example, any two points can be perfectly connected with a line (2 observations, 1 predictor, $R^2 =$ 1.0); any three points can be connected with a plane (3 observations, 2 predictors, $R^2 = 1.0$); and so forth. To adjust for this, SPSS follows the formula

$$R^2_{adj} = 1 - (1 - R^2)\left(\frac{n-1}{n-r}\right),$$

where n is the number of observations and r is the number of IVs plus 1 for the intercept (i.e., the number of unknown parameters). In cases when r is relatively close to n, the ratio on the right-hand side becomes relatively large, and the adjusted value becomes small; when n is very large compared to r, the right-hand side approaches 1 and the adjusted value is close to the original value.

The last value in the Model Summary table is the standard error of the R-square estimate, which is calculated as the square root of the MS-error from the ANOVA table below.

The ANOVA table contains the values used to calculate the statistics from the Model Summary table.

 # predictors

ANOVA[b]

Model		Sum of Squares	df	Mean Square	F	Sig.
1	Regression	9409.053	2	4704.527	575.495	.000[a]
	Residual	179.845	22	8.175		
	Total	9588.898	24			

a. Predictors: (Constant), Citations per paper (x2), Years on faculty (x1)
b. Dependent Variable: Impact score (y)

N-1-#predictors

Notice that (a) SS-regression/SS-total = R^2 (9409/9589 = .981); (b) *df*-regression + *df*-error = *df*-total; (c) MS = SS/*df*; and (d) MS-regression/MS-error = *F*.

Finally, the Coefficients table contains the standardized and unstandardized betas, as well as hypothesis tests for each.

Coefficients[a]

Model		Unstandardized Coefficients		Standardized Coefficients	t	Sig.	Correlations		
		B	Std. Error	Beta			Zero-order	Partial	Part
1	(Constant)	16.450	1.325		12.418	.000			
	Years on faculty (x1)	3.439	.117	.928	29.430	.000	.982	.988	.859
	Citations per paper (x2)	1.569	.350	.142	4.486	.000	.493	.691	.131

a. Dependent Variable: Impact score (y)

The unstandardized slopes are in the raw units (e.g., years, # of citations), and the standardized slopes are in standardized units (i.e., z-scores). We can use these parameters to predict faculty impact score either in raw terms:

$$impact = 16.45 + 3.44 * years + 1.57 * citations$$

or in standardized terms:

$$z(impact) = 0 + .93 * z(years) + .14 * z(citations).$$

The value of the intercept represents the value of the DV when all of the IVs are equal to zero. In regression, the mean of the IV(s) always predicts the mean of the DV. And because all standardized variables have a zero mean, the intercept will always be equal to zero in standardized terms. The literal meaning of these betas is the amount of change expected in the DV for a one-unit change in the IV (holding all other IVs constant). So you could say that each additional year on faculty is expected to increase a professor's impact score by 3.44 points, or, alternatively, that a one standard deviation increase in time on faculty increases impact by .93 standard deviations.

CONNECTIONS: UNDERSTANDING THE MEANING OF PARTIAL AND SEMIPARTIAL CORRELATIONS

Partial and semipartial ("part") correlations can be some of the most confusing concepts you'll encounter in regression, but the underlying idea is straightforward: They are both measures of the amount of variance of a DV that is explained by an IV. The trick is remembering *which parts* of the IV and the DV we're talking about. In most cases, the IVs will each have some overlap with each other and with the DV, so there are both *unique* and *overlapping* pieces of the IV.

Because we requested the semipartial and partial correlations in the Statistics menu ("/STATISTICS ZPP"), these values get added to the far right side of the Coefficients table.

Correlations		
Zero-order	Partial	Part
.982	.988	.859
.493	.691	.131

For example, the box in the figure represents 100% of the variance in our DV, *impact*. The two predictors each explain some unique variance, and there is some overlapping variance.

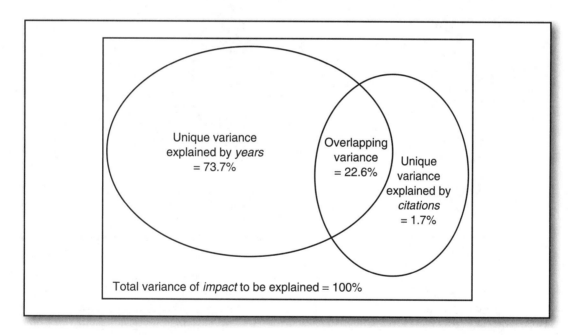

As a general rule in regression, and as we saw earlier with R and R-square for the model, the square of an r value (a correlation) can be interpreted as the percentage of variance accounted by that variable. Start with the zero-order correlations. The square of the zero-order correlations between the IVs and the DV represent the amount of variance that the *entire IV* explains of the DV. Hence, *years* explains $.982^2 = 96.4\%$ of the variance. This is shown in the figure as the sum of the unique part and the overlapping part: $73.7\% + 22.6\% = 96.4\%$ (with rounding error). Likewise, *citations* explains $.493^2 = 24.3\% = 22.6\% + 1.7\%$.

The semipartial ("part") correlations represent the amount of total variance of the whole DV that is explained by the *unique* part of the IV, where *unique* means each IV with the overlapping variance with the other IV(s) removed. Thus, the percentage of the whole of *impact* that is explained only by *years* is $.859^2 = 73.7\%$, and the part explained only by *citations* is $.131^2 = 1.7\%$.

Finally, the partial correlations represent the amount of variance that each IV uniquely explains *of the parts of the DV that are not accounted for by other predictors.* In other words, partial correlations are the correlations between the DV with all other IV(s) partialled out with the IV with all other IV(s) partialled out. The figure illustrates this concept using the partial correlation between *citations* and *impact*.

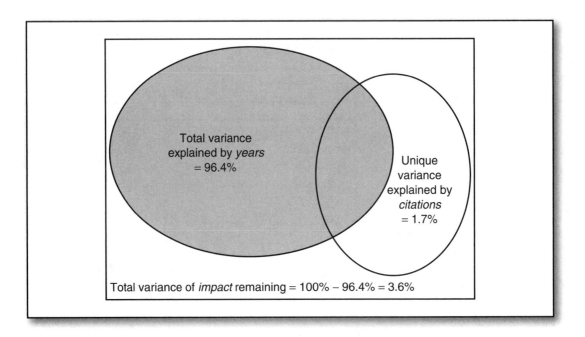

The partial correlation between *citations* and *impact* refers to how much variance *citations* explains uniquely (1.7%) out of the variance of *impact* that is not explained by *years* (100% − 96.4% = 3.6%). Thus, the squared partial correlation between *impact* and *citations* is 1.7%/3.6% = 47.2%, which is approximately equal to the squared value in the table (with rounding error). Likewise, the squared partial correlation between *impact* and *years* is 73.7%/(100% − 24.3%) = 97.3%.

The table summarizes the three different kinds of correlations calculated by SPSS.

Types of correlations computed by SPSS	Entire IV	IV with all other IVs removed
Entire DV	Zero-order	Semi-partial (AKA "part")
DV with all other IVs removed	—	Partial

SPSS can be used to compute versions of the DV and the IVs with other variables statistically removed or "partialled out." For example, to create a version of *citations* with *years* removed, regress *citations* on *years* and save the residuals, which represent the part of *citations* that is not explained by *years*:

```
REGRESSION /DEPENDENT cits /METHOD=enter years /SAVE
resid .
```

Do the same thing to remove *years* from the DV, *impact*:

```
REGRESSION /DEPENDENT impact /METHOD=enter years /SAVE
resid .
```

In the data file, be sure to label and rename the new variables so you remember what they are.

RES_1	Numeric	11	5	Citations w/ years removed (x1.x2)
RES_2	Numeric	11	5	Impact w/ years removed (y.x2)

Finally, compute a correlation matrix with these two "partiallized" variables and the original DV (/CORRELATIONS /VARIABLES=impact RES_1 RES_2 .).

Correlations

		Impact score (y)	Citations w/ years removed (x1. x2)	Impact w/ years removed (y. x2)
Impact score (y)	Pearson Correlation	1	.131	.190
	Sig. (2-tailed)		.533	.364
	N	25	25	25
Citations w/ years removed (x1.x2)	Pearson Correlation	.131	1	.691
	Sig. (2-tailed)	.533		.000
	N	25	25	25
Impact w/ years removed (y.x2)	Pearson Correlation	.190	.691	1
	Sig. (2-tailed)	.364	.000	
	N	25	25	25

Semi-partial correlation of *impact* with *citations*: Other predictors removed from *citations* **only**

Partial correlation of *impact* with *citations*: Other predictors removed from **both** *impact* and *citations*

Verify in the output that the correlation between *impact* and *citations w/o years* is .131—exactly the semipartial correlation—and the correlation between *impact w/o years* and *citations w/o years* is .691—exactly the partial correlation.

A CLOSER LOOK: HIERARCHICAL REGRESSION

The squared semipartial correlation represents the amount of unique variance of the DV explained by a predictor. But how much unique variance is significant? And how are we to decide how much variance warrants inclusion in the model? Each variable added to the model will explain *some* amount of variance (even just due to chance), but is that added variance worth the cost of an additional degree of freedom to the model and the reduction in parsimony? To some extent, the answer to these questions will be driven by your theory and hypotheses. But there is also a statistical answer to these questions in the *R-square change test,* which asks whether a predictor or set of predictors significantly improves the regression model compared to a simpler model without it. Comparing regression models in this way is known as *hierarchical* regression because the models being compared to each other are hierarchically nested within each other. This is often done in cases where certain variables are already known to explain some variance (e.g., demographics such as age, gender, or socioeconomic status), and others are hypothesized to explain variance *above and beyond* those known factors. In these cases, the known variables are entered in a block first, followed by blocks with each of the hypothesized variables.

For example, we saw in the initial regression run that *citations* explains far less variance in a faculty member's impact score than *years on faculty*. So a researcher might want to know whether adding *citations* to the regression model (for a final model with both *citations* and *years*) is a significant improvement compared to a model with only *years*. To do this in SPSS, specify each predictor as its own block to be entered sequentially. Begin by adding *years* in the first block, then adding *citations* in the second block.

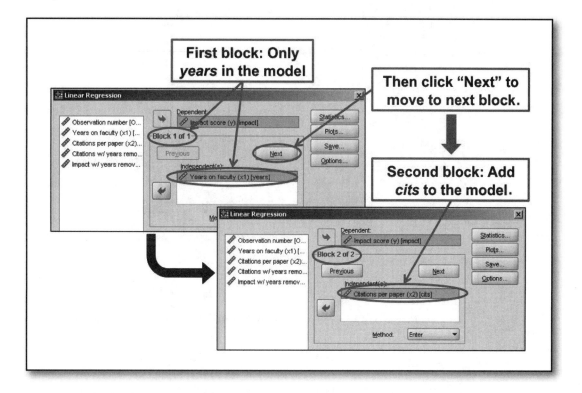

To test the difference between these two models (one with and one without *citations*), click on "Statistics" and check the "R squared change" box.

This block-wise entering of independent variables is represented in syntax with multiple "/METHOD=ENTER" lines.

```
REGRESSION

/STATISTICS COEFF OUTS R ANOVA CHANGE

/DEPENDENT impact

/METHOD=ENTER years

/METHOD=ENTER cits.
```

The output now contains statistics and coefficients for two nested models: *impact* predicted by *years* alone, and *impact* predicted by *years* + *cits*. The model summary contains the *R*-square values for each model, as well as the *R*-square change value from the previous model. For the first model, *R*-square and *R*-square change are equal because the previous "model" to the first one is the model with zero predictors. For the second model, *R*-square change is the difference between the two models.

Model 1: Only *years*
R-square change (from null) = R-square

Model Summary

Model	R	R Square	Adjusted R Square	Std. Error of the Estimate	R Square Change	F Change	df1	df2	Sig. F Change
1	.982[a]	.964	.963	3.86949	.964	617.416	1	23	.000
2	.991[b]	.981	.980	2.85915	.017	20.127	1	22	.000

a. Predictors: (Constant), Years on faculty (x1)
b. Predictors: (Constant), Years on faculty (x1), Citations per paper (x2)

Model 2: *Years + Cits*
R-square change (from Model 1) = R-square – R-square (Model 1)

The significant *p* value associated with the *F Change* value for the second model indicates that adding *cits* does significantly improve the model. Notice that the *R*-square change value (0.017, or 1.7%) is exactly the same as the squared semipartial correlation of *impact* with *cits*.

The Coefficients table contains standardized and unstandardized betas for both models.

Coefficients[a]

Model		Unstandardized Coefficients B	Unstandardized Coefficients Std. Error	Standardized Coefficients Beta	t	Sig.
1	(Constant)	20.020	1.433		13.968	.000
	Years on faculty (x1)	3.638	.146	.982	24.848	.000
2	(Constant)	16.450	1.325		12.418	.000
	Years on faculty (x1)	3.439	.117	.928	29.430	.000
	Citations per paper (x2)	1.569	.350	.142	4.486	.000

a. Dependent Variable: Impact score (y)

Notice that the beta for *years* is slightly reduced from Model 1 to Model 2. This confirms what we already knew from examining the semipartial correlations—that there is some overlapping variance explained by the two predictors. When added to the model, *cits* "grabs" some of the variance that had been attributed to *years* in the previous model.

A CLOSER LOOK: TESTING MODEL ASSUMPTIONS

All forms of the General Linear Model make the assumption that the residuals are normally distributed. This assumption can be informally checked by inspecting the Q-Q plot ("quantile-quantile plot"), which compares the cumulative distribution of the residuals to the distribution that would be expected if they were normal. Run the regression model again, but include the line "/SAVE = RESID" in the syntax to save the residuals (i.e., the errors) to the data file; then generate the Q-Q plot by clicking **Analyze → Descriptive Statistics → Q-Q Plots**.

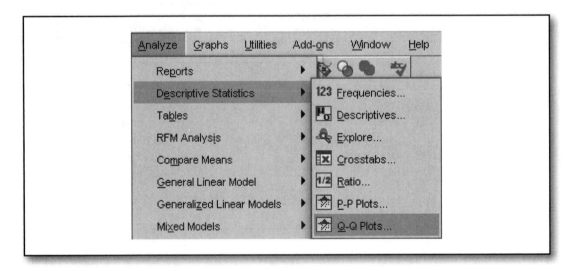

Then select the "unstandardized residuals" that we just created as the variable to plot.

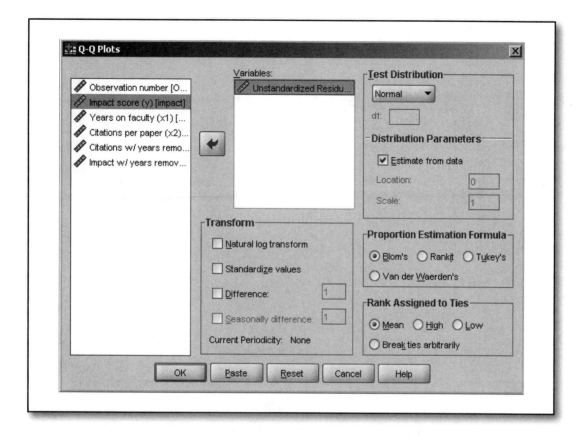

The full syntax is longer, but the only required pieces are

```
PPLOT
/VARIABLES=RES_3
/TYPE=Q-Q
/DIST=NORMAL.
```

SPSS produces two charts. First, the classic Q-Q plot showing the actual residuals plotted against what would be predicted by normal.

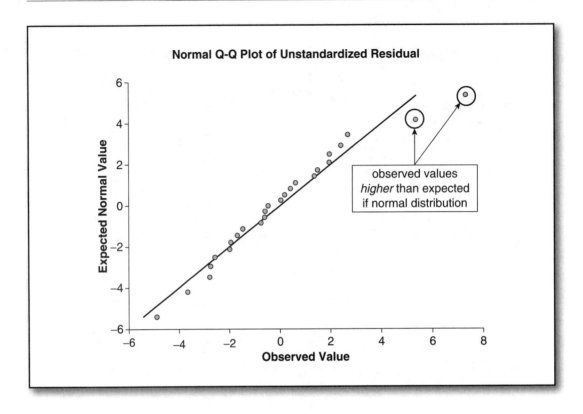

In this plot, the data from a perfectly normal distribution would fall perfectly along the 45-degree line. Points below the line show where the observed value is *greater* than normal, and points above the line show where the observed value is *less* than normal.

The second chart is a "detrended" Q-Q plot. It contains the same data from the figure above but is recoded so that each point is plotted as its deviation from the value expected under the normal assumption. Points above the line are higher than expected under normality; points below the line are lower than expected. Perfectly normal data would be arranged in a horizontal line at $y = 0$.

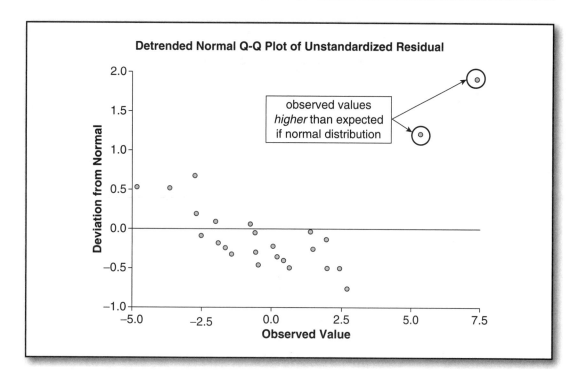

It is easier to see the two outliers on the right side of this plot: observed values of about 5 and about 7.5 that are roughly 1 and 2 standard deviations higher than normal, respectively.

The GLM also assumes that the error variances are equal at different levels of the independent variable(s). In ANOVA, this is equivalent to equality of error variances across groups; in regression, this means that the variance is equal across the continuous range of the IV(s). The most direct way to examine this assumption is to plot the residuals across the range of the predictors. As part of computing the regression model, SPSS generates a dummy variable called "*ZRESID" that contains the residuals. It won't be saved into the data file by default, but it can nonetheless be accessed from the syntax. For example, adding "/SCATTERPLOT = (*ZRESID, years)" to the regression syntax produces the scatterplot shown in the figure, with the residuals on the *y*-axis plotted along the range of *years* on the *x*-axis.

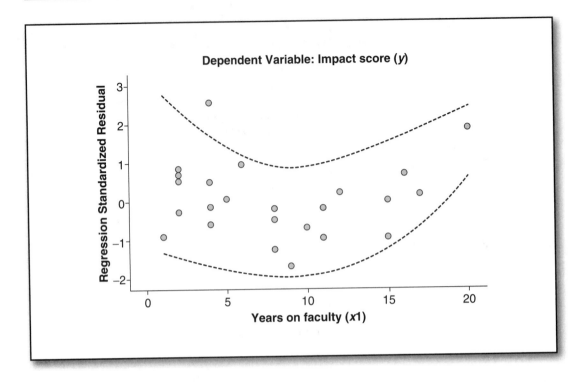

The dashed lines show the approximate range at each point on the IV. According to the assumption of equality of variance, the dashed lines should be parallel and straight, but they are (a) wider at the low end than the high end, indicating a violation of equality of variance, and (b) curved, indicating a possible quadratic relationship between *years* and *impact*.

To address the (roughly) quadratic relationship between the IV and DV, try squaring the IV, *years*, after centering (i.e., mean-correcting) it. The syntax is

```
COMPUTE years2 = (years-8.24) ** 2 .

exe .
```

This subtracts the mean (8.24) from *years*, then squares the centered result. Use the following syntax to test whether the quadratic years (*years2*) improves the model.

```
REGRESSION

/STATISTICS COEFF OUTS R ANOVA CHANGE

/DEPENDENT impact

/METHOD=ENTER years cits /METHOD=ENTER years2

/SCATTERPLOT=(*ZRESID, years) .
```

The results indicate that adding *years2* significantly improves the model, *R*-square change = 0.5%, *F*-change $(1, 22) = 8.05$, $p < .01$, and reduces the violation of homoscedasticity in residuals across the range of *years*.

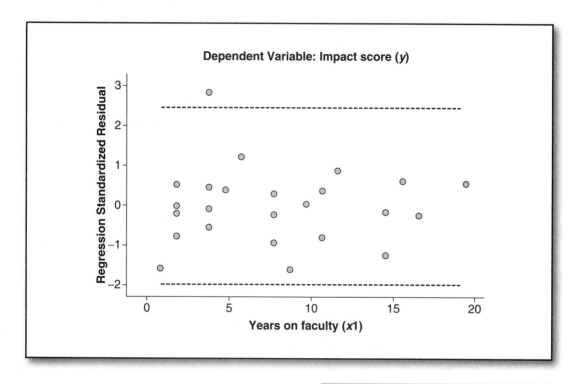

KEYWORDS

linear regression	R^2	adjusted R^2
multiple regression	standardized vs. unstandardized beta	zero-order correlation
beta weight		partial correlation
slope	predicted score	semipartial correlation
residual	regression model	Q-Q plot

12

Analysis of Covariance

Conceptual Background of Analysis of Covariance (ANCOVA)

Having learned that ANOVA and regression are both instances of the general linear model, you may not be surprised to learn that they can be combined into a single analysis. This technique—the *analysis of covariance,* or *ANCOVA*—is perfectly suited for studies with both continuous and categorical independent variables. The conceptual model can be written literally as a combination of ANOVA and regression models:

$$Obs_{ij} = Group_j + (IV_i * slope) + e_{ij},$$

where observation i within group j is described as the sum of group j's mean, plus person i's score on the continuous IV times a constant (the slope of the IV), plus error.

Analysis of covariance is a flexible technique that can be considered in at least two ways: as a special case of ANOVA or as a special case of regression. The underlying model is the same in both cases, but the focus is slightly different. In regression terms, ANCOVA can be translated to

$$Obs_{ij} = \beta_{0j} + (\beta_1 * IV_i) + e_{ij},$$

where β_1 is the slope of the IV, which is equal for all participants, and β_{0j} is the intercept that is *different for each group.* Thought of in this way, ANCOVA is just regression with one or more continuous IVs (and their interactions), but with several different intercepts (β_0s) depending on a categorical variable instead of just one.

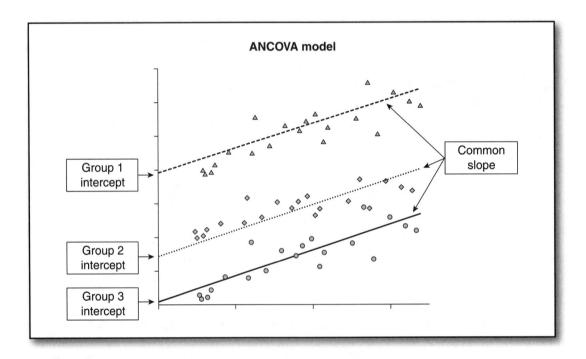

Another way to think of ANCOVA is as a special form of ANOVA. Here, observations are described in terms of group membership, but each person also varies around the group mean depending on a continuous variable:

$$Obs_{ij} = Group_j + (c * IV_i) + e_{ij},$$

where c is a constant (slope) that is the same for all individuals.

We emphasize that these two conceptualizations are identical; but depending on your particular theoretical or research question, it may be helpful to think of your model in one way or the other. For example, if you are primarily interested in the relationship among *reactance to authority, self-efficacy,* and *cigarette smoking* (all continuous), but you know that men tend to smoke more than women, you might use ANCOVA essentially as a regression (cigarette smoking regressed on reactance and self-efficacy) but with the categorical factor of gender included in the model as a control variable. Alternatively, if you are interested in the relationship of *ethnicity* and *nationality* (both categorical) to *cigarette smoking,* but you know that smoking varies with age, you might use ANCOVA but think of it as a two-way ANOVA (ethnicity-by-nationality predicting smoking) with a continuous covariate included in the model to control for age differences.

In both of these illustrative cases, there is at least one continuous and at least one categorical variable in the model at the same time. The difference is which variable counts as the variable of interest and which as the nuisance variable to be controlled for. Regardless, the models are statistically identical.

Computing ANCOVA in SPSS

To practice using ANCOVA in SPSS, download the data set "GPAClassRating.sav" from the website. This set contains overall ratings for a teaching assistant (*rating*) as a function of both the class that the assistant taught (*class*) and the GPA of the student making the rating (*GPA*). We would like to use ANCOVA to examine how a student's GPA affects his or her rating of the teaching assistant (TA), controlling for overall differences between classes. The conceptual model is

$$Rating_{ij} = Class_j + (\beta_1 * GPA_i) + e_{ij},$$

where the rating made by student i in class j is a function of the mean rating from class j, plus student i's GPA times the slope (β_1), plus error. We are primarily interested in β_1, which is interpreted as the average relationship between a student's GPA and the rating that student makes of a TA, controlling for differences between classes.

As ANCOVA is yet another example of the GLM, it can be found in SPSS by clicking **Analyze → General Linear Model → Univariate**. In the box that comes up, add *rating* as the Dependent Variable, *class* as a fixed factor, and *GPA* as a covariate. (Note that SPSS refers to continuous predictors as "covariates" and categorical predictors as "factors," but conceptually, they are both just independent variables.)

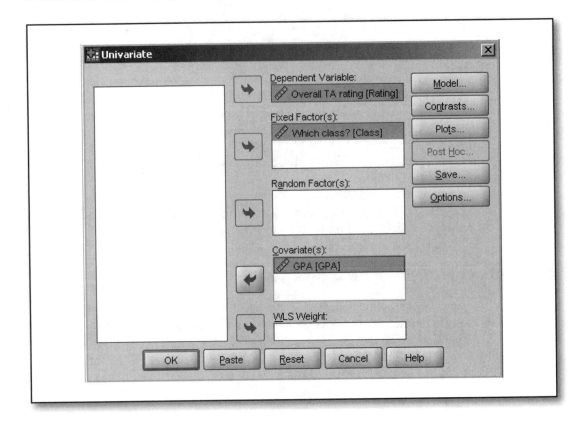

The default model (click "Model" to view) is "Full Factorial." This will include the main effects of all the IVs and the interactions *only among the categorical IVs (factors)*. SPSS does not include the interaction between the continuous and the categorical factors (here, the *class*-by-*GPA* interaction). The reason is that the ANCOVA model assumes that there is no interaction between the continuous and categorical factors; in other words, it assumes that the *slope of the continuous IV on the DV is the same across all the groups*. This is an assumption that should be tested, and we will review how to test it later.

As always, clicking the "Contrasts" button will reveal limited contrasts among the levels of the categorical IV(s). The LMATRIX command can be used in syntax to specify more flexible contrasts.

The "Plots" button allows you to specify mean plots of the factor but not of the covariate. See the section on visualization of ANCOVA results later in the chapter.

The "Save" button presents a number of optional variables to be saved into the data file. For example, just as in linear regression, SPSS will generate predicted values and residuals (errors) for each observation based on the model. These values can be saved if desired as separate variables (i.e., columns) in the data file.

Click the "Options" button to request several additional and useful pieces of output.

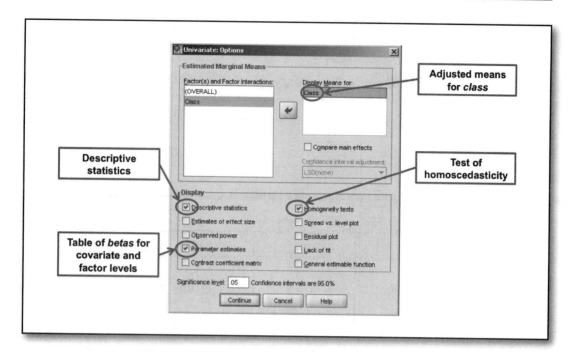

First, request the "estimated marginal means" (i.e., the adjusted group means) for *class* by moving that variable to the box in the top right corner of the Options menu. This will produce a table containing the *expected* value of each group's mean TA rating for a student with an average GPA (i.e., the group mean at the mean of the covariate). Second, check the "Parameter Estimates" to get the regression-like *betas* for all of the terms in the model, including the slope of the covariates and coefficients for each group. Finally, request descriptive statistics (including the actual group means) and homogeneity of variance tests.

The syntax for all of this output is

```
GLM Rating BY Class WITH GPA

/EMMEANS = TABLES(Class) WITH(GPA=MEAN)

/PRINT = HOMOGENEITY PARAMETER DESCRIPTIVE

/DESIGN = GPA Class .
```

The "/PRINT=DESCRIPTIVE" tag will display the mean *rating* for each of the three *class* levels (among other things). The "/EMMEANS" tag will print out the *expected* average *rating* for each class for someone with an average GPA. In other words, this will print out the mean *rating* for each *class* level but equating all the groups on *GPA* (i.e., controlling for GPA). This syntax is based on the general form for ANCOVA:

```
GLM [DV] BY [FACTOR(S)] WITH [COVARIATE(S)]

/DESIGN = [COVARIATE(S)] [FACTOR(S)] .
```

Understanding the Output of ANCOVA

The summary table of descriptive statistics is displayed first, containing group means, SDs, and Ns.

Descriptive Statistics

Dependent Variable:Overall TA rating

Which class?	Mean	Std. Deviation	N
Grad stats	4.3333	1.52753	8
Undergrad social	5.5000	1.92209	8
Grad social	4.9167	1.28560	8
Total	4.9167	1.60445	24

Note that the group means displayed in this table are the raw means and are not corrected for potential differences in GPA. For example, if there is a positive relationship between GPA and TA rating, and one of the classes happens to have a very high average GPA, then that class is also likely to have a high average TA rating as an artifact. The estimated marginal (EM) means below correct for those artifactual distortions.

Levene's test for equality of variances is presented next.

Levene's Test of Equality of Error Variances[a]

Dependent Variable:Overall TA rating

F	df1	df2	Sig.
1.918	2	21	.172

Tests the null hypothesis that the error variance of the dependent variable is equal across groups.

a. Design: Intercept + GPA + Class

This output presents the results of the test of equality of (*class*) group variances. The null hypothesis is that the groups are equal in variance, and the nonsignificant *p* value indicates that the assumption is not violated.

The next box displays the ANCOVA results.

Tests of Between-Subjects Effects

Dependent Variable:Overall TA rating

Source	Type III Sum of Squares	df	Mean Square	F	Sig.
Corrected Model	41.312[a]	3	13.771	15.389	.000
Intercept	6.366	1	6.366	7.114	.015
GPA	35.867	1	35.867	40.083	.000
Class	11.767	2	5.883	6.575	.006
Error	17.897	20	.895		
Total	639.375	24			
Corrected Total	59.208	23			

a. R Squared = .698 (Adjusted R Squared = .652)

The degrees of freedom are calculated in the same way as they are in regression in ANOVA: Continuous IVs (covariates) each use 1 degree of freedom, and categorical variables with *k* groups use *k* − 1 degrees of freedom. In this case, the model uses 1 + 2 = 3 degrees of freedom. There are *n* − 1 = 23 degrees of freedom total; hence, there are 23 − 3 = 20 degrees of freedom for the error variance. There is a significant effect of GPA, $F(1, 20) = 40.08$, $p < .01$, and a significant effect of *class*, $F(2, 20) = 6.58$, $p < .01$. We must examine plots or descriptive tables to interpret the direction of the significant effects.

In other forms of the ANOVA that we've seen so far, all possible interactions in the "full factorial" model are included by default. But there is no *class * GPA* interaction term included in the model here. That is because an explicit assumption of ANCOVA is that the interaction between the continuous and categorical independent variables is zero, or, in other words, that the slope of the continuous IV is equal across levels of the categorical IV. This assumption can and should be tested. See the section later in the chapter on evaluating the assumptions of ANCOVA for how to do so.

Because we requested the parameter estimates for the model ("/PRINT= PARAMETER"), they each appear in the next table along with standard errors and *t*-tests against the null that each estimate is no different from zero, as well as 95% confidence intervals for each.

Parameter Estimates

Dependent Variable:Overall TA rating

Parameter	B	Std. Error	t	Sig.	95% Confidence Interval	
					Lower Bound	Upper Bound
Intercept	1.878	.585	3.210	.004	.658	3.098
GPA	1.430	.226	6.331	.000	.959	1.901
[Class=1]	-1.358	.489	-2.779	.012	-2.377	-.339
[Class=2]	.285	.475	.601	.555	-.706	1.277
[Class=3]	0[a]	.	.	.	.	.

a. This parameter is set to zero because it is redundant.

The parameter for the continuous covariate, *GPA*, is interpreted exactly as a regression slope. Each one-unit change in the covariate produces a *B*-unit change in the DV. In this case, a one-point increase in *GPA* corresponds to a 1.43-point increase in TA rating. As noted earlier, that slope is assumed to be equal across the three groups (i.e., classes).

The parameters for each level of *class* correspond to the difference in *intercept* of each class from the overall intercept shown on the first line in the table. It will always be the case that one of the levels (the third class in this example) has no parameter of its own. That's because it would be redundant with the overall intercept; there is no need to add an additional parameter to the model when the overall intercept can double as the intercept for one of the groups and when the other groups' intercepts can be described as deviations from that mean. In this example, Class 3 has an intercept of 1.878, with Class 1 at 1.358 units less and Class 2 at .285 units more.

Taken together, the parameters can be used to write an equation to calculate the predicted TA rating value for any individual given his or her class and GPA:

$$Predicted\ rating = 1.878 + 1.43 * GPA - 1.358(Class1) + 0.285(Class2),$$

where *Class1* = 1 if the student is in Class 1 and 0 otherwise, and *Class2* = 1 if the student is in Class 2 and 0 otherwise. This equation can be rewritten to describe the predicted mean for each class separately according to *GPA*:

$$Predicted\ rating\ (Class\ 1) = 1.878 - 1.358 + 1.43 * GPA$$

$$Predicted\ rating\ (Class\ 2) = 1.878 + 0.285 + 1.43 * GPA$$

$$Predicted\ rating\ (Class\ 3) = 1.878 + 0 + 1.43 * GPA$$

Written in this way, it is clear that each class follows a linear regression model (with *rating* regressed on *GPA*) but with different slopes.

Finally, the estimated marginal means are printed because of the "/EMMEANS . . ." line in the syntax. This table contains the expected mean, standard error, and 95% CI of each of the groups evaluated at the mean of *GPA*.

Estimated Marginal Means

Which class?

Dependent Variable:Overall TA rating

Which class?	Mean	Std. Error	95% Confidence Interval	
			Lower Bound	Upper Bound
Grad stats	3.916[a]	.341	3.205	4.627
Undergrad social	5.560[a]	.335	4.862	6.257
Grad social	5.274[a]	.339	4.567	5.982

a. Covariates appearing in the model are evaluated at the following values: GPA = 2.37500.

These figures are calculated based on the equations on the previous page. For example, the mean of GPA is 2.375 so the expected value of Class 1 at the mean is $1.878 - 1.358 + (1.43 * 2.375) = 3.916$. As they are based on the earlier equations, these figures can be evaluated at any point along the range of the continuous IV (e.g., zero, minimum, maximum).

Notice that the differences between the estimated marginal means of the classes controlling for GPA are different from the differences between the raw group means displayed in the Descriptives box. For example, the raw difference between the two graduate courses (social psychology and statistics) is 0.58, but the GPA-corrected difference is 1.36. (See the *Making the Most of Syntax* section later in the chapter on custom hypothesis testing in ANCOVA for how to make specific group comparisons). The fact that the TA rating difference between classes changes depending on whether or not GPA is included in the model indicates that group differences in GPA between the two courses were masking a rather large difference in TA rating. This finding underscores the value of using ANCOVA to control for a covariate when it is confounded with the levels of the categorical IV.

Visualizing Results of the ANCOVA

We noted earlier that the GLM menu itself does not adequately plot the results of the ANCOVA. Fortunately, the flexible graphing options in SPSS do. Click on

Graphs → [**Legacy Dialogues (for newer versions of SPSS)**] → **Scatter/Dot**; then select "Simple Scatter," then "Define."

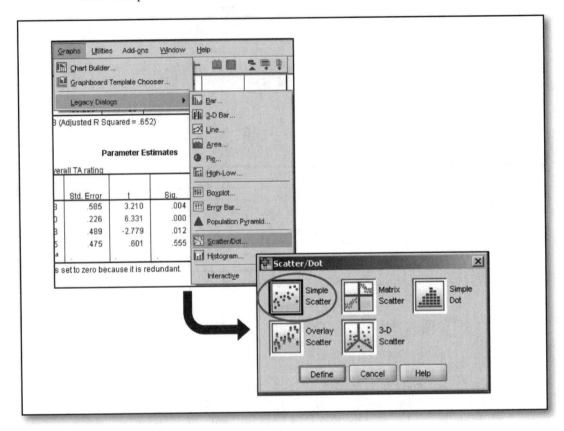

In the definition box, put the DV, *rating*, on the *y*-axis (by convention) and the continuous independent variable, *GPA*, on the *x*-axis (as though you were a simple scatterplot); then add the categorical variable, *class*, into the box labeled "Set Markers By."

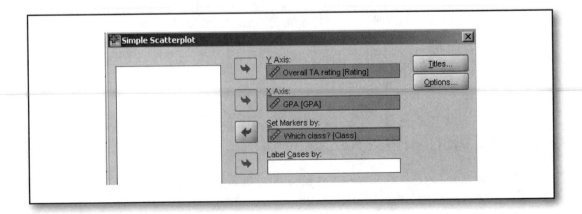

The syntax for this is

```
GRAPH /SCATTERPLOT(BIVAR)=GPA WITH Rating BY Class .
```

Note that the variable specification in this syntax mirrors that in the GLM line, with "[DV] WITH [continuous IV] BY [categorical DV]."

The graph will be appended to the end of the output file, but looks fairly ugly in its default form. Double-click anywhere on the graph to bring up the "Chart Editor" window.

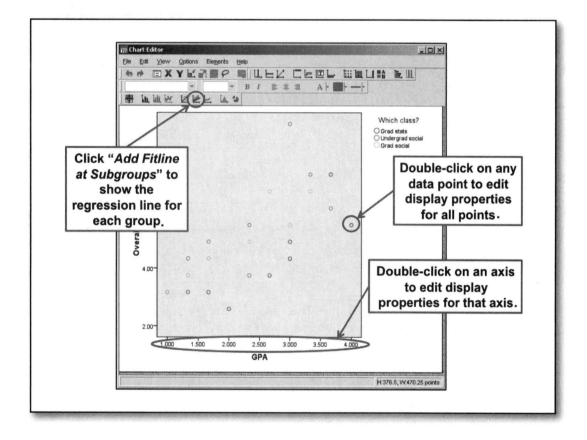

The most important addition for visualizing ANCOVA is the so-called fit line (i.e., regression line) at the level of the subgroups. We don't want a single *overall* fit line (with intercept at the overall intercept); instead, we want three lines—one for each group—with the same slope but different intercepts. Click the "Add Fit Line at Subgroups" button, or click **Elements → Fit Line At Subgroups**. Then double-click each element of the graph (e.g., lines, data points, axes) to edit the properties of those.

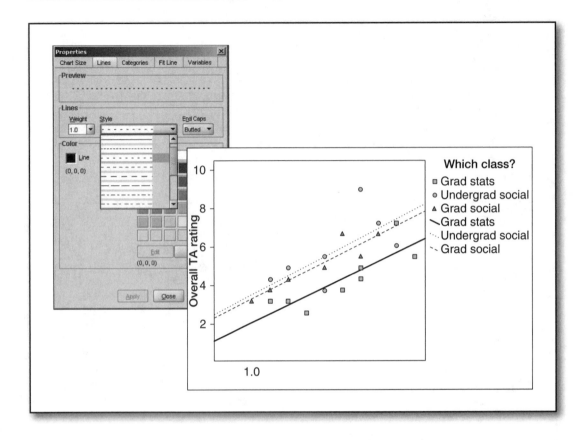

We edited this chart to be black-and-white print-friendly (e.g., different line and marker styles instead of the same style in different colors) and made the fonts larger.

MAKING THE MOST OF SYNTAX:
CUSTOM HYPOTHESIS TESTING IN ANCOVA

As in other forms of the GLM that we've seen, you can use the LMATRIX command to test arbitrary hypotheses among the group means and/or the slopes of the covariates. For example, in this case, we could test whether the slope of GPA on TA rating was less than 2 (testing the null hypothesis that each point increase in GPA related to a two-point increase in TA rating) using the syntax

```
/LMATRIX = GPA 1

/KMATRIX = 2
```

Or, we could test whether the mean TA ratings of the graduate statistics and graduate social psychology classes were equal (controlling for GPA differences) using

```
/LMATRIX = Class 1 0 -1
```

In both cases, testing custom hypotheses on one variable controls for the effect of the other. That control is one of the main reasons to use ANCOVA in the first place. For example, we found that there was a significant difference in TA rating between the two graduate classes (statistics vs. social psychology) when controlling for GPA (difference = 1.36).

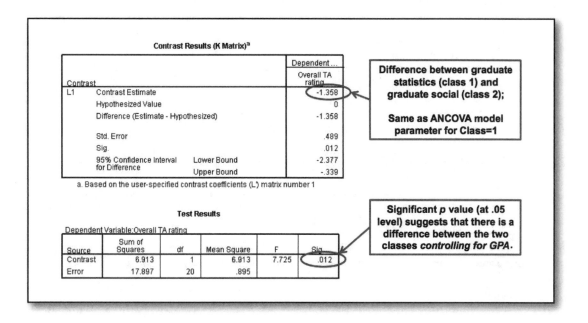

But when GPA was omitted from the model (GLM Rating BY Class /LMATRIX = Class 1 0 –1 /DESIGN = Class .), the difference did not emerge (difference = 0.583).

Contrast Results (K Matrix)[a]

Contrast		Dependent... Overall TA rating
L1	Contrast Estimate	-.583
	Hypothesized Value	0
	Difference (Estimate - Hypothesized)	-.583
	Std. Error	.800
	Sig.	.474
	95% Confidence Interval for Difference Lower Bound	-2.247
	Upper Bound	1.080

a. Based on the user-specified contrast coefficients (L') matrix number 1

Test Results

Dependent Variable:Overall TA rating

Source	Sum of Squares	df	Mean Square	F	Sig.
Contrast	1.361	1	1.361	.532	.474
Error	53.764	21	2.560		

In fact, you can see that there is no significant effect of *class* at all when differences in GPA are not controlled.

Tests of Between-Subjects Effects

Dependent Variable:Overall TA rating

Source	Type III Sum of Squares	df	Mean Square	F	Sig.
Corrected Model	5.444[a]	2	2.722	1.063	.363
Intercept	580.167	1	580.167	226.611	.000
Class	5.444	2	2.722	1.063	.363
Error	53.764	21	2.560		
Total	639.375	24			
Corrected Total	59.208	23			

a. R Squared = .092 (Adjusted R Squared = .005)

No significant effect of *class* when GPA is omitted from model.

GPA differences are suppressing true differences between the classes.

This example illustrates the increase in power to detect effects that can be gained by adding a covariate that systematically varies with the levels of the categorical independent measure.

A CLOSER LOOK: EVALUATING THE ASSUMPTIONS OF ANCOVA

Analysis of covariance makes the "homogeneity of regression" assumption that the slope of the covariate on the dependent variable is equal across groups. This is equivalent to saying that there is no interaction between the covariate (i.e., the continuous IV) and the factor (i.e., the categorical IV) or that the effect of one IV (the covariate) is equal at different levels of the other IV (the factor).

The easiest way to test this assumption is to add the interaction term to the model using syntax. This can be done by adding *GPA*class* to the "/DESIGN" tag as follows:

```
GLM Rating BY Class WITH GPA

/DESIGN = GPA Class GPA*Class .
```

Running this syntax produces only an ANOVA table with the tests of each of the terms.

Tests of Between-Subjects Effects

Dependent Variable:Overall TA rating

Source	Type III Sum of Squares	df	Mean Square	F	Sig.
Corrected Model	41.346ª	5	8.269	8.333	.000
Intercept	6.384	1	6.384	6.434	.021
GPA	35.313	1	35.313	35.585	.000
Class	.963	2	.481	.485	.623
Class * GPA	.034	2	.017	.017	.983
Error	17.862	18	.992		
Total	639.375	24			
Corrected Total	59.208	23			

a. R Squared = .698 (Adjusted R Squared = .615)

Homogeneity of regression assumption
Interaction between covariate and
categorical IV is not different from zero.

The nonsignificant p value for the *GPA*class* effect indicates that the assumption is met. Once this assumption is met, you can safely proceed with running your ANCOVA as above. Importantly, *remember to omit the interaction term* from the ANCOVA that you run as part of your formal data analysis. The interaction term was included only to test the assumption, not as a hypothesis test, and can affect the other terms of interest (the two main effects) if it is left in the model. This appears to be the case in this example because the significant difference in TA rating between classes disappeared when the interaction term was added to the model. Be sure that any ANCOVA result that you report in a research paper does not include the interaction term.

KEYWORDS

categorical factor

continuous covariate

regression intercept

homogeneity of regression assumption

adjusted means (estimated marginal means)

predicted score

fit line

13

Factor and Components Analysis

Conceptual Background of the Factor Analysis

Factor analysis and its cousin, principal components analysis, are part of a family of statistical techniques that has been around for more than 100 years. Although both procedures have been used for multiple purposes, perhaps the main application of principal components analysis is data reduction. Components analysis is frequently applied when a researcher has a larger number of continuously measured variables (typically, psychological test scores), and he or she wants to summarize those variables in terms of a smaller number of linear composites called "components." In a components analysis, the researcher does not need to propose any hypothetical entities (e.g., latent traits) that give rise to variation on the measured variables and account for the correlation among them.

In contrast, factor analysis is often used to explore the question of how many latent factors are required to explain the correlation within a set of observed variables. For example, a researcher may have collected data on 12 different tests of cognitive facility and, in turn, may be keenly interested in whether variation in scores on those tests reflects a single latent ability (e.g., "g," or general ability) or whether multiple factors are required to explain the relationships among the tests. Unlike components analysis, factor analysis typically does involve the researcher postulating one or more hypothetical entities called "latent traits" that explain the relationships among the measured variables.

Background Issues

Prior to conducting a factor or components analysis, a number of preliminary issues need to be considered. In particular, here we emphasize only two: the selection of variables to be factor analyzed and the number of subjects needed to conduct factor analysis.

It is often said that what you put in is what you get out of factor analysis. What this expression means is that if a researcher expects a factor to emerge in his or her data, he or she must have sufficient variables in the analysis to identify that factor. For example, if one is analyzing an eighth-grade mathematics achievement test, and the test contains geometry and calculus problems but not algebra items, there will be no chance for an algebra factor to emerge in the factor analysis. For this reason, many scholars have noted that the selection of variables is the key decision in performing any components or factor analysis. It is critically important that the researcher makes sure he or she has enough measured variables to represent the domains of interest. On the other hand, although a researcher wants to make sure that relevant content domains are properly represented among the measured variables, one of the great dangers of factor or components analysis is to include items that are overly redundant, such as "I'm very happy with myself" and "I'm usually happy with myself." Because such item pairs are likely to be highly correlated simply because of their semantic similarity, such items may seriously distort the results.

A second issue involves the number of observations required to perform a factor or component analysis. We comment briefly on this issue, but we do not wish this guide to serve as a reference for this important issue. The "number of subjects" question is exceedingly difficult to answer across a variety of research contexts. Although there have been dozens of proposed rules of thumb over the years, more recent research seems to indicate that the sample size needed depends heavily on the ultimate structure of the data. The fewer the factors, the cleaner the simple structure (see the next section), the higher the loadings, the fewer individuals are needed. We refer you to your statistics text or any number of books on multivariate analysis for further discussion.

Computing the Factor Analysis in SPSS

Use the data set "Factor.sav" from the website to follow along with a sample factor analysis. This set contains data from 1,000 subjects who each took a 12-test battery assessing cognitive ability. The scores on each test are continuously scored and normally distributed. The first four tests are hypothesized indicators of visual-spatial ability, the second four are proposed indicators of short-term memory functioning, and the remaining four are proposed indicators of social cognition. Given this, we decided to extract three factors and allow those factors to be correlated. The reason we allowed the factors to be correlated is that we hypothesize that the three distinct abilities are correlated due to general intelligence.

Conducting a factor analysis with SPSS is very straightforward and basically involves working through five command boxes. Load the data set; then click **Analyze** → **Dimension Reduction [or "Data Reduction" on earlier versions]** → **Factor** to bring up the factor analysis box.

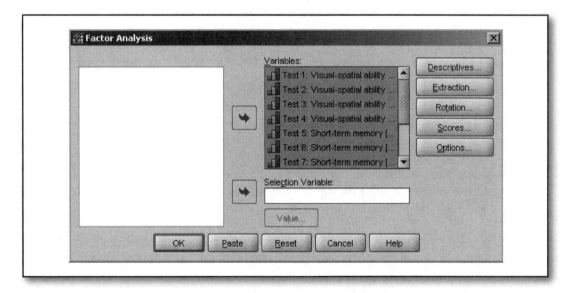

Move the variables of interest from the left box to the right "variables" box as shown in the figure. A researcher may also specify a selection variable such as gender or ethnicity, in which case the analysis will be performed separately based on the selection variable.

Click on "Descriptives" to select what will be shown in the output. In this case, we have chosen to show the univariate descriptive statistics and the initial (unrotated) factor solution. We have also selected to display the original correlation matrix, but not the significance level, determinant of the matrix, or the KMO test of sphericity.

Readers should consult their textbook for discussion of these technical terms. On the right-hand side, we did not select to see the inverse of the correlation matrix, or the anti-image. However, we almost always want to select the reproduced option. Basically, the reproduced matrix is the correlation matrix determined from the estimated model parameters, in this case, the estimated factor loadings. By comparing the original correlation matrix with the reproduced, a researcher can learn much regarding how well a particular exploratory factor solution recovers the original relations between the variables.

The next option box, "Extraction," is where the researcher selects the method of factor extraction. First, examine the "Method" menu. The option chosen from this menu will determine whether SPSS conducts a components or a factor analysis. The "Method" menu provides for several different types of analyses, such as principal components, generalized least squares, unweighted least squares, maximum likelihood, principal axis factoring, and the (seldom-used) alpha factoring. If the researcher selects principal components, then the matrix to be analyzed has ones on the diagonals, and a principal components analysis that attempts to explain as much item variance as possible will be conducted. The remaining options are factor analyses, with the most commonly selected being principal axis and maximum likelihood. With these procedures, the matrix to be analyzed has "communality estimates" (estimates of the amount of item variance that is shared with other items) on the diagonal. The goal of these is to find a set of latent factors that explains as much common variance as possible. Because we are conducting a factor analysis, we have selected "Principal axis factoring" from this menu.

The remaining options in this menu are fairly straightforward.

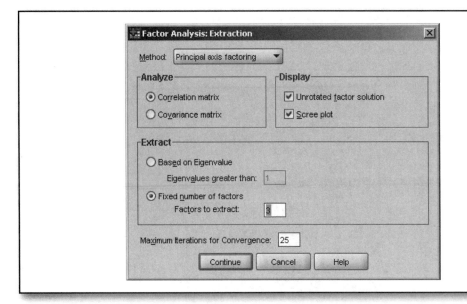

Specify under "Analyze" whether to use the correlation matrix or the covariance matrix for the analysis. The interpretation of the factor loadings depends critically on which option is selected, but most researchers routinely analyze a correlation matrix. The "Display" box controls the output of the unrotated factors and the scree plot. The scree plot, which shows a graph of eigenvalues on the *y*-axis and number of factors or components on the *x*-axis, is invaluable in judging the "number of factors to extract" question and should always be requested. Finally, the "Extract" box allows for either one of two methods of determining how many factors or components to extract in the initial solution. A researcher can extract based on the eigenvalue being greater than a certain number or specify the number of factors to extract based on a priori justification. The latter is by far the preferred method for both theoretical reasons (because it's always best to let theory dictate your data analysis) as well as a number of technical reasons beyond the present scope. In the present example, we have specified a priori to extract three factors because our battery is intended to assess three related but distinct types of cognitive abilities.

The "Rotation" box allows you to specify how the factors are rotated. It is well known that initial factor or component solutions are often uninterpretable and thus have to be "rotated" to facilitate meaningful interpretation. The basic choice in factor rotation is between orthogonal (uncorrelated factors) versus oblique (correlated factors) rotations. For orthogonal solutions, Varimax is commonly selected. If this is selected, note that (a) the factor structure and factor pattern will be equal, and thus it doesn't matter which is interpreted, and (b) there is no factor intercorrelation matrix reported because all correlations are zero. For oblique factor rotations, Direct Oblimin and Promax are the most commonly selected options. In either of these solutions, the factor structure and factor pattern matrices will differ and a factor intercorrelation matrix will be reported. Moreover, each of these options allows the researcher to control certain aspects of the rotation through the delta parameter for Direct Oblimin and the Kappa parameters for Promax. We suggest that researchers use the defaults unless they fully understand the mathematics underlying each of these rotations. Finally, the display box allows the researcher to control whether the rotated solution or a loading plot is shown in the output.

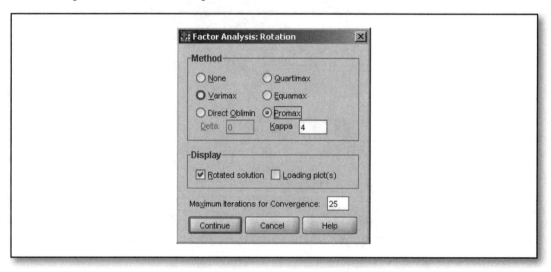

The "Scores" box performs only one function, namely, controlling how factor score estimation will be conducted, if desired. The three options are regression, Bartlett, and Anderson-Rubin method. Checking the top box saves the estimated factor scores back to the SPSS data file under the names "F1" for Factor 1, "F2" for Factor 2, and so on. Checking the bottom box displays the factor score coefficients.

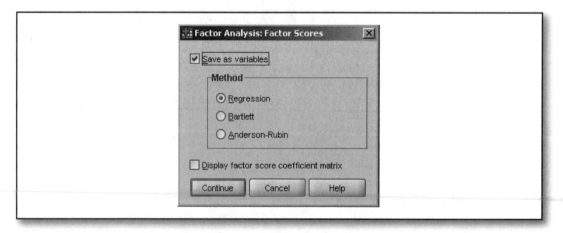

The final options box is called simply "Options," and it allows the user to control how missing data are to be handled in computing the original correlation matrix (listwise, pairwise, replace with mean). The coefficient display format is very handy in that it allows the researcher to sort the factor loading by the size of the loading, which, in turn, can greatly ease factor interpretation. The second check box allows the researcher to suppress factor loadings less than some value, say, .10. In factor analysis, loadings less than .30 are seldom considered important; thus, deleting them from the output can greatly simplify interpretation. Of course, the danger is that a researcher may miss a small but important cross-loading.

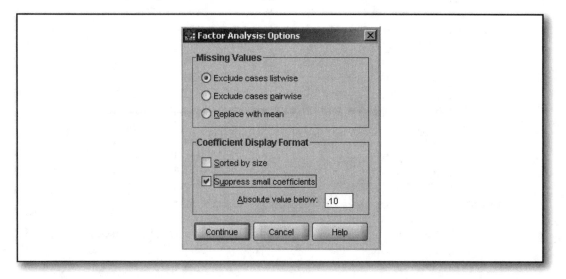

The syntax for this command is

```
FACTOR

/VARIABLES v1 v2 v3 v4 v5 v6 v7 v8 v9 v10 v11 v12

/ANALYSIS v1 v2 v3 v4 v5 v6 v7 v8 v9 v10 v11 v12

/PRINT UNIVARIATE INITIAL CORRELATION REPR EXTRACTION
ROTATION

/FORMAT BLANK(.10)

/PLOT EIGEN

/CRITERIA FACTORS(3) ITERATE(25)

/EXTRACTION PAF

/CRITERIA ITERATE(25)

/ROTATION PROMAX(4)

/SAVE REG(ALL)

/METHOD=CORRELATION.
```

Interpreting the SPSS Output of Factor Analysis

The first output derives from the descriptives box and displays the item means, standard deviation, and sample size.

Descriptive Statistics

	Mean	Std. Deviation	Analysis N
Test 1: Visual-spatial ability	.54	.499	1000
Test 2: Visual-spatial ability	.51	.500	1000
Test 3: Visual-spatial ability	.50	.500	1000
Test 4: Visual-spatial ability	.53	.500	1000
Test 5: Short-term memory	.47	.499	1000
Test 6: Short-term memory	.49	.500	1000
Test 7: Short-term memory	.50	.500	1000
Test 8: Short-term memory	.52	.500	1000
Test 9: Social cognition	.50	.500	1000
Test 10: Social cognition	.49	.500	1000
Test 11: Social cognition	.50	.500	1000
Test 12: Social cognition	.51	.500	1000

This is then followed by the original 12 × 12 correlation matrix. Because we specified for SPSS to use the correlation analysis in the "Extraction" menu (/METHOD=CORRELATION), these are the data that were actually entered into the analysis.

Correlation Matrix

		Test 1: Visual-spatial ability	Test 2: Visual-spatial ability	Test 3: Visual-spatial ability	Test 4: Visual-spatial ability	Test 5: Short-term memory	Test 6: Short-term memory	Test 7: Short-term memory	Test 8: Short-term memory	Test 9: Social cognition	Test 10: Social cognition	Test 11: Social cognition	Test 12: Social cognition
Correlation	Test 1: Visual-spatial ability	1.000	.135	.261	.237	.111	.087	.098	.088	.097	.095	.098	.121
	Test 2: Visual-spatial ability	.135	1.000	.184	.191	.047	-.006	.038	.065	.112	.066	.078	.118
	Test 3: Visual-spatial ability	.261	.184	1.000	.180	.070	.010	.086	.082	.092	.090	.038	.114
	Test 4: Visual-spatial ability	.237	.191	.180	1.000	.125	.103	.102	.116	.145	.127	.090	.045
	Test 5: Short-term memory	.111	.047	.070	.125	1.000	.180	.196	.215	.102	.043	.121	.077
	Test 6: Short-term memory	.087	-.006	.010	.103	.180	1.000	.172	.193	.082	.020	-.036	.056
	Test 7: Short-term memory	.098	.038	.086	.102	.196	.172	1.000	.236	.078	.000	.064	.020
	Test 8: Short-term memory	.088	.065	.082	.116	.215	.193	.236	1.000	.122	.037	.128	.088
	Test 9: Social cognition	.097	.112	.092	.145	.102	.082	.078	.122	1.000	.198	.214	.210
	Test 10: Social cognition	.095	.066	.090	.127	.043	.020	.000	.037	.198	1.000	.108	.196
	Test 11: Social cognition	.098	.078	.038	.090	.121	-.036	.064	.128	.214	.108	1.000	.160
	Test 12: Social cognition	.121	.118	.114	.045	.077	.056	.020	.088	.210	.196	.160	1.000

Next, the initial and final communality estimates (% of common variance) based on extracting three factors are displayed. Apparently, the three common factors proposed to underlie this set of items explains about 20% of the variance on each item.

Amount of variance explained by the (three) factors

Communalities

	Initial	Extraction
Test 1: Visual-spatial ability	.128	.251
Test 2: Visual-spatial ability	.077	.132
Test 3: Visual-spatial ability	.112	.245
Test 4: Visual-spatial ability	.125	.206
Test 5: Short-term memory	.103	.198
Test 6: Short-term memory	.088	.155
Test 7: Short-term memory	.099	.214
Test 8: Short-term memory	.123	.253
Test 9: Social cognition	.123	.267
Test 10: Social cognition	.079	.152
Test 11: Social cognition	.090	.150
Test 12: Social cognition	.101	.193

Extraction Method: Principal Axis Factoring.

Amount of variance explained by other variables (without factors)

The eigenvalues and following scree plot are useful in judging how many factors to extract. In the present case, the first three eigenvalues are larger than the others, but certainly the third is not much larger than the fourth.

Eigenvalues before and after extraction

Total Variance Explained

Factor	Initial Eigenvalues			Extraction Sums of Squared Loadings			Rotation Sums of Squared Loadings[a]
	Total	% of Variance	Cumulative %	Total	% of Variance	Cumulative %	Total
1	2.229	18.571	18.571	1.440	12.002	12.002	1.034
2	1.369	11.409	29.980	.567	4.724	16.726	1.089
3	1.196	9.967	39.946	.410	3.418	20.144	1.041
4	.964	8.032	47.979				
5	.883	7.357	55.336				
6	.875	7.296	62.631				
7	.822	6.852	69.483				
8	.799	6.657	76.140				
9	.757	6.308	82.448				
10	.743	6.196	88.644				
11	.691	5.755	94.398				
12	.672	5.602	100.000				

Extraction Method: Principal Axis Factoring.

a. When factors are correlated, sums of squared loadings cannot be added to obtain a total variance.

Percentage of variance explained by each factor

In turn, it is unclear whether the "elbow" of the scree plot occurs at the third or fourth eigenvalue.

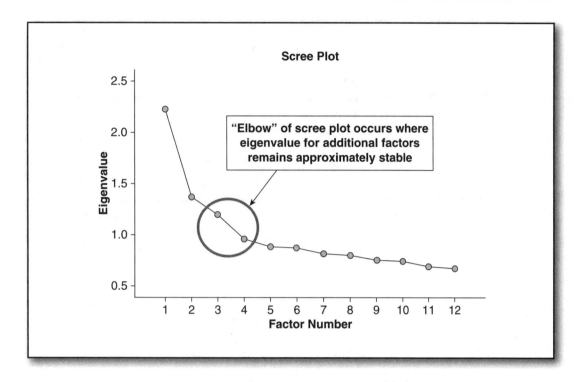

In practice, a researcher would want to estimate factor solutions in two to five dimensions and would scrutinize the resulting estimates in terms of interpretability, and then choose the best solution among those options.

Next are the initial factor matrix, the rotated factor pattern, and the factor structure.

Factor Matrix[a]

	Factor		
	1	2	3
Test 1: Visual-spatial ability	.415	-.106	-.261
Test 2: Visual-spatial ability	.291	-.172	-.132
Test 3: Visual-spatial ability	.383	-.187	-.293
Test 4: Visual-spatial ability	.408		-.190
Test 5: Short-term memory	.356	.284	
Test 6: Short-term memory	.249	.304	
Test 7: Short-term memory	.316	.337	
Test 8: Short-term memory	.387	.312	
Test 9: Social cognition	.411	-.147	.276
Test 10: Social cognition	.277	-.226	.155
Test 11: Social cognition	.301		.223
Test 12: Social cognition	.333	-.199	.207

Extraction Method: Principal Axis Factoring.
a. 3 factors extracted. 8 iterations required.

Pattern Matrix[a]

	Factor		
	1	2	3
Test 1: Visual-spatial ability		.491	
Test 2: Visual-spatial ability		.335	
Test 3: Visual-spatial ability		.524	
Test 4: Visual-spatial ability		.399	
Test 5: Short-term memory	.421		
Test 6: Short-term memory	.413		
Test 7: Short-term memory	.470		
Test 8: Short-term memory	.486		
Test 9: Social cognition			.506
Test 10: Social cognition			.379
Test 11: Social cognition			.384
Test 12: Social cognition			.436

Extraction Method: Principal Axis Factoring.
Rotation Method: Promax with Kaiser Normalization.
a. Rotation converged in 5 iterations.

Structure Matrix

	Factor		
	1	2	3
Test 1: Visual-spatial ability	.216	.500	.223
Test 2: Visual-spatial ability		.352	.220
Test 3: Visual-spatial ability	.135	.492	.190
Test 4: Visual-spatial ability	.248	.444	.237
Test 5: Short-term memory	.442	.186	.198
Test 6: Short-term memory	.389	.108	
Test 7: Short-term memory	.458	.174	
Test 8: Short-term memory	.500	.181	.220
Test 9: Social cognition	.217	.229	.514
Test 10: Social cognition		.207	.378
Test 11: Social cognition	.167	.154	.383
Test 12: Social cognition	.121	.217	.438

Extraction Method: Principal Axis Factoring.
Rotation Method: Promax with Kaiser Normalization.

The initial factor matrix is the *unrotated* solution, which can be thought of as the correlation between each item and each factor. Because we used "/FORMAT BLANK(.10)" in the syntax, all correlations less than 0.10 are not shown. It is the rotated factor pattern—containing (roughly) the partial correlations between each item and the rotated latent factors (i.e., the factor loadings) with the other factors removed—that is typically interpreted. In this case, the interpretation of the factor pattern is very simple—each set of four variables loads (i.e., is correlated with) a distinct latent factor. Although there is some variation of loading within each factor, this variation is relatively small and no item appears "definitive" of a factor. The factor structure matrix contains (roughly) the zero-order correlations between each item and each factor. The structure matrix will be equal to the pattern matrix only when an orthogonal (uncorrelated) solution is requested; in this case, we specified an oblique (correlated) solution, so the structure matrix is different from the pattern matrix.

In an oblique rotation such as the one conducted here, the algorithm will estimate the correlations among the factors in the population ("Factor Correlation Matrix").

Factor Correlation Matrix

Factor	1	2	3
1	1.000	.363	.337
2	.363	1.000	.456
3	.337	.456	1.000

Extraction Method: Principal Axis Factoring.
Rotation Method: Promax with Kaiser Normalization.

In the present case, the factor correlation matrix indicates that the three factors are indeed modestly related. This is not surprising. It is often the case that cognitive tests, even tests of distinct processes, remain correlated because of the general ability factor.

A CLOSER LOOK: REPORTING THE RESULTS IN A RESEARCH PAPER

We've described graphical methods to use in conjunction with several of the other statistics discussed in this book. Although factor and components analyses can be displayed graphically, the most common presentation format is in tables. We briefly review one graphical method here for two- and three-factor solutions and briefly outline some reporting guidelines for displaying results in tables.

To produce a plot of the rotated solution when conducting the factor analysis (**Analyze** → **Data Reduction** → **Factor**), click on the "Rotation" tab, and then select "Loading plots." Or just add "/PLOT ROTATION" to the syntax.

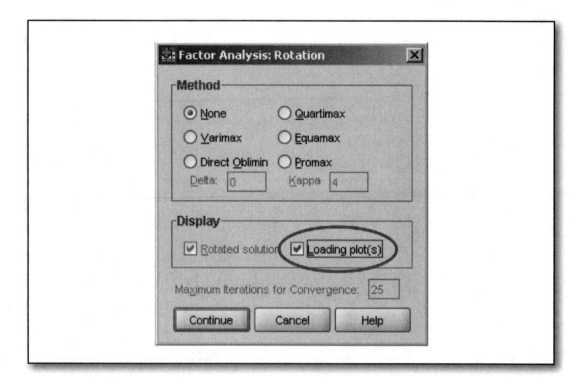

This option produces a scatterplot with one factor on each axis and data points representing the loadings of each item on the factors. Each point is plotted in space according to its loading on each of the factors. If an item loads highly on Factor 1 and close to zero on the others, it will be plotted with a large value on the axis corresponding to Factor 1 and small values on the other axes.

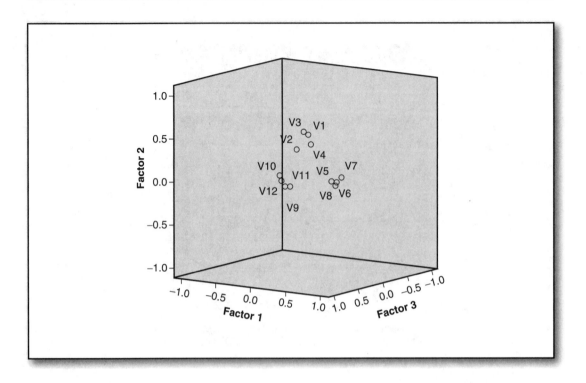

Consequently, it tends to look best with two-factor solutions and at most three-factor solutions. For example, here is the plot of only Factors 1 and 2. This plot is characteristic of a good factor solution: All of the items are close to one axis or the other, with no items along the diagonal (indicating cross-loading on the two factors).

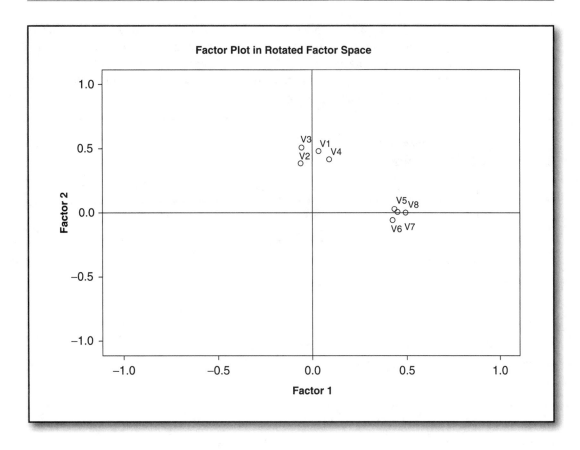

Factor Plot in Rotated Factor Space

The results of a factor or components analysis should always be reported in table form, and especially in cases when visualization is difficult (e.g., three factors) or impossible (four or more factors). One table should contain a matrix of factor loadings (the "Pattern Matrix" in SPSS) along with the communalities for each item (percent of variance explained) and eigenvalues for each factor. If an oblique rotation was used (as in the example here), the factor intercorrelation matrix should be presented in a second table.

In addition to any tables and figures, there are a number of analytic details to mention in the text of the paper. Be sure to specify whether you did a components or factor analysis (even though the results from these analyses can be quite similar) and which rotation method was used, if any. Specify how the number of factors was determined (e.g., by a priori theory, inspection of scree plots, etc.) and why a solution with fewer or more factors was not selected. Also in the text, interpret each factor by examining the items that loaded highly and the items that did not load as expected. Point out any cross-loadings and comment upon how they may contribute to the correlation among factors, as these items may represent a "blend" of two or more factors. Finally, note the presence of "doublets" or "triplets"—factors that consist of only two or three highly intercorrelated items—and consider the possibility that these factors may be artifacts of multiple items with highly similar content. In such cases, the factor is not necessarily a real, interpretable latent variable but rather merely reflects semantic similarity among the items. A solution to this problem can often be found by simply eliminating one of a pair of very highly intercorrelated items.

KEYWORDS

component	communality estimate	scree plot
factor	eigenvalue	pattern matrix
latent variable	factor rotation	structure matrix
factor loadings	orthogonal vs. oblique rotation	
extraction method		

14

Psychometrics

Conceptual Background of Psychometrics

Many research studies in the social sciences include questionnaire-type data. Accordingly, one motivation underlying the use of a psychometric analysis is to explore the psychometric properties of one's measures in a particular sample. In other words, a researcher may be keenly interested in exploring item means and variances, as well as scale score properties such as total test score mean and variance, and test score reliability in his or her particular sample. More ambitiously, a researcher may be considering developing a new measure of a psychological construct and may have administered items to a pilot sample. In this case, the investigator is keenly interested in whether the items intercorrelate as they should, which items are "good" measures of the construct, and which items are relatively "weak" or "poor" indicators. He or she will also be interested in scale score properties such as the coefficient alpha reliability. Finally, a third application of SPSS psychometric analysis is to explore the interrater reliability of a set of ratings. In this situation, two or more judges have responded to a set of items, and the researcher is interested in the reliability of each rater's scores and/or the aggregate score derived from two or more raters.

Preliminary Psychometrics in SPSS

The file "Extraversion.sav" on the website contains a data set consisting of 1,000 individuals who responded to an 8-item measure of the personality trait of extraversion. Each item is scored on a 1-to-5 scale with a 5 indicating higher levels of the trait.

Prior to launching a psychometric analysis, it is important that each item or variable be scored correctly. For example, on many personality, psychopathology, or health questionnaires, some items are "reverse keyed." This means that their direction of scoring is the reverse. For example, on a depression scale, there may be items like "I'm happy all the time" in which a low score, as opposed to a high score, indicates depression. This is not the place to discuss why questionnaire developers include both positively and negatively keyed items in their measures. However, we do note that psychometric analysis is easier when all the items are scored in the correct direction. To check this in the present data, ask for the correlation matrix among the eight items using **Analyze → Correlate → Bivariate**; then move the eight items from the left to the right "Variables" window.

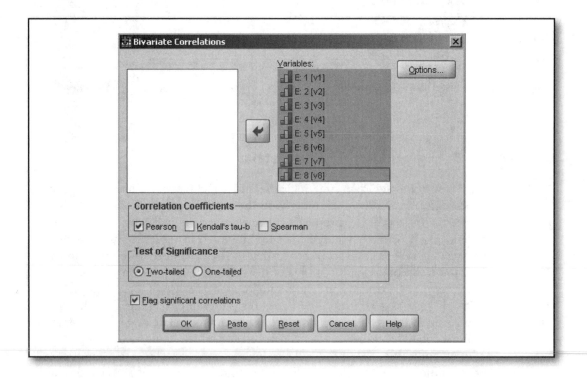

Alternatively, you can use the syntax "CORRELATIONS /VARIABLES=v1 v2 v3 v4 v5 v6 v7 v8 ."

The 8-by-8 correlation table clearly shows that in this case, all the items are positively intercorrelated—this is exactly what we want.

Correlations

		E: 1	E: 2	E: 3	E: 4	E: 5	E: 6	E: 7	E: 8
E: 1	Pearson Correlation	1	.279	.343	.312	.312	.250	.167	.155
E: 2	Pearson Correlation	.279	1	.247	.283	.527	.254	.241	.203
E: 3	Pearson Correlation	.343	.247	1	.496	.261	.338	.188	.205
E: 4	Pearson Correlation	.312	.283	.496	1	.297	.284	.238	.202
E: 5	Pearson Correlation	.312	.527	.261	.297	1	.382	.303	.284
E: 6	Pearson Correlation	.250	.254	.338	.284	.382	1	.112	.204
E: 7	Pearson Correlation	.167	.241	.188	.238	.303	.112	1	.305
E: 8	Pearson Correlation	.155	.203	.205	.202	.284	.204	.305	1

The fact that items are positively related is consistent with the idea that they all measure the same construct. If some items displayed negative correlations, we might have to consider reverse coding the item, or the possibility that the item is poor and should be discarded.

Now that we have established that the items are all scored in the correct direction, a second important preliminary analysis is to check response category usage. This can be easily accomplished through running frequencies: **Analyze → Descriptive Statistics → Frequencies**. The syntax is "FREQUENCIES VARIABLES=v1 v2 v3 v4 v5 v6 v7 v8 .". In the output, inspect whether there are any unused or rarely used response categories. This may indicate that the item content is too extreme or that the anchors are poorly worded. A researcher may also wish to study the item mean, variance, or skewness at this point as well.

E: 1

		Frequency	Percent	Valid Percent	Cumulative Percent
Valid	1	14	1.4	1.4	1.4
	2	104	10.4	10.4	11.8
	3	226	22.6	22.6	34.4
	4	519	51.9	51.9	86.3
	5	137	13.7	13.7	100.0
	Total	1000	100.0	100.0	

Frequencies for Item 1: Approximately normal

E: 2

		Frequency	Percent	Valid Percent	Cumulative Percent
Valid	1	8	.8	.8	.8
	2	46	4.6	4.6	5.4
	3	81	8.1	8.1	13.5
	4	446	44.6	44.6	58.1
	5	419	41.9	41.9	100.0
	Total	1000	100.0	100.0	

Frequencies for Item 2: Negatively skewed

In this case, we can see that Item 1 is approximately normal, whereas Item 2 has negative skew (i.e., long tail to the left).

See Chapter 2 on Descriptive Statistics for details on how to compute other informative preliminary summary statistics such as variance, skewness, and kurtosis.

Computing Formal Psychometric Analyses in SPSS

Having conducted these two basic data inspections using SPSS, we now turn to a formal psychometric analysis. Our main question here is, How well do these items measure a psychological construct? There are many approaches to addressing this issue, but here we will stick with the most ordinary conventional item- and scale-level analyses. To run a reliability analysis, click **Analyze** → **Scale** → **Reliability Analysis**.

Then place the items you wish to analyze into the box on the right, and for now, select the alpha option.

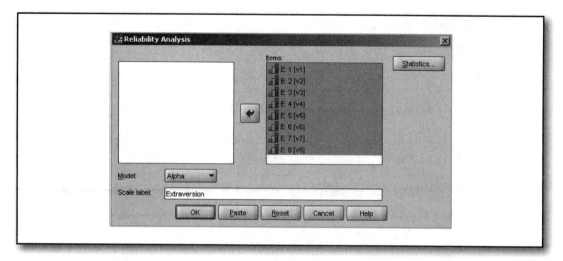

Pressing the "Statistics" button presents the following options. In this menu, we have selected to present descriptive statistics for each item, and the scale as a whole, and for the scale if each item were deleted (this should be clearer shortly).

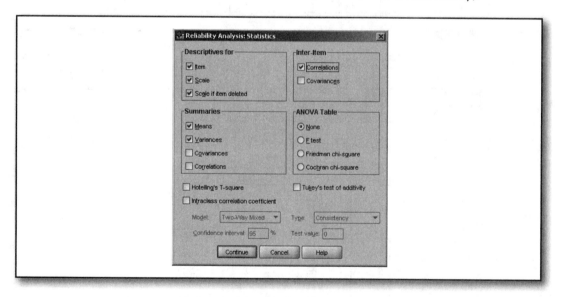

We also selected summary indexes such as reporting the mean and variance of raw scores (formed by summing together the individual item response scores). Finally, we requested that the program display the interitem correlation matrix (at this point, this is redundant with the previous analysis). The syntax for this is

```
RELIABILITY

/VARIABLES=v1 v2 v3 v4 v5 v6 v7 v8

/SCALE('Extraversion') ALL
```

```
/MODEL=ALPHA

/STATISTICS=DESCRIPTIVE SCALE CORR

/SUMMARY=TOTAL MEANS VARIANCE.
```

This series of commands produces the following results. First, the overall coefficient alpha for the scale is shown (.748). This is the primary value to report in your research paper as the reliability of the raw scale score. The standardized alpha of .751 is also displayed. Standardized alpha is an estimate of the internal consistency reliability assuming that each item has been standardized before summing into a raw score. The standardization removes the effects of differences between items in their variance.

Reliability Statistics

Cronbach's Alpha	Cronbach's Alpha Based on Standardized Items	N of Items
.748	.751	8

Next, the mean response, standard deviation of response, and the number of cases responding are shown for each item. Generally, people score high on these items. The intercorrelation matrix is presented below that and is identical to the analysis we computed earlier.

Item Statistics

	Mean	Std. Deviation	N
E: 1	3.66	.889	1000
E: 2	4.22	.841	1000
E: 3	4.05	.794	1000
E: 4	4.02	.952	1000
E: 5	4.12	.824	1000
E: 6	3.63	1.072	1000
E: 7	4.04	.885	1000
E: 8	3.74	.773	1000

Perhaps most interesting and informative are the item statistics (in the table called "Item-Total Statistics").

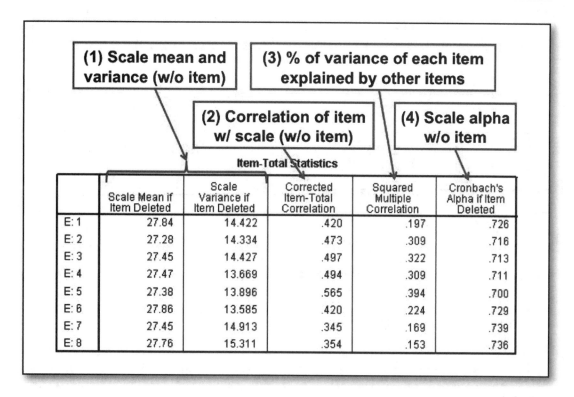

(1) Scale mean and variance (w/o item)

(3) % of variance of each item explained by other items

(2) Correlation of item w/ scale (w/o item)

(4) Scale alpha w/o item

Item-Total Statistics

	Scale Mean if Item Deleted	Scale Variance if Item Deleted	Corrected Item-Total Correlation	Squared Multiple Correlation	Cronbach's Alpha if Item Deleted
E: 1	27.84	14.422	.420	.197	.726
E: 2	27.28	14.334	.473	.309	.716
E: 3	27.45	14.427	.497	.322	.713
E: 4	27.47	13.669	.494	.309	.711
E: 5	27.38	13.896	.565	.394	.700
E: 6	27.86	13.585	.420	.224	.729
E: 7	27.45	14.913	.345	.169	.739
E: 8	27.76	15.311	.354	.153	.736

For each item, the following are provided: (a) the raw score scale mean and variance if the item were deleted from the scale; (b) the "corrected" item-total correlation (i.e., the correlation between the item and the scale score after the item has been subtracted from the scale score); (c) the squared multiple correlation, which indicates the degree to which an item is explainable via the other items on the scale (high R-squared values indicate a redundant item); and (d) the coefficient alpha reliability of the scale with the item eliminated from the scale. Generally, a researcher would want to eliminate items if the overall alpha would increase with the deletion, and retain the item otherwise.

Finally, SPSS displays the descriptive statistics for the overall scale.

Scale Statistics

Mean	Variance	Std. Deviation	N of Items
31.50	18.052	4.249	8

Here, the mean raw score, found by summing up the individual item scores within each person, was 31.5 with a variance of 18.05. Descriptive statistics are also provided for item means and variances in the table titled "Summary Item Statistics."

Summary Item Statistics

	Mean	Minimum	Maximum	Range	Maximum / Minimum	Variance	N of Items
Item Means	3.937	3.633	4.222	.589	1.162	.051	8
Item Variances	.781	.597	1.149	.552	1.924	.032	8

The figures in this table are mostly useful for diagnosing outlier items, such as those with means well above or below the "mean mean," resulting in a high variance across the means.

Interrater Reliability in SPSS

Another common psychometric question is whether multiple raters reach consensus about the properties of a set of items. For example, instead of having each subject complete a questionnaire assessing extraversion, we could have had a series of raters observe the behavior of each subject and make a single rating about the extraversion of each subject on a 5-point scale. The question of reliability arises in this case also, but here we are concerned about reliability *across raters* instead of reliability *across items*. A statistic called the *intraclass coefficient* (ICC) can be computed as a measure of the extent of agreement among a set of judges evaluating the same target. The ICC provides an index of the overall reliability among the judges.

The file "ExtraversionICC.sav" contains data from eight judges' ratings of the same 40 individuals on extraversion. Importantly, make note that the raw data are organized with one rater per column and the subjects on the rows. In other words, in an ICC analysis, the raters are analyzed as "items" would be in an alpha reliability analysis.

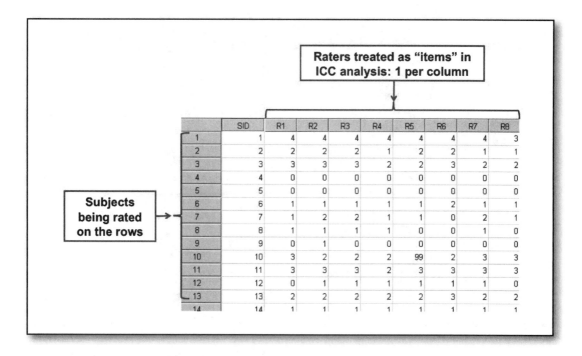

To compute the ICC, click **Analyze → Scale → Reliability Analysis**, and place the raters in the "items" box to the right.

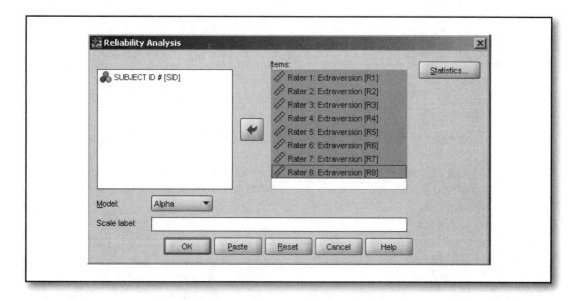

So far, this is identical to the alpha coefficient analysis, but not for long. Click "Statistics," and in the box that comes up, request the intraclass correlation coefficient using a two-way random model and absolute agreement.

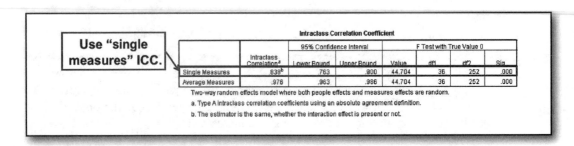

The other options (e.g., item and scale descriptives, inter-item correlations, etc.) can be useful for identifying poor "items" (i.e., raters) as noted earlier in alpha coefficient reliability analysis. They will not be covered again here.

The syntax for this is

```
RELIABILITY

/VARIABLES=R1 R2 R3 R4 R5 R6 R7 R8

/SCALE('Extraversion') ALL

/MODEL=ALPHA

/ICC=MODEL(RANDOM) TYPE(ABSOLUTE) CIN=95 TESTVAL=0.
```

The output simply contains a summary of the raters included and excluded, the alpha for the "scale" that consists of the eight raters (which should be ignored), and the ICC table.

Intraclass Correlation Coefficient

	Intraclass Correlation[a]	95% Confidence Interval		F Test with True Value 0			
		Lower Bound	Upper Bound	Value	df1	df2	Sig.
Single Measures	.838[b]	.763	.900	44.704	36	252	.000
Average Measures	.976	.963	.986	44.704	36	252	.000

Use "single measures" ICC.

Two-way random effects model where both people effects and measures effects are random.

a. Type A intraclass correlation coefficients using an absolute agreement definition.

b. The estimator is the same, whether the interaction effect is present or not.

The number to focus on is the "single measures" ICC. This number is calculated as the amount of variance that is due to between-subject variance, relative to the total variance (i.e., variance between the raters plus variance between subjects). Higher numbers indicate that more observed variance is attributed to the subjects than error in the judges' ratings. If the judges all agreed perfectly on every observation, the ICC would be "1." The "average measures" ICC is the reliability if you were to average across the eight raters.

A reader may wonder, Why use this fancy technique when I could just as easily calculate the average interrater correlation? If you only cared about *rank order*, and not about magnitude, then the average interrater correlation would be fine. But researchers *do* typically care about magnitude, and correlation is not sensitive to magnitude. For example, suppose four raters used a 10-point scale to rate four people on extraversion.

	Rater1	Rater2	Rater3	Rater4
1	2	1	1	7
2	4	3	2	8
3	6	5	3	9
4	8	7	4	10

All raters agree that the subjects increased in extraversion from Subject 1 through Subject 4. For example, Rater 1 gave "2, 4, 6, 8" and Rater 3 gave "1, 2, 3, 4" as their ratings. The correlations among the raters are perfect, 1.00. But there is almost no consensus on the magnitudes of the ratings. For example, Raters 2 and 3 gave Person 1 a "1," and Rater 4 gave the same person a "7" (out of 10). For this reason, the ICC of these ratings is .34, even though the coefficient alpha is .96. This example illustrates an important difference between alpha—a measure of covariation regardless of scale—and ICC—a measure of similarity of magnitude.

KEYWORDS

reverse keying	coefficient alpha	interrater reliability
reliability	intercorrelation matrix	intraclass coefficient (ICC)
scale score	item-total correlation	

15

Nonparametric Tests ❖

Conceptual Background of Nonparametric Tests

We've noted the assumptions of the general linear model in several places throughout this book. We've pointed out how to test the assumptions and even a few steps that you might take to attempt to correct violations of the assumptions. But what happens when your data are irreparably nonnormal? Or if your data never pretended to be normal in the first place, as is the case with rank-ordered data or single-subject response times? In those cases, one option is to abandon the general linear model entirely and work with an approach that makes fewer (or no) assumptions. One family of such approaches is known as "nonparametric" tests, because they are not assumed to follow a distribution parameter (e.g., *F* or *t*).

Recent versions of SPSS have offered an increasing number of nonparametric options. For now, we will review four different nonparametric tests that correspond to the one-sample *t*-test, independent- and paired-samples *t*-tests, and between- and within-subjects ANOVA. These are the Sign Test, Wilcoxon Rank-Sum Test, Wilcoxon Signed-Rank Test, Kruskal-Wallis One-Way Test, and Friedman's Rank Test, respectively.

Parametric test	Nonparametric analogue
One-sample *t*-test	Sign test
Independent samples t-test	Wilcoxon rank-sum test
Paired samples *t*-test	Wilcoxon signed-rank test
Between-subjects ANOVA	Kruskal-Wallis test
Within-subjects ANOVA	Friedman's rank test

The nonparametric tests all share the advantage of making fewer assumptions than the GLM, but that doesn't mean they are assumption free. For example, several of the tests assume that the distribution is *continuous,* meaning that there are no gaps in the range of possible values. Also, each of the nonparametric tests described here assume that the observations are independent or paired in a known way (similar to paired-samples *t*-tests). Because nonparametric tests rely on sample medians instead of means, they are more robust to outliers than traditional tests. However, these advantages come at a cost; in cases when your data meet assumptions of normality, parametric tests will be more powerful than nonparametric tests to detect an effect.

The Sign Test (for One-Sample Hypotheses)

The Sign Test is ideal for testing the median value of a sample that is not normally distributed. The concept is that a median can be defined for any continuous distribution, regardless of the shape of that distribution. All values in the sample can be assigned a "sign" based on whether they are above or below the median, and then a simple binomial probability can be computed for the observed pattern based on a hypothesized probability.

For example, suppose a candidate received the following percentages of the vote in 10 districts:

$$51, 56, 56, 41, 40, 30, 14, 33, 82, 31,$$

and we want to know whether that candidate received more than 50% of the vote on average. Under the null, the candidate received less than or equal to 50% of the vote, and the alternative is that she received more than 50%. We can assign a "sign" to each of the values based on this hypothesis, where "-" means the point is below the hypothesized median, and "+" means the point is above the hypothesized median:

$$+, +, +, -, -, -, -, -, +, -$$

So, there are four observations above the hypothesized median and six below, with a 50/50 chance of each observation being above or below given the null.

The file "NonPar.sav" contains the data on voting information for 10 districts in the variable called *districts.*

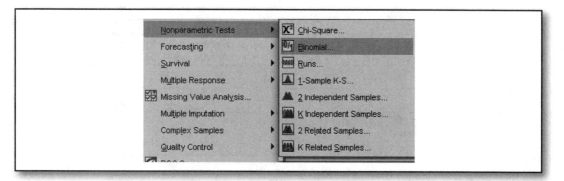

Use SPSS to compute the binomial probability by clicking **Analyze → Nonparametric Tests → Binomial**; then put the (one) test variable, *districts,* in the test variable list. Set "Define Dichotomy" (i.e., define the "sign") to "Cut point: 50." That will assign all values less than or equal to the cut point as one sign, and all values greater than the cut point as another. If the data have been predichotomized into "1"s and "0"s, you can select "Get from data." Leave the "Test Proportion" set to the default 50% (0.50), testing the null hypothesis that the cut point is at the median of the sample.

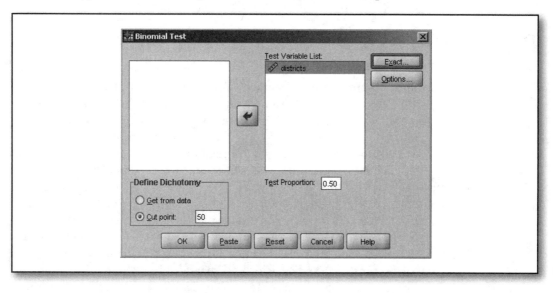

All other settings can be left at the default values. The syntax for this function is

```
NPAR TESTS /BINOMIAL (0.50) = districts (50) .
```

The output displays the observed distribution relative to the cutoff value as we calculated them earlier (six above and four below); their proportions (60%/40%); and the *two-tailed* test of the null hypothesis, which is that the candidate received *no more or less than 50% of the vote* across districts.

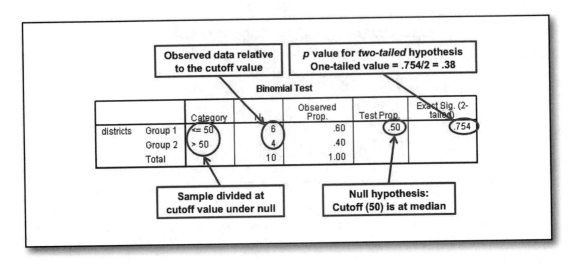

Divide the *p* value for the two-tailed hypothesis test (.754) in half in order to compute the one-tailed hypothesis (.754/2 = .38). In this case, we conclude that the candidate did not receive more than 50% of the vote on average.

The Wilcoxon Rank-Sum Test (for Independent Samples)

The logic of the Wilcoxon Rank-Sum Test is that if data from two groups are rank-ordered without regard to group membership, then the sum of the rank orders will be similar if the groups are drawn from identical distributions but will be different if the groups are drawn from different distributions. For example, consider two high schools each with five algebra classes. We want to know if one school has a larger average class size than the other. If one school's classrooms have 10, 20, 30, 40, and 50 students, and the other school's classrooms have 15, 25, 35, 45, and 55 students, then the (ascending) ranks of the two schools are 1, 3, 5, 7, 9 and 2, 4, 6, 8, 10, respectively. The sum of the ranks for the first school is 25 and the sum of the ranks of the second school is 30, so the two sums are only 5 points apart. In contrast, suppose one school's algebra classes have 10, 15, 20, 25, and 30 students, and the other school's classes have 35, 40, 45, 50, and 55 students. Now, the ranks for the two schools are 1, 2, 3, 4, 5, and 6, 7, 8, 9, 10 with sums of 15 and 40, which are separated by 25 points. The Wilcoxon Rank-Sum Test is a formal test of the difference in the sums of the ranks, with the null hypothesis that two independent samples drawn from the same distribution will have equal rank-sums.

The same data set used earlier ("NonPar.sav") contains the school class size data. The variable *class_size* contains the class sizes, and the two dummy variables, *class_gp1* and *class_gp2*, contain "1"s and "2"s corresponding to the two schools in the first and second examples noted earlier. Click on **Analyze → Nonparametric Tests → 2 Independent Samples**.

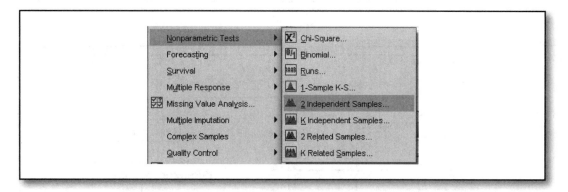

Just as in the two independent-samples *t*-test, place the test variable (*class_size*) in the box to the top right and the dummy variable, *class_gp1*, in the "Grouping Variable" window. Define the groups as having values "1" and "2" on the dummy variable.

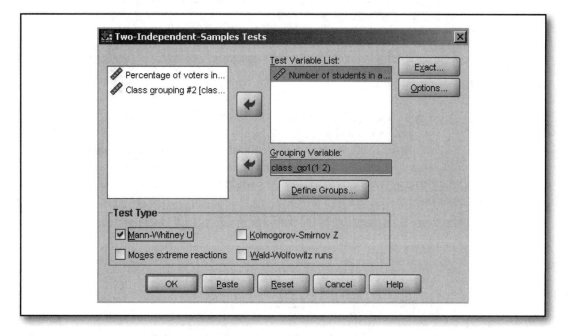

The Wilcoxon rank-sum value, *W*, will be calculated along with the Mann-Whitney *U*, which is selected by default. The two tests use different parameters but yield identical *p* values. Click "Options" and check "Descriptives" to see descriptive statistics on your test variable.

The syntax is "NPAR TESTS /M-W=class_size BY class_gp1(1 2) ." Adding descriptives adds the line "/STATISTICS=DESCRIPTIVE" to the syntax.

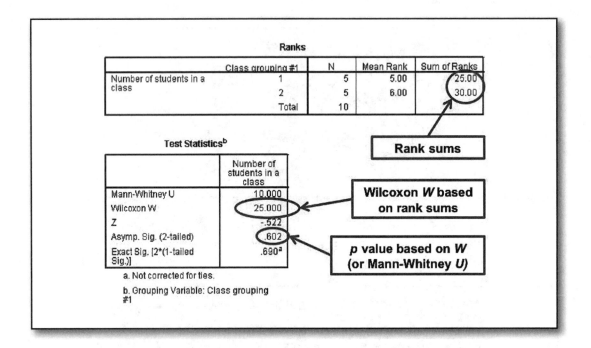

The output displays the sum (and the average) of the ranks, and two statistics computed based on them. The Mann-Whitney *U* is displayed first, then the Wilcoxon *W*. The *p* values for these test statistics are based on the smaller (lower-ranked) sample and can be looked up in a table or found in the SPSS output. Both the *U* and the *W* produce identical *p* values. In this case, we would conclude that the schools do not have different average class sizes.

For comparison, examine the other grouping variable, *class_gp2*.

```
NPAR TESTS

/M-W=class_size BY class_gp2(1 2)

/STATISTICS=DESCRIPTIVES .
```

Here, the class sizes in the second school are uniformly higher than in the first school, and the Wilcoxon Rank-Sum Test reveals a significant difference between the schools.

Ranks

	Class grouping #2	N	Mean Rank	Sum of Ranks
Number of students in a class	1	5	3.00	15.00
	2	5	8.00	40.00
	Total	10		

Test Statistics[b]

	Number of students in a class
Mann-Whitney U	.000
Wilcoxon W	15.000
Z	-2.611
Asymp. Sig. (2-tailed)	.009
Exact Sig. [2*(1-tailed Sig.)]	.008[a]

a. Not corrected for ties.

b. Grouping Variable: Class grouping #2

Class sizes
Class 1: 10, 15, 20, 25, 30
Class 2: 35, 40, 45, 50, 55

Ranks
Class 1: 1, 2, 3, 4, 5 (sum=15)
Class 2: 6, 7, 8, 9, 10 (sum=40)

Wilcoxon Signed-Rank Test (for Paired Samples)

In much the same way as a paired-samples *t*-test reduces to a one-sample *t*-test of the mean difference score, so, too, does the nonparametric equivalent of the paired-samples test, the Wilcoxon Signed-Rank Test, reduce to something similar to the one-sample Sign Test. The basic concept behind the test combines that of the two other nonparametric tests covered so far. In this test, you first rank the differences irrespective of sign, and then sum the ranks separately for positive and negative signs. The test statistic is a summed rank and is similar to the Wilcoxon *W*.

For example, suppose 10 individuals each completed a training program to improve their times to run a mile. The data are presented in the figure.

Measure	R1	R2	R3	R4	R5	R6	R7	R8	R9	R10
Before (m:s)	9:30	10:51	7:45	8:52	8:08	9:12	10:22	8:30	9:15	9:50
After (m:s)	8:51	10:41	7:52	7:51	7:22	9:12	9:52	8:41	8:46	10:01
Difference (s)	39	10	-7	61	46	0	30	-11	29	-11
Absolute difference	39	10	7	61	46	0	30	11	29	11
Rank	7	2	1	9	8	–	6	3.5	5	3.5
Signed-rank	7	2	-1	9	8	–	6	-3.5	5	-3.5

Sum of + ranks: 37
Sum of – ranks: 8

The differences are computed with improvements from before to after the program as positive numbers. Their absolute values are rank ordered (i.e., irrespective of sign). Subjects who did not change at all (i.e., difference = 0) are excluded, and ties are averaged (e.g., two subjects who tied for the third least change are each assigned "3.5"). After ranking, the signs are replaced and separate rank sums are computed for positive and negative values.

These data are in the variables *MileBefore* and *MileAfter* in the data file "NonPar.sav" on the webpage. In SPSS, click **Analyze → Nonparametric Tests → 2 Related Samples**.

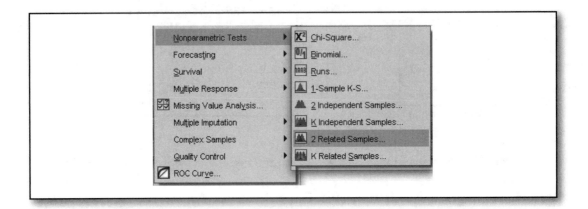

In the box, specify the pair of variables (*MileBefore* and *MileAfter*) as a "Test Pair" by clicking on the first variable, holding down the SHIFT key, then clicking the other.

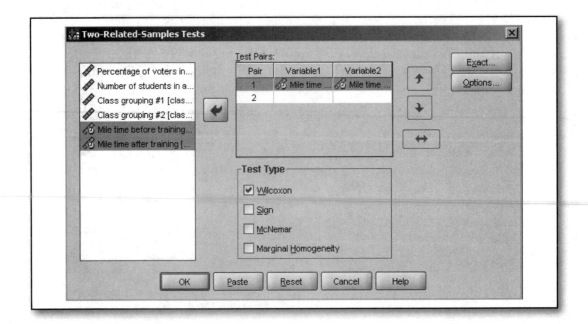

In the test type, specify "Wilcoxon" (by default) and request descriptives (if desired) in the "Options" menu.

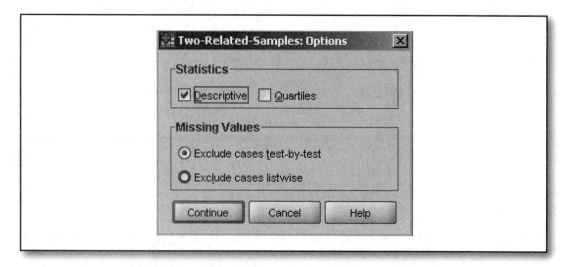

The syntax for this run of the Wilcoxon signed-rank test is

NPAR TESTS

/WILCOXON=MileBefore WITH MileAfter (PAIRED)

/STATISTICS DESCRIPTIVES .

The counts, means, and sums of the ranks for the positive and negative signs are displayed after the descriptives.

Ranks

		N	Mean Rank	Sum of Ranks
Mile time after training - Mile time before training	Negative Ranks	6[a]	6.17	37.00
	Positive Ranks	3[b]	2.67	8.00
	Ties	1[c]		
	Total	10		

a. Mile time after training < Mile time before training

b. Mile time after training > Mile time before training

c. Mile time after training = Mile time before training

As we had calculated, there were six participants who improved, three who became slower, and one who showed no change from before to after the training. The sum of the ranks are computed only for the positive (8) and negative (37) change scores. Finally, the last box displays the significance value for the signed-rank test of the differences.

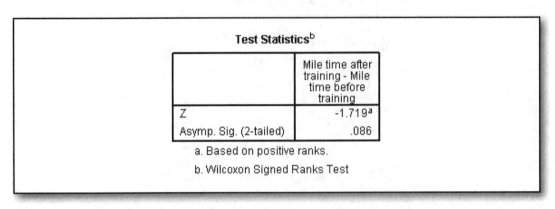

Test Statistics[b]

	Mile time after training - Mile time before training
Z	-1.719[a]
Asymp. Sig. (2-tailed)	.086

a. Based on positive ranks.

b. Wilcoxon Signed Ranks Test

The p value is associated with the *smaller* of the two rank sums (here, 8) and might be found in a table of critical values for the Wilcoxon Signed-Rank Test in your statistics textbook. Alternatively, SPSS also displays the p value in the table. The two-tailed test is not significant at traditional p value thresholds ($p = .09$), so we would conclude that the training program had no impact on mile times.

CONNECTIONS: A COMPARISON TO THE PAIRED-SAMPLES *T*-TEST

An astute reader may have noticed that the difference scores are approximately normally distributed. This is confirmed with a look at the P-P plot against a normal distribution.

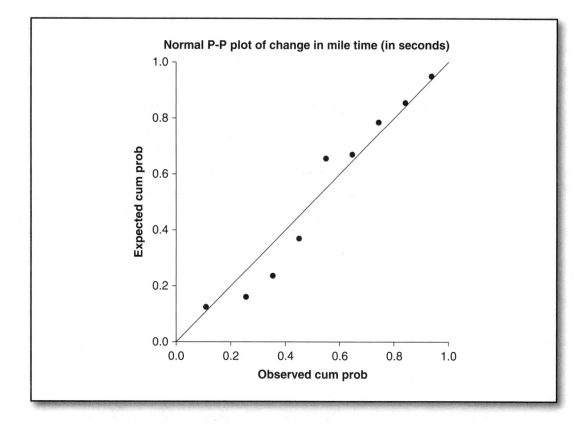

We noted earlier in this chapter that nonparametric tests are not as powerful as parametric tests when the data are normally distributed. As such, it is likely that the paired-samples *t*-test would provide a more powerful test of the hypothesis. To examine this possibility, run a paired-samples *t*-test (see Chapter 5 for more details) using the syntax

```
T-TEST PAIRS=MileBefore WITH MileAfter (PAIRED) .
```

The result of this test shows that there is a significant improvement in mile time—18.6 seconds—from before to after the training program.

Paired Samples Test

		Paired Differences							
					95% Confidence Interval of the Difference				
		Mean	Std. Deviation	Std. Error Mean	Lower	Upper	t	df	Sig. (2-tailed)
Pair 1	Mile time before training - Mile time after training	0:00:18.600	0:00:25.885	0:00:08.186	0:00:00.083	0:00:37.117	2.272	9	.049

Although the two *p* values are relatively close—.11 for the nonparametric test and .05 for the parametric test—this example illustrates a case where using a parametric test yields increased power because the assumption of normality is met.

The Kruskal-Wallis Test (for Between-Subjects Comparisons)

Just as the one-way ANOVA can be thought of as an extension of the independent-samples *t*-test, so, too, can the Kruskal-Wallis Test be thought of as an extension of the Wilcoxon Rank-Sum Test. The central idea is to rank order all observations, regardless of group membership, sum the ranks of the groups, and then make a comparison based on those sums. The summation formula that follows is slightly more complicated than that used in the rank-sum test, but the concept is the same. The resulting statistic is *H*, and it can be thought of as the "mean-square by ranks." Just like the mean-square terms that we learned about in earlier chapters, *H* is in squared units, and is approximated *chi-squared* distributed with $k - 1$ degrees of freedom (where k is the number of groups).

In case your statistics textbook does not contain it, the computational formula for the Kruskal-Wallis *H* is

$$H = \frac{12}{N(N + 1)} \sum \frac{R_i^2}{n_i} - 3(N + 1)$$

where N is the total number of observations, R_i is the sum of the ranks for group i, and n_i is the number of observations in group i.

For example, consider the data on three groups of taste-testers each rating a different kind of root beer on a 10-point scale. There are 21 subjects across three unequal groups. This data set is an ideal candidate to be analyzed using nonparametric methods because the *N*s per group are small, the group sizes are uneven and the data are not normally distributed.

	Raw measures			Ranked measures		
A	**B**	**C**	**A**	**B**	**C**
6.4	2.5	1.3	11	2	1
6.8	3.7	4.1	12	3	4
7.2	4.9	4.9	13	5.5	5.5
8.3	5.4	5.2	17	8	7
8.4	5.9	5.5	18	10	9
9.1	8.1	8.2	19	14	15.5
9.4	8.2		20	15.5	
9.7			21		
	Sum of ranks		**131**	**58**	**42**
	Number of ranks		**8**	**7**	**6**

The test statistic H can be computed as follows:

$$H = \frac{12}{N(N+1)} \sum \frac{R_i^2}{n_i} - 3(N+1) = \frac{12}{21(22)} \left(\frac{131^2}{8} + \frac{58^2}{7} + \frac{42^2}{6} \right) - 3(22) = 9.84$$

The significance value of $H = 9.84$ for 2 degrees of freedom can be looked up in a chi-squared table or computed in SPSS. The data shown in the table are in the data file "NonPar.sav" in the variables called *RootRate* (with all 21 ratings) and *RootGroup* (a dummy variable with values 1, 2, and 3, corresponding to groups A, B, and C, respectively). In SPSS, click on **Analyze → Nonparametric Tests → K Independent Samples**.

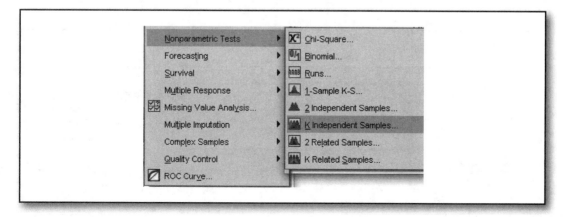

Then specify *RootRate* as the test variable and *RootGroup* as the grouping variable.

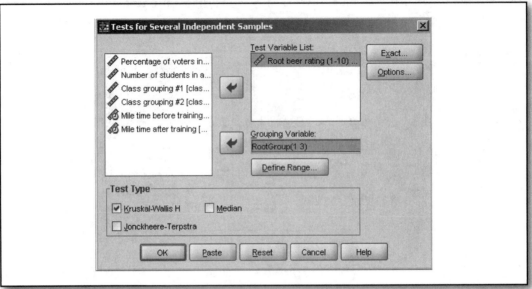

Unlike in the GLM menu, SPSS will not automatically figure out how many groups there are based on the dummy variable; you must specify the minimum and maximum index by clicking "Define Range." In this case, the groups are coded as "1," "2," and "3," so specify "1" and "3." Click "Options" and check the "Descriptives" box, or add "/ STATISTICS=DESCRIPTIVE" to the syntax, to see descriptive statistics for each of the groups.

The syntax for the Kruskal-Wallis Test for independent groups is

```
NPAR TESTS /K-W=RootRate BY RootGroup(1 3) .
```

The output first summarizes the mean rank for each group. The rank sum can be recovered by multiplying the mean rank by the *N* for each group.

Ranks

	Group (A, B, or C)	N	Mean Rank	Rank-sums
Root beer rating (1-10)	A	8	16.38	A: 8 * 16.38 = 131
	B	7	8.29	B: 7 * 8.29 = 58
	C	6	7.00	C: 6 * 7.00 = 42
	Total	21		

The numbers are exactly what we calculated by hand in the table. After that, SPSS displays the associated chi-squared test.

Test Statistics[a,b]

	Root beer rating (1-10)
Chi-Square	9.849
df	2
Asymp. Sig.	.007

a. Kruskal Wallis Test

b. Grouping Variable: Group (A, B, or C)

Based on this significant test, we can conclude that there are significant differences in the ratings of the root beers. The appropriate next step following a significant Kruskal-Wallis Test is to follow up with pairwise tests between the group medians using the Wilcoxon Rank-Sum Test. This is analogous to using pairwise *t*-tests to probe a significant one-way ANOVA.

Friedman's Rank Test (for Within-Subject Comparisons)

The last kind of nonparametric test we will discuss is Friedman's Rank Test for within-subject comparisons. This test is analogous to the repeated-measures ANOVA for within-subjects variables. It assumes multiple and related observations from each participant, and capitalizes on the correlations between them. The general idea behind the test is that the multiple conditions are rank ordered *within* each subject, and then the ranks are summed across the participants. Just like the within-subjects ANOVA, this procedure controls for between-subject variability because the comparisons are made on a within-person basis.

The computational formula of the test is similar to the Kruskal-Wallis, and is also chi-squared distributed. The test statistic is Friedman's Chi-Squared and is computed as

$$\chi_f^2 = \frac{12}{Nk(k+1)} \sum R_i^2 - 3N(k+1)$$

where N is the total sample size, k is the number of within-subjects conditions, and R_i is the sum of the ranks for condition i.

For example, suppose the following five coffee shops each attempted to brew coffee using four different brewing methods: drip coffee, espresso, French press, and percolator. The dependent measure is the amount of caffeine in milligrams per tablespoon of coffee. Because each coffee shop used its own blend of beans, the average amount of caffeine across the shops varies. What we're interested to know is whether there is an effect of the *method* of brewing, controlling for these differences across shops.

Coffee shop	Method: Caffeine (mg/tbsp)			
	Drip	Espresso	French Press	Percolator
Perugino	94	88	89	97
Café Vero	79	77	84	92
Village Coffee Roaster	85	87	81	87
Profeta	84	92	87	89
Quick Fix	88	81	79	80

These caffeine values can then be rank ordered within each coffee shop, and the ranks are summed. Ties are averaged across two positions (e.g., two values sharing second place each receive a "2.5").

Coffee shop	Ranks: Caffeine within-shop			
	Drip	Espresso	French Press	Percolator
Perugino	3	1	2	4
Café Vero	2	1	3	4
Village Coffee Roaster	2	3.5	1	3.5
Profeta	1	4	2	3
Quick Fix	4	3	1	2
Rank-sum	**12**	**12.5**	**9**	**16.5**

Following the formula for Friedman's Chi-Squared, we get

$$\chi_F^2 = \frac{12}{Nk(k+1)}\sum R_i^2 - 3N(k+1) = \frac{12}{20(5)}(12^2 + 12.5^2 + 9^2 + 16.5^2) - 15(5) = 3.42.$$

This value is chi-squared distributed with $k - 1 = 3$ degrees of freedom.

In SPSS, this quantity can be computed by clicking **Analyze → Nonparametric Tests → K Related Samples**.

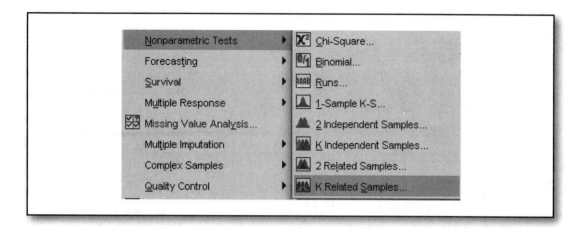

Move the four brewing types to the "Test Variables" list (*Caff_Drip, Caff_Espr, Caff_FrPr*, and *Caff_Perc*), and be sure that "Friedman" is checked in the "Test Type" box.

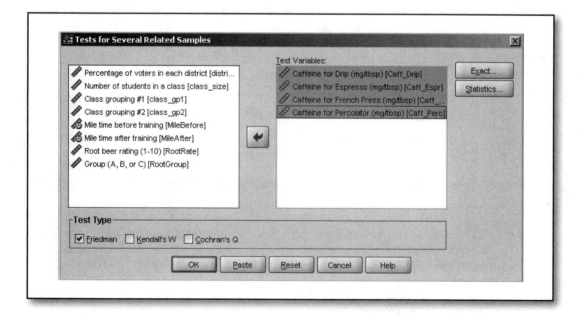

Display descriptives by checking the "Descriptives" box in the "Options" menu, or add "/STATISTICS=DESCRIPTIVES" to the syntax.

The full syntax for this function is

```
NPAR TESTS
/FRIEDMAN=Caff_Drip Caff_Espr Caff_FrPr Caff_Perc
/STATISTICS DESCRIPTIVES .
```

The results display the descriptives for each cell (which can be useful for interpreting significant test results) and the mean ranks. The rank sums can be recovered by multiplying the mean ranks by the cell size.

Ranks

	Mean Rank
Caffeine for Drip (mg/tbsp)	2.40
Caffeine for Espresso (mg/tbsp)	2.50
Caffeine for French Press (mg/tbsp)	1.80
Caffeine for Percolator (mg/tbsp)	3.30

Rank-sums

Drip:	5 * 2.4 = 12
Espresso:	5 * 2.5 = 12.5
French Press:	5 * 1.8 = 9
Percolator:	5 * 3.3 = 16.5

Finally, the chi-squared test is reported with 3 degrees of freedom. The value is identical to the one we computed by hand earlier.

Test Statistics[a]

N	5
Chi-Square	3.490
df	3
Asymp. Sig.	.322

a. Friedman Test

In this case, we found no evidence for differences in caffeine between the brewing methods. However, had we found evidence of differences among the brewing methods, the next step would be to proceed with Wilcoxon Signed-Rank Tests to compare pairs of brewing methods to each other.

KEYWORDS

test parameter	Mann-Whitney U	Friedman's Rank Test
sign test	Wilcoxon Signed-Rank Test	
Wilcoxon Rank-Sum Test	Kruskal-Wallis Test	

16

Matrix Algebra ❖

Conceptual Background of Matrix Algebra

The general linear model is the conceptual and statistical backbone of nearly all of the tests covered in the book. Everything from *t*-tests, ANOVA, correlation, regression, and even factor analysis can be described in terms of the GLM. In its most general form, the GLM equation is

$$\mathbf{Y} = \mathbf{X}\boldsymbol{\beta} + \boldsymbol{\varepsilon},$$

where $\mathbf{Y}$ is a vector of data with the dependent measure, $\mathbf{X}$ is the "design matrix" that specifies the type of test to be run (e.g., ANOVA vs. regression) by its form, $\boldsymbol{\beta}$ is the parameter vector that contains parameters of the model (e.g., group means or regression slopes), and $\boldsymbol{\varepsilon}$ is the vector of residual errors. (In matrix algebra, variables that represent vectors or matrices are typically denoted in **bold** to indicate that they are more than just scalars).

Any of the models using the GLM can be written in a similar form but with slight modification to the design matrix and (consequently) to the parameter vector as appropriate. For example, a one-way ANOVA GLM for 6 subjects in 2 groups is written as

$$
\begin{bmatrix} DV_{11} \\ DV_{21} \\ DV_{31} \\ DV_{12} \\ DV_{22} \\ DV_{32} \end{bmatrix} = \begin{bmatrix} 1 & 0 \\ 1 & 0 \\ 1 & 0 \\ 0 & 1 \\ 0 & 1 \\ 0 & 1 \end{bmatrix} \begin{bmatrix} mean_1 \\ mean_2 \end{bmatrix} + \begin{bmatrix} e_{11} \\ e_{21} \\ e_{31} \\ e_{12} \\ e_{22} \\ e_{32} \end{bmatrix},
$$

where DV_{ij} is the value of the dependent measure for subject i in group j, the $mean_j$ is the mean of group j, and e_{ij} is the error for subject i in group j. Similarly, a regression model for six subjects is written as

$$
\begin{bmatrix} DV_1 \\ DV_2 \\ DV_3 \\ DV_4 \\ DV_5 \\ DV_6 \end{bmatrix} = \begin{bmatrix} 1 & IV_1 \\ 1 & IV_2 \\ 1 & IV_3 \\ 1 & IV_4 \\ 1 & IV_5 \\ 1 & IV_6 \end{bmatrix} \begin{bmatrix} \beta_0 \\ \beta_1 \end{bmatrix} + \begin{bmatrix} e_1 \\ e_2 \\ e_3 \\ e_4 \\ e_5 \\ e_6 \end{bmatrix},
$$

where DV_i is the value of the dependent measure for subject i, IV_i is the independent measure for subject i, β_0 and β_1 are the intercept and slope of the regression line, and e_i is the error for subject i. These examples illustrate how seemingly different statistical tests are each special cases of the same general model.

One great advantage of all of these tests sharing a conceptual model is that learning to compute any one of them teaches you to compute all of them. Mathematically speaking, the specific contents of the design matrix and the parameter vector are irrelevant to solving the general linear equation. Regardless of the contents of **Y**, **X**, and **β**, we solve for **β** first by ignoring ε (for now), and rewriting the equation as

$$\mathbf{Y} = \mathbf{X}\boldsymbol{\beta}.$$

Next, we divide both sides by **X**, which is accomplished in matrix algebra by multiplying both sides by the inverse of **X**. (Just like dividing by 2 is the same as multiplying by ½).

$$(\mathbf{X}^{-1})\mathbf{Y} = (\mathbf{X}^{-1})\mathbf{X}\boldsymbol{\beta} = \boldsymbol{\beta}.$$

In order to solve for **β** in this way, you need to be able to calculate the inverse of **X** (written as $\mathbf{X}^{-1}$). But for reasons beyond the present scope, not all design matrices are invertible. In these cases, the general linear equation can still be solved using the *pseudo-inverse* of **X**, written as $(\mathbf{X'X})^{-1}\mathbf{X'}$, where $\mathbf{X'}$ is the transpose of **X**, yielding the solution as

$$(\mathbf{X'X})^{-1}\mathbf{X'Y} = (\mathbf{X'X})^{-1}(\mathbf{X'X})\boldsymbol{\beta} = \boldsymbol{\beta}.$$

In cases when **X** is invertible, the solution is the same regardless of whether the inverse or the pseudo-inverse is used. For this reason, using the pseudo-inverse to solve for $\boldsymbol{\beta}$ is more robust to variation in the form of the design matrix than using the inverse. Consequently, many software packages (including SPSS) will always left-multiply **Y** by the pseudo-inverse to solve the general linear equation.

In this chapter, we use the matrix algebra capabilities of SPSS to solve the general linear model. This will illustrate what happens "behind the scenes" in SPSS when you run any of the tests based on the GLM and will show you how to compute several common terms (e.g., sum-of-squares) using matrix algebra.

Overview of Matrix Algebra in SPSS

SPSS allows users to directly manipulate matrices and vectors using syntax. Any matrix algebra commands must be bookended by the terms "MATRIX" and "END MATRIX."

```
MATRIX .

[list of commands]

END MATRIX .
```

Between these two lines, you can import or define data, manipulate variables using matrix algebra, print results to the output window, or save variables to the data file using a variety of commands.

The data to be manipulated can be either defined in syntax or imported from a data file (i.e., an SPSS .sav file). To define a matrix or vector, use the "COMPUTE" command, name the variable; then put data in curly brackets ("{" and "}") with columns separated by commas and rows separated by semicolons. For example, to enter the design matrix for the one-way ANOVA with six subjects in two groups noted earlier, type

```
COMPUTE des_mat = {1, 0; 1, 0; 1, 0; 0, 1; 0, 1; 0, 1} .
```

Then print the design matrix to the output window using the "PRINT" command:

```
PRINT des_mat .
```

The design matrix in rectangular form should be displayed in the output window.

```
                    Run MATRIX procedure:

                    DES_MAT
                       1   0
                       1   0
                       1   0
                       0   1
                       0   1
                       0   1


                    ------ END MATRIX -----
```

Data can also be imported from an SPSS file using the command "GET data .". This stores all of the cases from all of the variables in one large matrix called *data*. From there, the *data* matrix can be split into different variables using the "COMPUTE" command. For example, to store the first two columns of the data matrix as variables called *column1* and *column2*, run the following syntax:

```
GET data.

COMPUTE column1 = data(:,1) .

COMPUTE column2 = data(:,2) .
```

When indexing a matrix or vector, use (row, column) format. For example, *data(:, 2)* is all rows of column #2 in *data*, and *data(4,2)* is the value in the fourth row of the second column of *data*.

Once the data are made available to the matrix editor by using "COMPUTE" to name them, they can be manipulated using standard mathematical operators (e.g., +, *) and a handful of specific matrix operations such as "GINV(X)" for the pseudo-inverse (or "generalized inverse") of X, "MSUM(X)" for the sum of all the values in the vector X, and "FCDF(v, df1, df2)" to look up the cumulative probability of obtaining an *F* value of *v* or lower in a distribution with *df1* and *df2* degrees of freedom.

For example, we can multiply the variable *des_mat* by two and view it:

```
COMPUTE des_mat2 = 2*des_mat .

PRINT des_mat2 .
```

or even compute and view the pseudo-inverse:

```
COMPUTE inv_mat = ginv(des_mat) .

PRINT inv_mat .
```

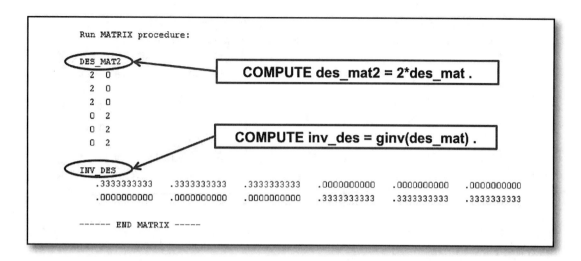

A complete guide to many of the useful matrix algebra functions provided by SPSS can be found by clicking on **Help → Command Syntax Reference**, then viewing the section on "MATRIX-END MATRIX" in the index.

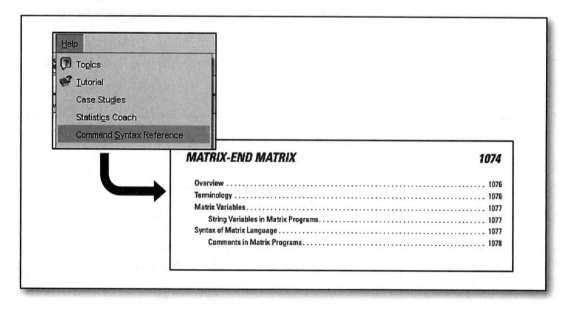

MAKING THE MOST OF SYNTAX:
SOLVING THE GENERAL LINEAR EQUATION IN SPSS

We will practice using matrix algebra via syntax on the data set used in Chapter 6, "Wedding.sav." To refresh your memory, this was a data set about how many songs a wedding guest will dance to (*dances*) as a function of the guest's relationship to the couple (*relation;* 1=Friend, 2=Family, 3=Family friend, 4=Co-worker). We will compute a one-way ANOVA where *dances* is the dependent variable and *relation* is the independent variable with four levels. The general linear model for this test is

$$
\begin{bmatrix} Dance_{11} \\ \cdots \\ Dance_{n1} \\ Dance_{12} \\ \cdots \\ Dance_{n2} \\ Dance_{13} \\ \cdots \\ Dance_{n4} \end{bmatrix}
=
\begin{bmatrix} 1 & 0 & 0 & 0 \\ \cdots & \cdots & & \\ 1 & 0 & 0 & 0 \\ 0 & 1 & 0 & 0 \\ \cdots & \cdots & & \\ 0 & 1 & 0 & 0 \\ 0 & 0 & 1 & 0 \\ \cdots & \cdots & & \\ 0 & 0 & 0 & 1 \end{bmatrix}
\begin{bmatrix} Friend_m \\ Family_m \\ Fam.friend_m \\ Coworker_m \end{bmatrix}
+
\begin{bmatrix} e_{11} \\ \cdots \\ e_{n1} \\ e_{12} \\ \cdots \\ e_{n2} \\ e_{13} \\ \cdots \\ e_{n4} \end{bmatrix},
$$

where $Dance_{ij}$ is the number of dances that subject i in group j is expected to have; $Friend_m$, $Family_m$, and so on are the means of those groups; and e_{ij} is the residual error for subject i in group j.

First, we want to extract the data from the spreadsheet to make it available to the matrix algebra processor. We'll do this in three steps: first, by extracting all the data into a matrix called *data* ("GET"); then defining the variables *dances* and *relation* as the first and second columns in the data matrix, respectively ("COMPUTE"); and finally by checking that they were extracted and made available to the matrix editor as desired ("PRINT").

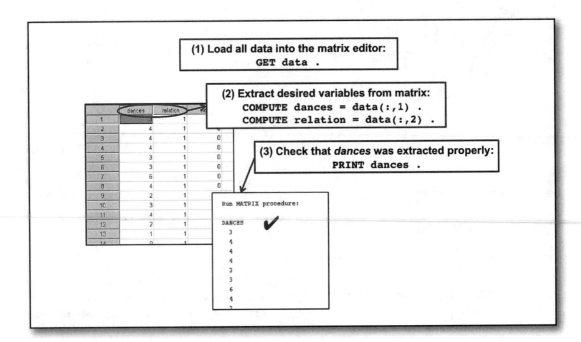

So far we have the following syntax:

```
MATRIX .
GET data .
COMPUTE dances = data(:,1) .
COMPUTE relation = data(:,2) .
PRINT dances .
END MATRIX .
```

Next, we want to define a new variable that will contain the design matrix. We could type it into the syntax by hand, but that would take a while because it has four columns (corresponding to the four groups) and 200 rows (corresponding to the 200 guests). Fortunately, the group membership is coded in the variable *relation*, and SPSS has a function called "DESIGN" that automatically creates a design matrix from a categorical coding variable. Use that function; then check that the matrix has been created properly using

```
COMPUTE X = DESIGN(relation) .
PRINT X .
```

The output should be a 200 × 4 design matrix with ones indicating group membership and zeros indicating otherwise.

```
X
       1  0  0  0
       1  0  0  0
       1  0  0  0
       1  0  0  0
       1  0  0  0
       1  0  0  0
       1  0  0  0
       1  0  0  0

          ...

       0  0  0  1
       0  0  0  1
       0  0  0  1
       0  0  0  1
       0  0  0  1

    ------ END MATRIX -----
```

Next, we can calculate the degrees of freedom based on the size of the design matrix. Recall that the two degrees of freedom for an *F*-test correspond to $k - 1$ and $N - k$, where k is the number of groups and N is the total sample size. A nice feature of the general linear model is that the design matrix always contains N rows and k columns. So we can use the built-in functions "NROWS" and "NCOLS" to define variables with the degrees of freedom:

```
COMPUTE df_bet = NCOL(X)-1 .

COMPUTE df_err = NROW(X)-NCOL(X) .

PRINT df_bet .

PRINT df_err .
```

This produces the correct degrees of freedom for this model, 3 and 196.

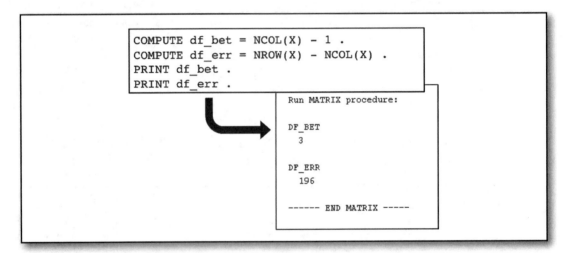

Next, we want to solve the GLM equation by rearranging

$$\mathbf{Y} = \mathbf{X}\boldsymbol{\beta} \Rightarrow \mathbf{X}^{-1}\mathbf{Y} = \mathbf{X}^{-1}\mathbf{X}\boldsymbol{\beta}.$$

In SPSS, first we will compute $\mathbf{X}^{-1}$ as the pseudo-inverse of $\mathbf{X}$, the design matrix, then left-multiply it by $\mathbf{Y}$, the DV:

```
COMPUTE invX = GINV(X) .

COMPUTE beta = invX * dances .

PRINT beta .
```

The output of this can be compared to the descriptive statistics derived from running the one-way ANOVA using the GLM syntax that we learned in Chapter 6:

```
GLM dances BY relation

/PRINT=DESCRIPTIVE

/DESIGN = relation .
```

Group means found using matrix algebra	Group means found using the GLM function from Chapter 6		

Run MATRIX procedure:
 	
BETA
  3.400000000
  4.380000000
  2.140000000
  4.560000000
 	
------ END MATRIX -----
	Descriptive Statistics		

	Dependent Variable:How many dances anticipated?		
	Type of relationship with the bride/groom	Mean	
	Friend	3.40	
	Family	4.38	
	Family friend	2.14	
	Co-worker	4.56	
	Total	3.62	

Now that we have successfully recovered the group means (which are the values in β), we have all parts of the general linear equation except for the residuals, ε. These can be found easily by rearranging

$$\mathbf{Y} = \mathbf{X}\boldsymbol{\beta} + \boldsymbol{\varepsilon} \Rightarrow \boldsymbol{\varepsilon} = \mathbf{Y} - \mathbf{X}\boldsymbol{\beta}.$$

In syntax, the errors are computed using

```
COMPUTE e = dances-X*beta .
```

Then, the sum-of-squares errors can be found using a nifty built-in function called "MSSQ," or matrix sum-of-squares. This function squares each member of a matrix (or a vector as in this case), then sums them all.

```
COMPUTE ss_with = MSSQ(e) .

PRINT ss_with .
```

Alternatively, a standard matrix algebra way of computing the sum-of-squares of a vector is to matrix-multiply the vector by its transpose (the "T" function in syntax), as in "COMPUTE SS_WITH = T(e) * e."

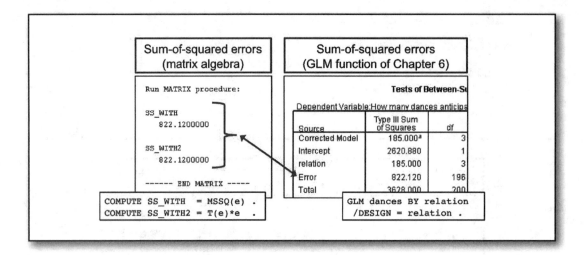

In either case, you can see that the sum-of-squares error is the same as the figure derived by the GLM command run on these same data from Chapter 6.

At this point, we have computed the sum-of-squares error and both degrees of freedom (error and between groups). We need only the sum-of-squares between groups to be able to calculate the two mean-square terms and then the *F.* So what is the sum-of-squares between groups? It is the total variation of the groups from the grand mean, calculated as the sum of the squared deviations of each individual's group mean from the grand mean. And because we already know the group means (calculated in β), we just need to find the grand mean to calculate the last sum-of-squares. Of course, the grand mean is just the average of the four group means.

```
COMPUTE GM = MSUM(beta) / NCOL(X) .

COMPUTE ss_bet = MSSQ( (X*beta)-GM ) .

PRINT ss_bet .
```

Running this syntax produces the sum-of-squares between groups, 185, which is the same as the figure calculated by the GLM function in Chapter 6.

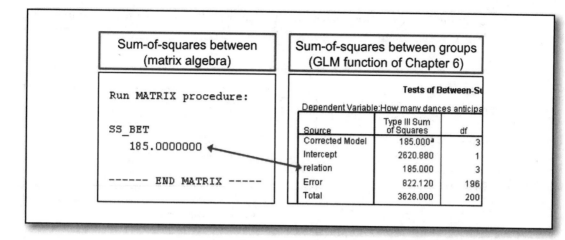

From here, we can compute the mean-square terms based on the sum-of-squares and degrees of freedom, and the *F* as the ratio of the two mean-squares:

```
COMPUTE ms_bet = ss_bet / df_bet .

COMPUTE ms_with = ss_with / df_err .

COMPUTE Fval = ms_bet / ms_with .
```

Next, compute the *p* value by using the "FCDF" function (which looks up the cumulative probability of finding an *F* less than or equal to *Fval* with *df_bet* and *df_err* degrees of freedom), then reversing that to find the probability of finding a value *greater* than *Fval*.

```
COMPUTE Pval = 1-FCDF(Fval, df_bet, df_err) .
```

Finally, use the "TITLE" tag as part of the "PRINT" command to label the various pieces of output:

```
PRINT ss_bet / title "Sum-of-squares between groups" .

PRINT ss_with / title "Sum-of-squares error" .

PRINT ms_bet / title "Mean squared between groups" .

PRINT ms_with / title "Mean squared error" .

PRINT Fval / title "Value of the F ratio" .

PRINT Pval / title "p-value" .
```

In the end, the output is identical to that from the GLM syntax function or the point-and-click menus.

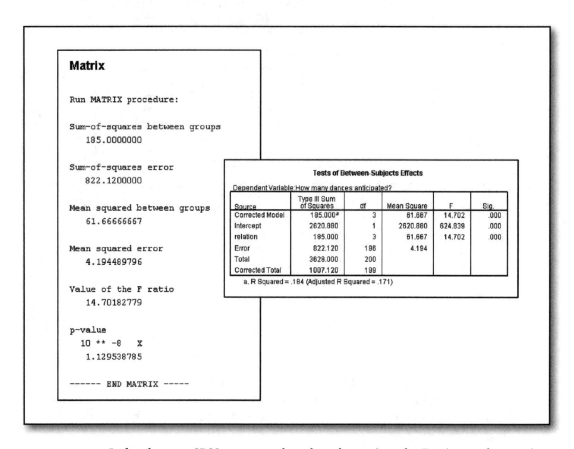

```
Matrix

Run MATRIX procedure:

Sum-of-squares between groups
  185.0000000

Sum-of-squares error
  822.1200000

Mean squared between groups
  61.66666667

Mean squared error
  4.194489796

Value of the F ratio
  14.70182779

p-value
  10 ** -8   X
  1.129538785

------ END MATRIX -----
```

Tests of Between-Subjects Effects

Dependent Variable:How many dances anticipated?

Source	Type III Sum of Squares	df	Mean Square	F	Sig.
Corrected Model	185.000[a]	3	61.667	14.702	.000
Intercept	2620.880	1	2620.880	624.839	.000
relation	185.000	3	61.667	14.702	.000
Error	822.120	196	4.194		
Total	3628.000	200			
Corrected Total	1007.120	199			

a. R Squared = .184 (Adjusted R Squared = .171)

In fact, because SPSS computes the values that go into the *F* ratio exactly as we just did, the output from your matrix algebra calculates should always be exactly the same as the output from the GLM functions. If it's not, check your work because you probably made a mistake in your matrix algebra!

A CLOSER LOOK: CUSTOM HYPOTHESIS TESTING USING MATRIX ALGEBRA

The Wald test is a general formula for testing hypotheses in ANOVA. In this model, hypotheses are expressed as a vector of coefficients, **h**, which is multiplied by the group means in the vector **β**, and compared to the test value *a*. Any hypothesis that can be expressed as a linear combination of the group means can be written as **h** and therefore can be tested using the Wald test.

The derivation of the Wald test is too complicated to describe in detail here, so we refer you to your statistics textbook for more details. For now, all you need to know is that the computational formula for the Wald is

$$F = \frac{(\mathbf{h}\boldsymbol{\beta} - a)'(\mathbf{h}(x'x)^{-1}\mathbf{h}')^{-1}(\mathbf{h}\boldsymbol{\beta} - a)/q}{\sigma_e^2},$$

where $\mathbf{h}$ is the hypothesis vector, $\boldsymbol{\beta}$ is the model parameter vector, a is the test value, x is the design matrix, q is the number of rows in the hypothesis ($\mathbf{h}$), and the denominator is the mean-square error. The Wald value is F-distributed with degrees of freedom q and $N - k$, corresponding to the number of rows in $\mathbf{h}$ and the degrees-of-freedom error, respectively.

For example, suppose we wanted to replicate the hypothesis tested in Chapter 6 regarding the difference between friends, on one hand, and co-workers and family together, on the other. Because of the order that the groups are coded, this hypothesis can be written as

$$\mathbf{h} = [-1\ 0.5\ 0\ 0.5]$$

with the test value a set to zero (because we're testing the null hypothesis that the mean number of dances for *friends* is equal to the average of *co-workers* and *family*, with nothing left over).

This can be computed in syntax continuing from above (and using some of the output), we can compute $\mathbf{h}\boldsymbol{\beta} - a$ with

```
COMPUTE h = {-1, 0.5, 0, 0.5} .

COMPUTE a = 0 .

COMPUTE hba = (h*beta)-a .
```

The middle part of the numerator, the inverse of $\mathbf{h}$ times $(\mathbf{X}'\mathbf{X})^{-1}$ times $\mathbf{h}'$, is computed as

```
COMPUTE h_xpxi_h = h * GINV(T(X)*X) * T(h) .
```

The entire numerator is the mean-square contrast. The quantity $(\mathbf{h}\boldsymbol{\beta} - a)'*(\mathbf{h}(\mathbf{X}'\mathbf{X})^{-1}\mathbf{h}')^{-1}*(\mathbf{h}\boldsymbol{\beta} - a)$ is the sum-of-squares for the contrast, and q is the degrees of freedom for the contrast.

```
COMPUTE q = NROW(h) .

COMPUTE ms_contr = (T(hba) * GINV(h_xpxi_h) * hba) / q .
```

And finally the value of the Wald and the *p* value are

```
COMPUTE wald = ms_contr / ms_with .

COMPUTE PvalWald = 1-FCDF(wald, q, df_err) .

PRINT wald .

PRINT PvalWald .
```

The output from this can be compared to the output from the custom hypothesis test that we computed in Chapter 6:

```
GLM dances BY relation

/LMATRIX = relation -1 .5 0 .5

/DESIGN = relation .
```

As you can see, the Wald value is exactly the *F* value that was calculated by the custom hypothesis test.

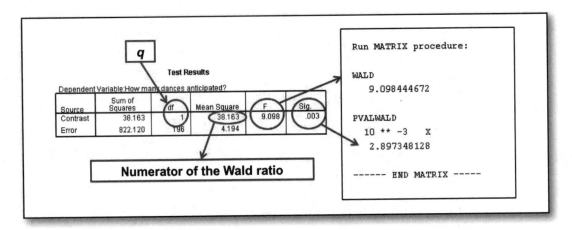

It is also possible to verify that the "Contrast Estimate" is the same as **hβ**, the "Hypothesized Value" is the same as *a*, the "Difference" is the same as **hβ** − *a*, and that the mean-square for the contrast is the same as the value calculated above.

Once this syntax is operational, it can be modified easily to test any linear hypothesis **h** among the group means; simply replace the values here with your desired contrast. For example, the three-row contrast

```
COMPUTE h = {1, 0, 0, -1; 0, 1, 0, -1; 0, 0, 1 -1} .
```

is known as the "omnibus" hypothesis and is equivalent to the main effect of *relation*.

Appendix: Commented Syntax for One-Way ANOVA Using Matrix Algebra in SPSS

The symbols "/*" together indicate the beginning of a comment in syntax. In the figure, we present the complete matrix algebra formulation of the GLM presented earlier with comments detailing the purpose of each line. Together with the data file "Wedding .sav," this syntax verbatim will run without error when pasted into the syntax window on your computer.

```
MATRIX .    /* All matrix algebra calculations must begin with
"MATRIX"

GET data .

  /* Import of the data in the active spreadsheet to variable data

COMPUTE dances = data(:,1) .    /* First column: dances

COMPUTE relation = data(:,2) . /* Second column: relation

COMPUTE X = DESIGN(relation) .

  /* Create a design matrix based on the grouping variable relation

COMPUTE df_bet = NCOL(X) - 1 .

  /* Between-groups degrees of freedom = # columns in matrix - 1
COMPUTE df_err = NROW(X) - NCOL(X) .

  /* Degrees of freedom error = # of subjects - # of groups

COMPUTE invX = GINV(X) .        /* Pseudo-inverse of X (X⁻¹)

COMPUTE beta = invX * dances . /* Solve for beta = X⁻¹Y

COMPUTE e  = dances - X*beta . /* Solve for e = Y - X*beta

COMPUTE SS_WITH = MSSQ(e) .     /* SS-within: matrix sum-of-squares

COMPUTE SS_WITH2 = T(e)*e .     /* SS-within: e'e (e-transpose-e)

COMPUTE GM = msum(beta) / ncol(X) .

  /* Grand mean is sum of group means divided by number of groups
COMPUTE SS_BET = MSSQ(  (X*beta) - GM ) .

  /* Sum-of-squares between is sum of squared deviations from GM
```

(Continued)

(Continued)

```
COMPUTE ms_bet = ss_bet / df_bet .     /* MS-bet = SS-bet / df-bet

COMPUTE ms_with = ss_with / df_err . /* MS-err = SS-err / df-err

COMPUTE Fval = ms_bet / ms_with .     /* F-ratio = MS-bet / MS-err

COMPUTE Pval = 1-FCDF(Fval, df_bet, df_err) .

   /* Use the F cumulative distribution function to find P(F≤Fval)

/* Print the calculated figures to the output window with titles

PRINT ss_bet / title "Sum-of-squares between groups" .

PRINT ss_with / title "Sum-of-squares error" .

PRINT ms_bet / title "Mean squared between groups" .

PRINT ms_with / title "Mean squared error" .

PRINT Fval / title "Value of the F ratio".

PRINT Pval / title "p-value" .

COMPUTE h = {-1, 0.5, 0, 0.5} .        /* Hypothesis: [-1  0.5  0  0.5]

COMPUTE a = 0 .                        /* Test value: 0

COMPUTE hba = (h*beta) - a .           /* Weighted means vs. test value

COMPUTE h_xpxi_h =  h * GINV(T(X)*X) * T(h) .

   /* The middle part of the numerator is h(X'X)⁻¹h'

COMPUTE q = NROW(h) .

   /* Degrees of freedom contrast is the number of rows in h

COMPUTE ms_contr = (T(hba) * GINV(h_xpxi_h) * hba) / q .

   /* The full numerator: (hβ-a)'*(h(X'X)⁻¹h')⁻¹*(hβ-a) / q

COMPUTE wald = ms_contr / ms_with .   /* Wald = MS-contrast / MS-err

COMPUTE PvalWald = 1-FCDF(wald, q, df_err) .

   /* Use the F cumulative distribution function to find P(F ≤ Fval)

PRINT wald / title "Wald value" .           /* Print the Wald value

PRINT PvalWald / title "p-value" .          /* Print the p-value

PRINT ms_contr / title "MS-contrast" .

   /* Print the numerator of the Wald (AKA the MS-contrast)

END MATRIX .      /* All matrix operations end with END MATRIX
```

KEYWORDS

general linear equation

data vector

design matrix

parameter vector

residual error vector

matrix inverse

pseudo-inverse

left-multiply

Wald test

hypothesis vector

Appendix

General Formulation of Contrasts Using LMATRIX

I n Chapter 7, we walked through a single example of how to use the LMATRIX function to compute a few custom contrasts in syntax. But the "LMATRIX" function in SPSS is a powerful tool that can compute nearly any contrast among any combination of group means. In the most general terms, the steps for figuring out the right syntax are as follows:

1. Write down the contrast coefficients for each cell in a table like the one shown in the figure. The first factor should be along the rows, and the second factor should be along the columns.

Two-factor case

Factor 2

		L1	L2	L3	L4	
Factor	L1	a	b	c	d	$a+b+c+d$
1	L2	e	f	g	h	$e+f+g+h$
		$a+e$	$b+f$	$c+g$	$d+h$	$a+b+c+d+e+f+g+h$

If you have a three-way ANOVA, make separate tables for each level of the first factor, with the second factor levels in the rows and the third factor levels in the columns. (For example, suppose we wanted to look at the *gender* of the guests in addition to their side and relationship to the couple. Then there would be two 2 × 4 tables like the one shown in the figure, one for males and one for females.)

Three-factor case

Factor 1, L1

Factor 3

		L1	L2	L3	L4	
Factor	L1	a	b	c	d	$a+b+c+d$
2	L2	e	f	g	h	$e+f+g+h$
		$a+e$	$b+f$	$c+g$	$d+h$	$a+b+c+d+e+f+g+h$

Factor 1, L2

Factor 3

		L1	L2	L3	L4	
Factor	L1	i	j	k	l	$i+j+k+l$
2	L2	m	n	o	p	$m+n+o+p$
		$i+m$	$j+n$	$k+o$	$l+p$	$i+j+k+l+m+n+o+p$

2. Compute the marginal sums across the rows and across the columns. If you have a three-way ANOVA, make a new table that is identical in form to the ones you made for each level of the first factor and contains a sum of all the other tables.

Three-factor case

Factor 1, L1

Factor 3

		L1	L2	L3	L4	
Factor	**L1**	*a*	*b*	*c*	*d*	*a+b+c+d*
2	**L2**	*e*	*f*	*g*	*h*	*e+f+g+h*
		a+e	*b+f*	*c+g*	*d+h*	*a+b+c+d+e+f+g+h*

Factor 1, L2

Factor 3

		L1	L2	L3	L4	
Factor	**L1**	*i*	*j*	*k*	*l*	*i+j+k+l*
2	**L2**	*m*	*n*	*o*	*p*	*m+n+o+p*
		i+m	*j+n*	*k+o*	*l+p*	*i+j+k+l+m+n+o+p*

Factor 1, Marginal sums

Factor 3

		L1	L2	L3	L4	
Factor	**L1**	*a+i*	*b+j*	*c+k*	*d+l*	*a+b+c+d+i+j+k+l*
2	**L2**	*e+m*	*f+n*	*g+o*	*h+p*	*e+f+g+h+m+n+o+p*
		a+e+i+m	*b+f+j+n*	*c+g+k+o*	*d+h+l+p*	**sum all a thru p**

3. After the "/LMATRIX = " tag, list out all of the factors and all of the interactions *in the same order as they are listed in the GLM and DESIGN tags.* For example,

```
/LMATRIX = IV1 IV2 IV1*IV2
```

for two factors, or

```
/LMATRIX = IV1 IV2 IV3 IV1*IV2 IV1*IV3 IV1*IV2*IV3
```

for three factors.

4. Write down the cell values and marginal sums for each term based on the tables you generated in Step 2. With two factors (one with 2 levels and the other with 4 levels), the general form (based on the tables) is

```
/LMATRIX =   IV1 [a+b+c+d]  [e+f+g+h]

 IV2 [a+e]  [b+f]  [c+g]  [d+h]

 IV1*IV2 [a]  [b]  [c]  [d]  [e]  [f]  [g]  [h]
```

With three factors, the general form is

```
/LMATRIX =   IV1 [sum a thru h]  [sum i thru p]

 IV2 [a+b+c+d+i+j+k+l]  [e+f+g+h+m+n+o+p]

 IV3 [a+e+i+m]  [b+f+j+n]  [c+g+k+o]  [d+h+l+p]

 IV1*IV2 [a+b+c+d]  [e+f+g+h]  [i+j+k+l]  [m+n+o+p]

 IV1*IV3 [a+e]  [b+f]  [c+g]  [d+h]  [i+m]  [j+n]  [k+o]  [l+p]

 IV2*IV3 [a+i]  [b+j]  [c+k]  [d+l]  [e+m]  [f+n]  [g+o]  [h+p]

 IV1*IV2*IV3 [a]  [b]  [c]  [d]  [e]  [f]  [g]  [h]  [i]  [j]  [k]  [l]
             [m]  [n]  [o]  [p]
```

5. Remove any term (and its coefficients) if all the coefficients are equal to 0.

For example, suppose we wanted to compute the following contrast based on the data set "Wedding.sav" from Chapters 6 and 7, which tests whether the difference in dancing between co-workers and family on the bride's side is different between male and female guests.

Male guests

Relationship

		Friend	Family	Family friend	Co-worker	
Side	Bride	0	-1	0	1	0
	Groom	0	0	0	0	0
		0	-1	0	1	0

Female guests

Relationship

		Friend	Family	Family friend	Co-worker	
Side	Bride	0	1	0	-1	0
	Groom	0	0	0	0	0
		0	1	0	-1	0

All guests

Relationship

		Friend	Family	Family friend	Co-worker	
Side	Bride	0	0	0	0	0
	Groom	0	0	0	0	0
		0	0	0	0	0

The corresponding syntax is

```
/LMATRIX = gender*relation 0 -1 0 1 0 1 0 -1
gender*side*relation 0 -1 0 1 0 0 0 0 0 1 0 -1 0 0 0 0
```

Subject Index

Syntax Index

SAGE Research Methods Online
The essential tool for researchers

**Sign up now at
www.sagepub.com/srmo
for more information.**

An expert research tool

- An **expertly designed taxonomy** with more than 1,400 unique terms for social and behavioral science research methods

- **Visual and hierarchical search tools** to help you discover material and link to related methods

- Easy-to-use navigation tools
- Content organized by complexity
- Tools for citing, printing, and downloading content with ease
- Regularly updated content and features

A wealth of essential content

- The most comprehensive picture of quantitative, qualitative, and mixed methods available today

- More than **100,000 pages of SAGE book and reference material** on research methods as well as editorially selected material from SAGE journals

- More than **600 books** available in their entirety online

Launching 2011!